AF651903

# The Transnational Dimension of Cyber Crime and Terrorism

# The Transnational Dimension of Cyber Crime and Terrorism

**Rajan Nagia**

CYBER TECH PUBLICATIONS
4264/3, Ansari Road, Daryaganj, New Delhi-110002 (India)
Ph.: 011-23244078, 011-43559448 Fax: 011-23280028
E-Mail: cyberpublicationsdelhi@yahoo.com
Website: www.cybertechpublications.com

**THE TRANSNATIONAL DIMENSION OF CYBER CRIME AND TERRORISM**

**Rajan Nagia**

© Reserved

First Edition 2010

All rights reserved. No part of this publication may be reproduced, stored in a retrieval system or transmitted, in any form or by any means, electronic, mechanical, photo copying, recording or otherwise, without the prior permission of the publisher.

*Published by :*

**G.S. Rawat** for **Cyber Tech Publications**
4264/3, Ansari Road, Daryaganj, New Delhi-110002 (India)
Ph.: 011-23244078, 011-43559448 Fax: 011-23280028
E-Mail: cyberpublicationsdelhi@yahoo.com
Website: www.cybertechpublications.com

*Printed at:* Asian Offset Printers, Delhi-53

# Preface

In a world of intertwined global networks, is there a need for a coordinated, sustained, and institutionalized approach to protecting critical network infrastructures?" We propose that the answer to this question is yes, and that there is a need not for one, but for several such "coordinated, sustained, and institutionalized" approaches. Both critical network infrastructures and the attacks that threaten them take a wide range of forms; they both also cross borders in complex and sometimes surprising ways. Software written in India controls emergency gas leak repairs in Britain; an e mail from Kenya might cross the Atlantic in route to South Africa; and a hacker operating from an unidentified country might use computers in Latvia and the United States to attack a South Korean government site. No single national or international approach can create trust in so many different infrastructure systems.

We believe, therefore, that the best way to create trust in global networks is to rely not on a single line of defence, but on a series of overlapping defences that include both national and international strategies, public and private efforts, formal and informal channels, and multilateral and bilateral cooperation. The goal of such defences, taken together, should be to help create trust by giving each nation the confidence that when an attack breaches one or more defences, other defences will step into the gap and halt the attack, contain the damage, or deter the attacker from striking again.

In this book, we focus specifically on opportunities for international cooperation to add to that series of overlapping defences, and on one aspect of trust: security. We do not address other components of trust such as data integrity, software reliability, or engineering standards except as they relate to security, although we anticipate with great interest the discussion of these issues in other papers in this workshop.

The first factor driving the need for defence is the growing dependence of business and society on critical network infrastructures. Communication has become the lifeblood of modern societies. The rise of e commerce has made these networks responsible for a growing share of national wealth and hopes for greater prosperity. Furthermore, in some nations, pre-existing critical services have come to rely on electronic networks – emergency services, navigation systems for shipping and air traffic, electric power grids, and water control systems. While these dependencies vary from nation to nation, nearly all nations already or will in the future depend on these critical network infrastructures.

The second factor in the need for defence is that these networks are vulnerable to attack. Many were designed without security in mind, and new vulnerabilities are reported routinely in the most widely used and in even the most recently updated systems.

*—Author*

# CONTENTS

# 1

# Introduction

Business, government and industry have all become addicted to information. Their reliance on information creates opportunities for terrorism. Imagine a day without the Internet. What would the impact be? Just what is considered to be cyber terrorism?

Cyber terrorism is the premeditated use of disruptive activities, or the threat thereof, against computers and/or networks, with the intention to cause harm or further social, ideological, religious, political or similar objectives, or to intimidate any person in furtherance of such objectives.

If your look at the projected eCommerce number for this year, the Internet being down for just one day could disrupt nearly $6.5 billion worth of transactions. More than just eCommerce transactions flow over the Internet. eMail, voice communications, some banking machines, credit card authorizations for physical stores and the list goes on and on. Information is the life blood of commerce, regulatory oversight and even social status. The importance of the information and the ability to access it, transfer it and act upon it has increased to the point that it is unfathomable for all but the smallest of businesses to operate without computers or networks. As the value of the computing infrastructure increases so to does the value of disruption. The financial implications are one thing, but the psychological impact of the Internet disruption could be even more damaging.

How likely is this to happen? It is not, if it will happen, but when. The likelihood of a cyber terrorism attack disrupting the

Internet increases every day. The increased reliance on the Internet by business, government and society has made it a prime target for terrorist intent on disrupting our economy and way of life.

Security professionals have expressed their increasing concern over not cnly the increase in frequency of attacks against the Internet, but also the increase in the level of sophistication of these attacks. While the complexity of the attacks is increasing, the skill level of the intruder that launched the attack is decreasing. This is a very troubling trend. As the terrorists learn from every attack what works and what doesn't, where the vulnerabilities are, how we respond, and the methods we use to detect these attacks, they gain the knowledge that will increase their odds for success. Could the northeast black out in August have been the first cyber attack? A question that is in the back of many people's minds.

## WHAT IS THE CURRENT STATE OF ATTACK?

Despite significant investment in technology and infrastructure, cyber terrorism represents one of the greatest challenges in combating terrorism. Every day the Internet and countless other computer systems are under attack. In the 2002 research study conducted by the Computer Crime Research Center, 90% of respondents detected computer security breaches within the last twelve months. In another more recent study conducted by CIO Online, 92% of companies have experienced computer attacks and/or breaches in the last 12 months. If that is not shocking enough, security professionals are worried about the increased sophistication of threats against computer systems.

Here are some interesting statistics.

- In the first half of 2002, there were more than 180,000 Internet based attacks on business.
- Attacks against the Internet increase at an annual rate above 60%.
- The average business will experience 32 break-in attempts this week.
- Reported systems vulnerabilities and security incidents are doubling each year.

- The reported number of vulnerabilities and security incidents represent an estimated 10% of the actual total.

Most studies to date have shown that critical information infrastructures are potentially vulnerable to a cyber terrorist attack. The increasing complexity of information systems creates new vulnerabilities and challenges for IT management. Even if the technology is armor plated, insiders acting alone or in concert with other terrorists may be able to exploit their access capabilities to wreak considerable harm.

## *What would the impact be?*

The intention of a cyber terrorism attack could range from economic disruption through the interruption of financial networks and systems or used in support of a physical attack to cause further confusion and possible delays in proper response. Although cyber attacks have caused billions of dollars in damage and affected the lives of millions, we have yet witness the implications of a truly catastrophic cyber terrorism attack. What would some of the implications be?

### *Direct Cost Implications*

- Loss of sales during the disruption
- Staff time, network delays, intermittent access for business users
- Increased insurance costs due to litigation
- Loss of intellectual property - research, pricing, etc.
- Costs of forensics for recovery and litigation
- Loss of critical communications in time of emergency

### *Indirect Cost Implications*

- Loss of confidence and credibility in our financial systems
- Tarnished relationships& public image globally
- Strained business partner relationships - domestic and internationally
- Loss of future customer revenues for an individual or group of companies

- Loss of trust in the government and computer industry

New legislation is requiring system breaches to be reported (SB1386 California). Other proposed legislation would allow damages to be sought by victims of attacks that are launched from hacked web systems. California's SB 1386 is a sweeping measure that mandates public disclosure of computer-security breaches in which confidential information of any California resident may have been compromised. The bill further goes on to define personal information as an individual's first name or initial and last name in combination with a SSN, a driver's license number, or any account numbers, credit card numbers, debit card numbers, and associated passwords or codes. Think of the liability an organization would incur if their systems were compromised and thousands of individuals personal information were exposed and even exploited for financial gain - (funding terrorism).

With the "LoveBug" virus costing nearly $10 billion, it is hard to fathom the financial implications of a much more serious and comprehensive attack. Each and every day corporations in the U.S. and abroad spend millions combating the threats of cyber attacks and cyber terrorism. Corporate efforts reach tens (if not hundreds) of billions of dollars annually and with the increased frequency of attacks, the cost will significantly increase in the coming years. As we face more and more complex attacks from professional cyber warriors, corporations will increasing seek help from the governments around the world to thwart these efforts and stem the financial bleeding.

## *When will it happen?*

As discussed earlier as the value of our information infrastructure further increases and the capabilities of the cyber terrorists' increase, the likelihood of a significant incident increases. Factoring in the increased value of the Internet before, during, and after a Presidential election along with the psychological impact that type of an event would have, coupled with the ever increasing capabilities of the attackers - that would be "PRIME TIME" for such an incident. Would such an attack have a significant direct impact on the election - NO. But if a terrorist were planning to send a message, I can think of no better time.

## THWARTING CYBER TERRORISM

Corporate America must be forced to wage an all-out war against cyber terrorism. Securing the information infrastructures will require a substantial effort on everyone's part. Close collaboration between government and the private sector is critical. Even more critical is the close collaboration within the computer, networking and software industries. These industries must work closely and continue efforts to enhance technology security capabilities. Security is designed in, not added on. Until the weakest links in the network are protected we all are vulnerable and may be impacted. The government sector must institute tougher penalties for cyber crimes and increased funding for law enforcement efforts to fight it. Easier said than done. This must be accomplished with a high degree of collaboration globally. Getting countries to agree on anything these days seems to be an almost unachievable task. Is cyber terrorism the shape of future conflict? Is a digital underground developing right now? Will our scientists, software engineers, and technical resources be able to stay one step ahead of these faceless terrorists? Only time will tell!

Computer and information security, data protection, and privacy are all growing problems. No single technology or product will eliminate threats and risk. I do not believe we have even begun to think of the social and economic implications of a considerable cyber terrorism attack against our infrastructure. Securing our computers, information, and communications networks secure our economy and our country. A global strategy and policy for combating this type of terrorism is need now.

2

# Cyberterrorism and its Solutions: An Indian Perspective

The aim of this article is to analyse the adverse impact of "Cyber Terrorism" on the national interest of India. Cyber terrorism is a catastrophic phenomenon that has not yet attracted the attention of the Indian Legislature. The law in this regard is not sufficient and the problem of cyber terrorism can be tackled properly either by making a separate law in this regard or by making suitable amendments in the already existing Information Technology Act, 2000. In the absence of the political and legislative will to fill in this lacuna, the judiciary has to play a proactive role and construe the provisions of existing laws in a liberal and purposive manner.

## INTRODUCTION

The traditional concepts and methods of terrorism have taken new dimensions, which are more destructive and deadly in nature. In the age of information technology the terrorists have acquired an expertise to produce the most deadly combination of weapons and technology, which if not properly safeguarded in due course of time, will take its own toll. The damage so produced would be almost irreversible and most catastrophic in nature. In short, we are facing the worst form of terrorism popularly known as "Cyber Terrorism". The expression "cyber terrorism" includesan intentional negative and harmful use of the information technology for producing destructive and harmful effects to the property, whether tangible or intangible, of others. For instance, hacking of a computer system and then deleting the useful and valuable business information of the rival competitor is a part and parcel of cyber terrorism. The definition of "cyber terrorism" cannot be made exhaustive as the nature of crime is such that it must be left to be inclusive in nature. The nature of "cyberspace " is such that new methods and technologies are invented regularly; hence it is not advisable to put the definition in a straightjacket formula or pigeons hole. In fact, the first effort of the Courts should be to interpret the definition as liberally as possible so that the menace of cyber terrorism can be tackled stringently and with a punitive hand. The law dealing with cyber terrorism is, however, not adequate to meet the precarious intentions of these cyber terrorists and requires a rejuvenation in the light and context of the latest developments all over the world. The laws of India have to take care of the problems originating at the international level because the Internet, through which these terrorist activities are carried out, recognises no boundaries. Thus, a cyber terrorist can collapse the economic structure of a country from a place with which India may not have any reciprocal arrangements, including an "extradition treaty". The only safeguard in such a situation is to use the latest technology to counter these problems. Thus, a good combination of the latest security technology and a law dealing with cyber terrorism is the need of the hour.

## FORMS OF CYBER TERRORISM

It is very difficult to exhaustively specify the forms of cyber terrorism. In fact, it would not be a fruitful exercise to do the same. The nature of cyber terrorism requires it to remain inclusive and open ended in nature, so that new variations and forms of it can be accommodated in the future. The following can be safely regarded as the forms of cyber terrorism applying the definition and the concepts discussed above:

### *(I) Privacy violation:*

The law of privacy is the recognition of the individual's right to be let alone and to have his personal space inviolate. The right to privacy as an independent and distinctive concept originated in the field of Tort law, under which a new cause of action for damages resulting from unlawful invasion of privacy was recognised. *In recent times, however, this right has acquired a constitutional status, the violation of which attracts both civil as well as criminal consequences under the respective laws.* The intensity and complexity of life have rendered necessary some retreat from the world. Man under the refining influence of culture, has become sensitive to publicity, so that solitude and privacy have become essential to the individual. *Modern enterprise and invention have, through invasions upon his privacy, subjected him to mental pain and distress, far greater than could be inflicted by mere bodily injury.* Right to privacy is a part of the right to life and personal liberty enshrined under Article 21 of the Constitution of India. With the advent of information technology the traditional concept of right to privacy has taken new dimensions, which require a different legal outlook. To meet this challenge recourse of Information Technology Act, 2000 can be taken.

The various provisions of the Act aptly protect the online privacy rights of the netizens. Certain acts have been categorised as offences and contraventions, which have tendency to intrude with the privacy rights of the netizens. These rights are available against private individuals as well as against cyber terrorists. Section 1 (2) read with Section 75 of the Act provides for an extra-territorial application of the provisions of the Act. Thus, if a person (including a foreign national) contravenes the privacy of an individual by means of computer, computer system or computer network located in India, he would be liable under the provisions of the Act. This makes it clear that the long arm jurisdiction is equally available against a cyber terrorist, whose act has resulted in the damage of the property, whether tangible or intangible.

### (II) Secret information appropriation and data theft:

The information technology can be misused for appropriating the valuable Government secrets and data of private individuals and the Government and its agencies. A computer network owned by the Government may contain valuable information concerning defence and other top secrets, which the Government will not wish to share otherwise. The same can be targeted by the terrorists to facilitate their activities, including destruction of property. It must be noted that the definition of property is not restricted to moveables or immoveables alone. In R.K. Dalmia v Delhi Administration the Supreme Court held that the word "property" is used in the I.P.C in a much wider sense than the expression "movable property". There is no good reason to restrict the meaning of the word "property" to moveable property only, when it is used without any qualification. Whether the offence defined in a particular section of IPC can be committed in respect of any particular kind of property, will depend not on the interpretation of the word "property" but on the fact whether that particular kind of property can be subject to the acts covered by that section. Thus, if any person without permission of the owner or any other person who is incharge of a computer, computer system or computer network -

(a) accesses or secures access to such computer, computer system or computer network.

(b) downloads, copies or extracts any data, computer data base or information from such computer, computer system or computer network including information or data held or stored in any removable storage medium;

(c) damages or causes to be damaged any computer, computer system or computer network, data, computer data base or any other programmes residing in such computer, computer system or computer network;

he shall be liable to pay damages by way of compensation not exceeding one crore rupees to the person so affected. The expression "Computer Database" means a representation of information, knowledge, facts, concepts or instructions in text, image, audio, video that are being prepared or have been prepared in a formalised manner or have been produced by a computer, computer system or computer network and are intended for use in a computer, computer system or computer network.

The expression "Damage" means to destroy, alter, delete, add, modify or re-arrange any computer resource by any means. These provisions make it clear that secret information appropriation and data theft by the cyber terrorists will be dealt with punitive sting and monetary impositions.

## (III) Demolition of e-governance base:

The aim of e-governance is to make the interaction of the citizens with the government offices hassle free and to share information in a free and transparent manner. It further makes the right to information a meaningful reality. In a democracy, people govern themselves and they cannot govern themselves properly unless they are aware of social, political, economic and other issues confronting them. To enable them to make a proper judgment on those issues, they must have the benefit of a range of opinions on those issues. Right to receive and impart information is implicit in free speech. This, right to receive information is, however, not absolute but is subject to reasonable restrictions which may be imposed by the Government in public interest. In P.U.C.L. V U.O.I the Supreme Court specified the grounds on which the government can withhold information relating to various matters, including trade secrets. The Supreme Court observed: " Every right- legal or moral- carries with it a corresponding objection. It is subject to several exemptions/ exceptions indicated in broad terms. Generally, the exemptions/ exceptions under those laws entitle the Govt to with hold information relating to the following matters:

(1) International relations;
(2) National security (including defiance) and public safety;
(3) Investigation, detection and prevention of crime;
(4) Internal deliberations of the Govt;
(5) Information received in confidence from a source outside the Govt;
(6) Information, which, if disclosed, would violate the privacy of the individual;
(7) Information of an economic nature (including Trade Secrets) which, if disclosed, would confer an unfair advantage on some person or concern, or, subject some person or Govt, to an unfair disadvantage;
(8) Information, which is subject to a claim of legal professional privilege, e.g. communication between a legal adviser and the client; between a physician and the patient;

(9) Information about scientific discoveries".

It must be noted that the primary aim of all cyber terrorist activities is to collapse a sound communication system, which includes an e-governance base. Thus, by a combination of virus attacks and hacking techniques, the e-governance base of the government can be caused to be collapsed. This would be more deleterious and disastrous as compared to other tangible damages, which were caused by the traditional terrorist activities. Similarly, the terrorists to the common detriment of the nation at large can illegally obtain information legitimately protected from public scrutiny by the government in the interest of security of the nation. Thus, a strong e-governance base with the latest security methods and systems is the need of the hour.

## *(IV) Distributed denial of services attack:*

The cyber terrorists may also use the method of distributed denial of services (DDOS) to overburden the Government and its agencies electronic bases. This is made possible by first infecting several unprotected computers by way of virus attacks and then taking control of them. Once control is obtained, they can be manipulated from any locality by the terrorists. These infected computers are then made to send information or demand in such a large number that the server of the victim collapses.

Further, due to this unnecessary Internet traffic the legitimate traffic is prohibited from reaching the Government or its agencies computers. This results in immense pecuniary and strategic loss to the government and its agencies. It must be noted that thousands of compromised computers can be used to simultaneously attack a single host, thus making its electronic existence invisible to the genuine and legitimate netizens and end users. The law in this regard is crystal clear. If any person without permission of the owner or any other person who is incharge of a computer, computer system or computer network :

(a) introduces or causes to be introduced any computer contaminant or computer virus into any computer, computer system or computer network;

(b) disrupts or causes disruption of any computer, computer system or computer network;

(c) denies or causes the denial of access to any person authorised to access any computer, computer system or computer network by any means;

The shall be liable to pay damages by way of compensation not exceeding one crore rupees to the person so affected . The expression "Computer Contaminant" means any set of computer instructions that are designed -

(a) to modify, destroy, record, transmit data or programme residing within a computer, computer system or computer network; or

(b) by any means to usurp the normal operation of the computer, computer system, or computer network. Thus, distribute denial of services by the cyber terrorists will be tackled by invoking the provisions of sections 43,65 and 66 collectively.

### *(V) Network damage and disruptions:*

The main aim of cyber terrorist activities is to cause networks damage and their disruptions. This activity may divert the attention of the security agencies for the time being thus giving the terrorists extra time and makes their task comparatively easier. This process may involve a combination of computer tampering, virus attacks, hacking, etc. The law in this regard provides that if any person without permission of the owner or any other person who is incharge of a computer, computer system or computer network -

(a) accesses or secures access to such computer, computer system or computer network

(b) introduces or causes to be introduced any computer contaminant or computer virus into any computer, computer system or computer network;

(c) damages or causes to be damaged any computer, computer system or computer network, data, computer data base or any other programmes residing in such computer, computer system or computer network;

(d) disrupts or causes disruption of any computer, computer system or computer network;

(e) denies or causes the denial of access to any person authorised to access any computer, computer system or computer network by any means;

The shall be liable to pay damages by way of compensation not exceeding one crore rupees to the person so affected. The expression "Computer Virus" means any computer instruction, information, data or programme that destroys, damages, degrades or adversely affects the performance of a computer resource or attaches itself to another computer resource and operates when a programme, data or instruction is executed or some other event takes place in that computer resource. The person tampering with such computer source documents shall be punishable with imprisonment up to 3 years or with fine, which may extend up to Rs.2 lakhs, or with both. Further, if a person causes wrongful loss or damage to any person, by destroying, deleting or altering any information residing in his (owner's) compute resource or diminishes its value or utility or affects it injuriously by any means, he commits hacking and thus, violates the privacy of the owner. The person hacking shall be punishable with imprisonment up to 3 years or with fine, which may extend up to Rs.2 lakhs, or with both. However, an innocent infringer will not be liable if he proves that he committed the act without any intention or knowledge. A network service provider will be liable for various violations and contraventions mentioned under the Act if he makes available any third party information or data to a person for the commission of an offence or contravention. However, a network service provider will not be liable if he proves that the offence or contravention was committed without his knowledge or he had exercised all due diligence to prevent such commission. Thus, these provisions can be safely invoked for meeting challenges posed by network damage and disruptions caused by cyber terrorists.

## The Roads Ahead

The menace of cyber terrorism can be effectively curbed, if not completely eliminated, if the three sovereign organs of the

Constitution work collectively and in harmony with each other. Further, a vigilant citizenry can supplement the commitment of elimination of cyber terrorism.

## *(1) Legislative commitment:*

The legislature can provide its assistance to the benign objective of elimination of cyber terrorism by enacting appropriate statutes dealing with cyber terrorism. It must be noted that to give effect to the provisions of Information Technology Act, 2000 appropriate amendments have been made in the I.P.C, 1860, the Indian Evidence Act, 1872, the Bankers' Books Evidence Act, 1891 and the Reserve Bank of India Act, 1934. On the same lines a new chapter dealing with "Cyber terrorism" can be added to the already existing criminal statues to make them compatible with modern forms of terrorisms. Similarly, a new chapter dealing with cyber terrorism can be incorporated in the Information Technology Act, 2000 by way of its amendment to bring harmonization among various laws. The repealment of POTA and its likely replacement with a new ordinance is an opportunity for the legislature to make the terrorist law effective to deal with cyber terrorism.

## *(2) Executives concern:*

The Central Government and the State Governments can play their role effectively by making various rules and regulations dealing with cyber terrorism and its facets from time to time. The Central Government can, by notification in the Official Gazette and in the Electronic Gazette, makes rules to carry out the provisions of the Information Technology Act. Similarly, the State Government can, by notification in Official Gazette, makes rules to carry out the provisions of the Act. In exercise of the powers conferred by section 90 of the Information Technology Act, 2000 (Central Act 21 of 2000), the Government of Karnataka has made the Information Technology (Karnataka) Rules 2004. The Rules define "Cyber Café" as premises where the Cyber Café Owner/Network Service Provider provides the computer services including Internet access to the public. Rule 3 (1) provides that the owner of the Cyber Café shall take sufficient precautions so that computers and computer systems in the Cyber Café are not used for any illegal or criminal activity. Rule 3 (2) mandates that the Cyber Café Owner/Network Service Provider shall not allow any User to use his Computer, Computer System and/or Computer Network without the identity of the User being established before him before use.

The Rule provides that the intending User may establish his Identity by producing any Photo Identity Card issued by any School or College or a Photo Credit Card of any Bank or Passport or Voters Identity Card or PAN Number Card issued by Income-Tax authorities or Photo Identity Card issued by the Employer or Driving License to the satisfaction of Cyber Café Owner. Rule 4(1) provides that after the identity of the User is established, the owner of the Cyber Café or the manager or the attendant or on his behalf any authorised person managing the Cyber Café shall obtain and maintain the following information in the Log Register for each user: (i) Name of the User, (ii) Age and Sex of the User, (iii) Present residential address of the User, (iv) Log in time, and (v) Log out time. Rule 4 (2) provides that if a User cannot produce any Photo Identity Card to establish his identity to the satisfaction of the Cyber Café Owner/ Network Service Provider, he may be photographed by the Cyber Café Owner/Network Service Provider after obtaining his consent using a 'Web Camera' hooked onto one of the computers or computer systems in the Cyber Café and the User shall be explained that his photograph will be taken and stored in the hard disk of the computer, for verification by Law enforcement authorities, whenever required.

This is in addition to the entries made in the log register. The Rule further provides that in case the User does not agree for storing his photograph he shall not be allowed to use any computer, computer system and /or computer network or access to the Internet in the Cyber Café. Rule 4(3) provides that all time clocks in Cyber Cafes must be regularly checked and synchronized with Indian Standard Time (IST). Rule 4(4) provides that maintaining proper account of the User as explained shall be the responsibility of the Cyber Café Owner/Network Service provider. Rule 5(5) provides that the Log Register and the Photograph of the User shall be maintained by the Cyber Café Owner/Network Service Provider for a minimum period of ONE YEAR and the same shall be provided to Law enforcement agencies as and when required. Rule 4(6) provides that the Cyber Police authorities may on complaint inspect Cyber Cafes at all reasonable time to ensure compliance of these rules. If any Cyber Café Owner/Network Service Provider fails to maintain Log Register and records he shall be liable for penalties as provided in the Act or any other Law, for the time being in force. These provisions are sufficient to take care of illegal use of cyber café for terrorist activities. Further, the government can also block web sites propagating cyber terrorism. It must be noted that the Indian Computer Emergency Response Team (CERT-In) has been designated as the single authority for issuing of instructions in the context of blocking of web sites. CERT-In has to instruct the Department of Telecommunications to block the web sites after verifying the authenticity of the complaint and satisfying that action of blocking of website is absolutely essential. There is no explicit provision in the IT Act, 2000 for blocking of websites. In fact, blocking is considered to be censorship; hence it can be challenged if it restricts the freedom of speech and expression. But websites promoting hate, contempt, slander or defamation of others, promoting gambling, promoting racism, *violence and terrorism*, pornography and violent sex can reasonably be blocked since all such websites cannot claim the Fundamental Right of free speech and expression. The blocking of such website may be equated to "balanced flow of information" and not censorship. If the blocking of a website is arbitrary, unreasonable and unfair and is based on extraneous and irrelevant materials and reasons, then it would be vulnerable to the attack of unconstitutionality, being in violation of Articles 14, 19 and 21 of the Constitution of India.

### *(3) Judicial response:*

The judiciary can play its role by adopting a stringent approach towards the menace of cyber terrorism. It must, however, first tackle the jurisdiction problem because before invoking its judicial powers the courts are required to satisfy themselves that they possess the requisite jurisdiction to deal with the situation. Since the Internet "is a cooperative venture not owned by a single entity or government, there are no centralized rules or laws governing its use. The absence of geographical boundaries may give rise to a situation where the act legal in one country where it is done may violate the laws of another country. This process further made complicated due to the absence of a uniform and harmonised law governing the jurisdictional aspects of disputes arising by the use of Internet. It must be noted that, generally, the scholars point towards the following "theories" under which a country may claim prescriptive jurisdiction:

(a) a country may claim jurisdiction based on "objective territoriality" when an activity takes place within the country,

(b) a "subjective territoriality" may attach when an activity takes place outside a nation's borders but the "primary effect" of the action is within the nation's borders,

(c) a country may assert jurisdiction based on the nationality of either the actor or the victim,

(d) in exceptional circumstances, providing the right to protect the nation's sovereignty when faced with threats recognised as particularly serious in the international community.

In addition to establishing a connecting nexus, traditional international doctrine also calls for a "reasonable" connection between the offender and the forum. Depending on the factual context, courts look to such factors, as whether the activity of individual has a "substantial and foreseeable effect" on the territory, whether a "genuine link" exists between the actor and the forum, the character of the activity and the importance of the regulation giving rise to the controversy, the extent to which exceptions are harmed by the regulation, and the importance of the regulation in the international community. The traditional jurisdictional paradigms may provide a framework to guide analysis for cases arising in cyberspace. It must be noted that by virtue of section 1(2) read with section 75 of the Information Technology Act, 2000 the courts in India have "long arm jurisdiction" to deal with cyber terrorism.

## *(4) Vigilant citizenry:*

The menace of cyber terrorism is not the sole responsibility of State and its instrumentalities. The citizens as well as the netizens are equally under a solemn obligation to fight against the cyber terrorism. In fact, they are the most important and effective cyber terrorism eradication and elimination mechanism. The only requirement is to encourage them to come forward for the support of fighting against cyber terrorism. The government can give suitable incentives to them in the form of monetary awards. It must, however, be noted that their anonymity and security must be ensured before seeking their help. The courts are also empowered to maintain their anonymity if they provide any information and evidence to fight against cyber terrorism.

## CONCLUSION

The problem of cyber terrorism is multilateral having varied facets and dimensions. Its solution requires rigorous application of energy and resources. It must be noted that law is always seven steps behind the technology. This is so because we have a tendency to make laws when the problem reaches at its zenith. We do not appreciate the need of the hour till the problem takes a precarious dimension. At that stage it is always very difficult, if not impossible, to deal with that problem. This is more so in case of offences and violations involving information technology. One of the argument, which is always advanced to justify this stand of non-enactment is that "the measures suggested are not adequate to deal with the problem". It must be appreciated that "something is better than nothing". The ultimate solution to any problem is not to enact a plethora of statutes but their rigorous and dedicated enforcement. The courts may apply the existing laws in a progressive, updating and purposive manner. It must be appreciated that it is not the "enactment" of a law but the desire, will and efforts to accept and enforce it in its true letter and spirit, which can confer the most strongest, secure and safest protection for any purpose. The enforcement of these rights requires a "qualitative effort" and not a "quantitative effort". Thus, till a law dealing expressly with cyber terrorism is enacted, we must not feel shy and hesitant to use the existing provisions.

# 3

# Cyberterrorism: How Real is the Threat?


## SUMMARY

- The potential threat posed by cyberterrorism has provoked considerable alarm. Numerous security experts, politicians, and others have publicized the danger of cyberterrorists hacking into government and private computer systems and crippling the military, financial, and service sectors of advanced economies.
- The potential threat is, indeed, very alarming. And yet, despite all the gloomy predictions, no single instance of real cyberterrorism has been recorded. This raises the question: just how real is the threat?
- Psychological, political, and economic forces have combined to promote the fear of cyberterrorism. From a psychological perspective, two of the greatest fears of modern time are combined in the term "cyberterrorism." The fear of random, violent victimization blends well with the distrust and outright fear of computer technology.
- Even before 9/11, a number of exercises identified apparent vulnerabilities in the computer networks of the U.S. military and energy sectors. After 9/11, the security and terrorism discourse soon featured cyberterrorism prominently, promoted by interested actors from the political, business, and security circles.

- Cyberterrorism is, to be sure, an attractive option for modern terrorists, who value its anonymity, its potential to inflict massive damage, its psychological impact, and its media appeal.
- Cyberfears have, however, been exaggerated. Cyberattacks on critical components of the national infrastructure are not uncommon, but they have not been conducted by terrorists and have not sought to inflict the kind of damage that would qualify as cyberterrorism.
- Nuclear weapons and other sensitive military systems, as well as the computer systems of the CIA and FBI, are "air-gapped," making them inaccessible to outside hackers. Systems in the private sector tend to be less well protected, but they are far from defenseless, and nightmarish tales of their vulnerability tend to be largely apocryphal.
- But although the fear of cyberterrorism may be manipulated and exaggerated, we can neither deny nor ignore it. Paradoxically, success in the "war on terror" is likely to make terrorists turn increasingly to unconventional weapons, such as cyberterrorism. And as a new, more computer-savvy generation of terrorists comes of age, the danger seems set to increase.

## INTRODUCTION

The threat posed by cyberterrorism has grabbed the attention of the mass media, the security community, and the information technology (IT) industry. Journalists, politicians, and experts in a variety of fields have popularized a scenario in which sophisticated cyberterrorists electronically break into computers that control dams or air traffic control systems, wreaking havoc and endangering not only millions of lives but national security itself. And yet, despite all the gloomy predictions of a cyber-generated doomsday, no single instance of real cyberterrorism has been recorded.

Just how real is the threat that cyberterrorism poses? Because most critical infrastructure in Western societies is networked through computers, the potential threat from cyberterrorism is, to be sure, very alarming. Hackers, although not motivated by the same goals that inspire terrorists, have demonstrated that individuals can gain access to sensitive information and to the operation of crucial services. Terrorists, at least in theory, could thus follow the hackers' lead and then, having broken into government and private computer systems, cripple or at least disable the military, financial, and service sectors of advanced economies. The growing dependence of our societies on information technology has created a new form of vulnerability, giving terrorists the chance to approach targets that would otherwise be utterly unassailable, such as national defense systems and air traffic control systems. The more technologically developed a country is, the more vulnerable it becomes to cyberattacks against its infrastructure.

Concern about the potential danger posed by cyberterrorism is thus well founded. That does not mean, however, that all the fears that have been voiced in the media, in Congress, and in other public forums are rational and reasonable. Some fears are simply unjustified, while others are highly exaggerated. In addition, the distinction between the potential and the actual damage inflicted by cyberterrorists has too often been ignored, and the relatively benign activities of most hackers have been conflated with the specter of pure cyberterrorism.

This report examines the reality of the cyberterrorism threat, present and future. It begins by outlining why cyberterrorism angst has gripped so many people, defines what qualifies as "cyberterrorism" and what does not, and charts cyberterrorism's appeal for terrorists. The report then looks at the evidence both for and against Western society's vulnerability to cyberattacks, drawing on a variety of recent studies and publications to illustrate the kinds of fears that have been expressed and to assess whether we need to be so concerned. The conclusion looks to the future and argues that we must remain alert to real dangers while not becoming victims of overblown fears.

## Cyberterrorism Angst

The roots of the notion of cyberterrorism can be traced back to the early 1990s, when the rapid growth in Internet use and the debate on the emerging "information society" sparked several studies on the potential risks faced by the highly networked, high-tech-dependent United States. As early as 1990, the National Academy of Sciences began a report on computer security with the words, "We are at risk. Increasingly, America depends on computers. . . . Tomorrow's terrorist may be able to do more damage with a keyboard than with a bomb." At the same time, the prototypical term "electronic Pearl Harbor" was coined, linking the threat of a computer attack to an American historical trauma.

Psychological, political, and economic forces have combined to promote the fear of cyberterrorism. From a psychological perspective, two of the greatest fears of modern time are combined in the term "cyberterrorism." The fear of random, violent victimization blends well with the distrust and outright fear of computer technology. An unknown threat is perceived as more threatening than a known threat. Although cyberterrorism does not entail a direct threat of violence, its psychological impact on anxious societies can be as powerful as the effect of terrorist bombs. Moreover, the most destructive forces working against an understanding of the actual threat of cyberterrorism are a fear of the unknown and a lack of information or, worse, too much misinformation.

After 9/11, the security and terrorism discourse soon featured cyberterrorism prominently. This was understandable, given that more nightmarish attacks were expected and that cyberterrorism seemed to offer al Qaeda opportunities to inflict enormous damage. But there was also a political dimension to the new focus on cyberterrorism. Debates about national security, including the security of cyberspace, always attract political actors with agendas that extend beyond the specific issue at hand—and the debate over cyberterrorism was no exception to this pattern. For instance, Yonah Alexander, a terrorism researcher at the Potomac Institute—a think tank with close links to the Pentagon—announced in December 2001 the existence of an "Iraq Net." This network supposedly consisted of more than one hundred websites set up across the world by Iraq since the mid-nineties to launch denial-of-service (DoS) attacks against U.S. companies (such attacks render computer systems inaccessible, unusable, or inoperable). "Saddam Hussein would not hesitate to use the cyber tool he has. . . . It is not a question of if but when. The entire United States is the front line," Alexander claimed. (See Ralf Bendrath's article "The American Cyber-Angst and the Real World," published in 2003 in *Bombs and Bandwidth*, edited by Robert Latham.) Whatever the intentions of its author, such a statement was clearly likely to support arguments then being made for an aggressive U.S. policy toward Iraq. No evidence of an Iraq Net has yet come to light.

Combating cyberterrorism has become not only a highly politicized issue but also an economically rewarding one. An entire industry has emerged to grapple with the threat of cyberterrorism: think tanks have launched elaborate projects and issued alarming white papers on the subject, experts have testified to cyberterrorism's dangers before Congress, and private companies have hastily deployed security consultants and software designed to protect public and private targets. Following the 9/11 attacks, the federal government requested $4.5 billion for infrastructure security, and the FBI now boasts more than one thousand "cyber investigators."

Before September 11, 2001, George W. Bush, then a presidential candidate, warned that "American forces are overused and underfunded precisely when they are confronted by a host of new threats and challenges—the spread of weapons of mass destruction, the rise of cyberterrorism, the proliferation of missile technology." After the 9/11 attacks, President Bush created the Office of Cyberspace Security in the White House and appointed his former counterterrorism coordinator, Richard Clarke, to head it. The warnings came now from the president, the vice president, security advisors, and government officials: "Terrorists can sit at one computer connected to one network and can create worldwide havoc," cautioned Tom Ridge, director of the Department of Homeland Security, in a representative observation in April 2003. "[They] don't necessarily need a bomb or explosives to cripple a sector of the economy or shut down a power grid." These warnings certainly had a powerful impact on the media, on the public, and on the administration. For instance, a survey of 725 cities conducted in 2003 by the National

League of Cities found that cyberterrorism ranked alongside biological and chemical weapons at the top of a list of city officials' fears.

The mass media have added their voice to the fearful chorus, running scary front-page headlines such as the following, which appeared in the *Washington Post* in June 2003: "Cyber-Attacks by Al Qaeda Feared, Terrorists at Threshold of Using Internet as Tool of Bloodshed, Experts Say." Cyberterrorism, the media have discovered, makes for eye-catching, dramatic copy. Screenwriters and novelists have likewise seen the dramatic potential, with movies such as the 1995 James Bond feature, *Goldeneye*, and 2002's *Code Hunter* and novels such as Tom Clancy and Steve R. Pieczenik's *Netforce* popularizing a wide range of cyberterrorist scenarios.

The net effect of all this attention has been to create a climate in which instances of hacking into government websites, online thefts of proprietary data from companies, and outbreaks of new computer viruses are all likely to be labeled by the media as suspected cases of "cyberterrorism." Indeed, the term has been improperly used and overused to such an extent that, if we are to have any hope of reaching a clear understanding of the danger posed by cyberterrorism, we must begin by defining it with some precision.

## What Is Cyberterrorism?

There have been several stumbling blocks to creating a clear and consistent definition of the term "cyberterrorism." First, as just noted, much of the discussion of cyberterrorism has been conducted in the popular media, where journalists typically strive for drama and sensation rather than for good operational definitions of new terms. Second, it has been especially common when dealing with computers to coin new words simply by placing the word "cyber," "computer," or "information" before another word. Thus, an entire arsenal of words—cybercrime, infowar, netwar, cyberterrorism, cyberharassment, virtual warfare, digital terrorism, cybertactics, computer warfare, cyberattack, and cyber-break-ins—is used to describe what some military and political strategists describe as the "new terrorism" of our times. Fortunately, some efforts have been made to introduce greater semantic precision. Most notably, Dorothy

Denning, a professor of computer science, has put forward an admirably unambiguous definition in numerous articles and in her testimony on the subject before the House Armed Services Committee in May 2000:

> Cyberterrorism is the convergence of cyberspace and terrorism. It refers to unlawful attacks and threats of attacks against computers, networks and the information stored therein when done to intimidate or coerce a government or its people in furtherance of political or social objectives. Further, to qualify as cyberterrorism, an attack should result in violence against persons or property, or at least cause enough harm to generate fear. Attacks that lead to death or bodily injury, explosions, or severe economic loss would be examples. Serious attacks against critical infrastructures could be acts of cyberterrorism, depending on their impact. Attacks that disrupt nonessential services or that are mainly a costly nuisance would not.

It is important to distinguish between cyberterrorism and "hacktivism," a term coined by scholars to describe the marriage of hacking with political activism. ("Hacking" is here understood to mean activities conducted online and covertly that seek to reveal, manipulate, or otherwise exploit vulnerabilities in computer operating systems and other software. Unlike hacktivists, hackers tend *not* to have political agendas.) Hacktivists have four main weapons at their disposal: virtual blockades; e-mail attacks; hacking and computer break-ins; and computer viruses and worms.

A virtual blockade is the virtual version of a physical sit-in or blockade: political activists visit a website and attempt to generate so much traffic toward the site that other users cannot reach it, thereby disrupting normal operations while winning publicity—via media reports—for the protesters' cause. "Swarming" occurs when a large number of individuals simultaneously access a website, causing its collapse. Swarming can also amplify the effects of the hacktivists' second weapon: e-mail bombing campaigns (bombarding targets with thousands of messages at once, also known as "ping attacks"). Maura Conway reported in her essay "Reality Bytes" (*First Monday* 7, no. 11 [November 2002]) on an e-mail bombing campaign launched in July 1997 against the Institute for Global Communications (IGC), a San Francisco–based Internet service provider (ISP) that hosted the web pages of *Euskal Herria* (in English, the *Basque Country Journal*), a publication edited by supporters of the Basque separatist group ETA. The attackers wanted ETA's site removed from the Internet. They bombarded IGC's website with thousands of e-mails, clogging the system, and threatened to attack other organizations using IGC services. IGC pulled the *Euskal Herria* site just a few days later.

The Spanish government was suspected of being behind the e-mail bombing, but the identity of the attackers remains uncertain. Whether or not the suspicion is well founded, it underlines the fact that the hacktivists' tools are widely available and can be as easily employed by governments as by small groups of political activists.

Many cyberprotesters use the third weapon in the hacktivists' arsenal: web hacking and computer break-ins (hacking into computers to access stored information, communication facilities, financial information, and so forth). In her report "Is Cyber Terror Next?" (http://www.ssrc.org/sept11/essays/denning.htm), Denning notes that the Computer Emergency Response Team Coordination Center (CERT/CC), a federally funded research and development center operated by Carnegie Mellon University, reported 2,134 cases of computer break-ins and hacks in 1997. The number of incidents rose to 21,756 in 2000 and to almost 35,000 during the first three quarters of 2001 alone. In 2003, CERT/CC received more than half a million e-mail messages and more than nine hundred hotline calls reporting incidents or requesting information. In the same year, no fewer than 137,529 computer security incidents were reported. Given that many, perhaps most, incidents are never reported to CERT/CC or any agency or organization, the actual figures are probably much higher. Moreover, Denning notes that each single incident that is reported involves thousands of victims. This rise in cyberattacks reflects the growing popularity of the Internet, the vast number of vulnerable targets, and the development of sophisticated and easy-to-use hacking tools.

The fourth category of hacktivist weaponry comprises viruses and worms, both of which are forms of malicious code that can infect computers and propagate over computer networks. Their impact can be enormous. The Code Red worm, for example, infected about a million servers in July 2001 and caused $2.6 billion in damage to computer hardware, software, and networks, and the I LOVE YOU virus unleashed in 2000 affected more than twenty million Internet users and caused billions of dollars in damage. Although neither the Code Red worm nor the I LOVE YOU virus was spread with any political goals in mind (both seem to have been the work of hackers, not hacktivists), some computer viruses and worms have been used to propagate political messages and, in some cases, cause serious damage. During the NATO operation to evict Serbian forces from Kosovo, businesses, public entities, and academic institutes in NATO member-states received virus-laden e-mails from a range of Eastern European countries. The e-mail messages, which had been poorly translated into English, consisted chiefly of unsubtle denunciations of NATO for its unfair aggression and defenses of Serbian rights. But the real threat was from the viruses. This was an instance of cyberwarfare launched by Serbian hacktivists against the economic infrastructure of NATO countries.

In February 2000, the sites of Amazon.com, e-Bay, Yahoo, and a host of other well-known companies were stopped for several hours due to DoS attacks. On October 22, 2002, the *Washington Post* reported that "the heart of the Internet network sustained its largest and most sophisticated attack ever." A DoS attack struck the thirteen "root servers" that provide the primary road map for almost all Internet communications worldwide. It caused no slowdowns or outages because of safeguards built into the system, but a longer and more extensive attack could have inflicted serious damage.

Hacktivism, although politically motivated, does not amount to cyberterrorism. Hacktivists do want to protest and disrupt; they *do not* want to kill or maim or terrify. However, hacktivism does highlight the threat of cyberterrorism, the potential that individuals with no moral restraint may use methods similar to those developed by hackers to wreak havoc. Moreover, the line between cyberterrorism and hacktivism may sometimes blur, especially if terrorist groups are able to recruit or hire computer-savvy hacktivists or if hacktivists decide to escalate their actions by attacking the systems that operate critical elements of the national infrastructure, such as electric power networks and emergency services.

## THE APPEAL OF CYBERTERRORISM FOR TERRORISTS

Cyberterrorism is an attractive option for modern terrorists for several reasons.

- First, it is cheaper than traditional terrorist methods. All that the terrorist needs is a personal computer and an online connection. Terrorists do not need to buy weapons such as guns and explosives; instead, they can create and deliver computer viruses through a telephone line, a cable, or a wireless connection.
- Second, cyberterrorism is more anonymous than traditional terrorist methods. Like many Internet surfers, terrorists use online nicknames—"screen names"—or log on to a website as an unidentified "guest user," making it very hard for security agencies and police forces to track down the terrorists' real identity. And in cyberspace there are no physical barriers such as checkpoints to navigate, no borders to cross, and no customs agents to outsmart.
- Third, the variety and number of targets are enormous. The cyberterrorist could target the computers and computer networks of governments, individuals, public utilities, private airlines, and so forth. The sheer number and complexity of potential targets guarantee that terrorists can find weaknesses and vulnerabilities to exploit. Several studies have shown that critical infrastructures, such as electric power grids and emergency services, are vulnerable to a cyberterrorist attack because the infrastructures and the computer systems that run them are highly complex, making it effectively impossible to eliminate all weaknesses.
- Fourth, cyberterrorism can be conducted remotely, a feature that is especially appealing to terrorists. Cyberterrorism requires less physical training, psychological investment, risk

of mortality, and travel than conventional forms of terrorism, making it easier for terrorist organizations to recruit and retain followers.

- Fifth, as the I LOVE YOU virus showed, cyberterrorism has the potential to affect directly a larger number of people than traditional terrorist methods, thereby generating greater media coverage, which is ultimately what terrorists want.

## A Growing Sense of Vulnerability

*Black Ice: The Invisible Threat of Cyber-Terror*, a book published in 2003 and written by *Computerworld* journalist and former intelligence officer Dan Verton, describes the 1997 exercise code-named "Eligible Receiver," conducted by the National Security Agency (NSA). (The following account draws from "Black Ice," *Computerworld*, August 13, 2003.) The exercise began when NSA officials instructed a "Red Team" of thirty-five hackers to attempt to hack into and disrupt U.S. national security systems. They were told to play the part of hackers hired by the North Korean intelligence service, and their primary target was to be the U.S. Pacific Command in Hawaii. They were allowed to penetrate any Pentagon network but were prohibited from breaking any U.S. laws, and they could only use hacking software that could be downloaded freely from the Internet. They started mapping networks and obtaining passwords gained through "brute-force cracking" (a trial-and-error method of decoding encrypted data such as passwords or encryption keys by trying all possible combinations). Often they used simpler tactics such as calling somebody on the telephone, pretending to be a technician or high-ranking official, and asking for the password. The hackers managed to gain access to dozens of critical Pentagon computer systems. Once they entered the systems, they could easily create user accounts, delete existing accounts, reformat hard drives, scramble stored data, or shut systems down. They broke the network defenses with relative ease and did so without being traced or identified by the authorities.

The results shocked the organizers. In the first place, the Red Team had shown that it was possible to break into the U.S. Pacific military's command-and-control system and, potentially, cripple it.

In the second place, the NSA officials who examined the experiment's results found that much of the private-sector infrastructure in the United States, such as the telecommunications and electric power grids, could easily be invaded and abused in the same way.

The vulnerability of the energy industry is at the heart of *Black Ice.* Verton argues that America's energy sector would be the first domino to fall in a strategic cyberterrorist attack against the United States. The book explores in frightening detail how the impact of such an attack could rival, or even exceed, the consequences of a more traditional, physical attack. Verton claims that during any given year, an average large utility company in the United States experiences about 1 million cyberintrusions. Data collected by Riptech, Inc.—a Virginia-based company specializing in the security of online information and financial systems—on cyberattacks during the six months following the 9/11 attacks showed that companies in the energy industry suffered intrusions at twice the rate of other industries, with the number of severe or critical attacks requiring immediate intervention averaging 12.5 per company.

Deregulation and the increased focus on profitability have made utilities and other companies move more and more of their operations to the Internet in search of greater efficiency and lower costs. Verton argues that the energy industry and many other sectors have become potential targets for various cyberdisruptions by creating Internet links (both physical and wireless) between their networks and supervisory control and data acquisition (SCADA) systems. These SCADA systems manage the flow of electricity and natural gas and control various industrial systems and facilities, including chemical processing plants, water purification and water delivery operations, wastewater management facilities, and a host of manufacturing firms. A terrorist's ability to control, disrupt, or alter the command and monitoring functions performed by these systems could threaten regional and possibly national security.

According to Symantec, one of the world's corporate leaders in the field of cybersecurity, new vulnerabilities to a cyberattack are being discovered all the time. The company reported that the number of "software holes" (software security flaws that allow malicious hackers to exploit the system) grew by 80 percent in 2002. Still, Symantec claimed that no single cyberterrorist attack was recorded (applying the definition that such an attack must originate in a country on the State Department's terror watch list). This may reflect the fact that terrorists do not yet have the required know-how. Alternatively, it may illustrate that hackers are not sympathetic to the goals of terrorist organizations—should the two groups join forces, however, the results could be devastating.

Equally alarming is the prospect of terrorists themselves designing computer software for government agencies. Remarkably, as Denning describes in "Is Cyber Terror Next?" at least one instance of such a situation is known to have occurred:

In March 2000, Japan's Metropolitan Police Department reported that a software system they had procured to track 150 police vehicles, including unmarked cars, had been developed by the Aum Shinryko cult, the same group that gassed the Tokyo subway in 1995, killing 12 people and injuring 6,000 more. At the time of the discovery, the cult had received classified tracking data on 115 vehicles. Further, the cult had developed software for at least 80 Japanese firms and 10 government agencies. They had worked as subcontractors to other firms, making it almost impossible for the organizations to know who was developing the software. As subcontractors, the cult could have installed Trojan horses to launch or facilitate cyber terrorist attacks at a later date.

Despite stepped-up security measures in the wake of 9/11, a survey of almost four hundred IT professionals conducted for the Business Software Alliance during June 2002 revealed widespread concern. (See Robyn Greenspan, "Cyberterrorism Concerns IT Pros," Internetnews.com, August 16, 2002.) About half (49 percent) of the IT professionals felt that an attack is likely, and more than half (55 percent) said the risk of a major cyberattack on the United States has increased since 9/11. The figure jumped to 59 percent among those respondents who are in charge of their company's computer and Internet security. Seventy-two percent agreed with the statement "there is a gap between the threat of a major cyberattack and the government's ability to defend against it," and the agreement rate rose to 84 percent among respondents who are most knowledgeable about security. Those surveyed were concerned about attacks not only on the government but also on private targets. Almost three-quarters (74 percent) believed that national financial institutions such as major national banks would be likely targets within the next year, and around two-thirds believed that attacks were likely to be launched within the next twelve months against the computer systems that run communications networks (e.g., telephones and the Internet), transportation infrastructure (e.g., air traffic control computer systems), and utilities (e.g., water stations, dams, and power plants).

A study released in December 2003 (and reported in the *Washington Post* on January 31, 2004) appeared to confirm the IT professionals' skepticism about the ability of the government to defend itself against cyberattack. Conducted by the House Government Reform Subcommittee on Technology, the study examined computer security in federal agencies over the course of a year and awarded grades. Scores were based on numerous criteria, including how well an agency trained its employees in security and the extent to which it met established security procedures such as limiting access to privileged data and eliminating easily guessed passwords. More than half the federal agencies surveyed received a grade of D or F. The Department of Homeland Security, which has a division devoted to monitoring cybersecurity, received the lowest overall score of the twenty-four agencies surveyed. Also earning an F was the Justice Department, the agency charged with investigating and prosecuting cases of hacking and other forms of cybercrime. Thirteen agencies improved their scores slightly compared with the previous year, nudging the overall government grade from an F up to a D. Commenting on these results, Rep. Adam H. Putnam (R-Fl.), chairman of the House Government Reform Subcommittee on Technology, declared that "the threat of cyberattack is real. . . . The damage that could be inflicted both in terms of financial loss and, potentially, loss of life is considerable."

Such studies, together with the enormous media interest in the subject, have fueled popular fears about cyberterrorism. A study by the Pew Internet and American Life Project found in 2003 that nearly half of the one thousand Americans surveyed were worried that terrorists could launch attacks through the networks connecting home computers and power utilities. The Pew study found that 11 percent of respondents were "very worried" and 38 percent were "somewhat worried" about an attack launched through computer networks. The survey was taken in early August, before the major blackout struck the Northeast and before several damaging new viruses afflicted computers throughout the country.

## Is the Cyberterror Threat Exaggerated?

Amid all the dire warnings and alarming statistics that the subject of cyberterrorism generates, it is important to remember one simple statistic: so far, there has been no recorded instance of a terrorist cyberattack on U.S. public facilities, transportation systems, nuclear power plants, power grids, or other key components of the national infrastructure. Cyberattacks are common, but they have not been conducted by terrorists and they have not sought to inflict the kind of damage that would qualify them as cyberterrorism.

When U.S. troops recovered al Qaeda laptops in Afghanistan, officials were surprised to find its members more technologically adept than previously believed. They discovered structural and engineering software, electronic models of a dam, and information on computerized water systems, nuclear power plants, and U.S. and European stadiums. But the evidence did *not* suggest that al Qaeda operatives were planning cyberattacks, only that they were using the Internet to communicate and coordinate physical attacks. Neither al Qaeda nor any other terrorist organization appears to have tried to stage a serious cyberattack. For now, the most damaging attacks and intrusions, experts say, are typically carried out either by disgruntled corporate insiders intent on embezzlement or sabotage or by individual hackers—typically young and male—seeking thrills and notoriety. According to a report issued in 2002 by IBM Global Security Analysis Lab, 90 percent of hackers are amateurs with limited technical proficiency, 9 percent are more skilled at gaining unauthorized access but do not damage the files they read, and only 1 percent are highly skilled and intent on copying files or damaging programs and systems. Most hackers, it should be noted, concentrate on writing programs that expose security flaws in computer software, mainly in the operating systems produced by Microsoft. Their efforts in this direction have sometimes embarrassed corporations but have also been responsible for alerting the public and security professionals to major security flaws in software.

Moreover, although there are hackers with the ability to damage systems, disrupt e-commerce, and force websites offline, the vast majority of hackers do not have the necessary skills and knowledge. The ones who do, generally do not seek to wreak havoc. Douglas Thomas, a professor at the University of Southern California, spent seven years studying computer hackers in an effort to understand better who they are and what motivates them. Thomas interviewed hundreds of hackers and explored their "literature." In testimony on July 24, 2002, before the House Subcommittee on Government Efficiency, Financial Management and Intergovernmental Relations, Thomas argued that "with the vast majority of hackers, I would say 99 percent of them, the . 'sk [of cyberterrorism] is negligible for the simple reason that those hackers do not have the skill or ability to organize or execute an attack that would be anything more than a minor inconvenience." His judgment was echoed in *Assessing the Risks of Cyberterrorism, Cyber War, and Other Cyber Threats*, a 2002 report for the Center for Strategic and International Studies, written by Jim Lewis, a sixteen-year veteran of the State and Commerce Departments. "The idea that hackers are going to bring the nation to its knees is too far-fetched a scenario to be taken seriously," Lewis argued. "Nations are more robust than the early analysts of cyberterrorism and cyberwarfare give them credit for. Infastructure systems [are] more flexible and responsive in restoring service than the early analysts realized, in part because they have to deal with failure on a routine basis."

Many computer security specialists believe it is virtually impossible to use the Internet to inflict death on a large scale and scoff at the notion that terrorists would bother trying. The resilience of computer systems to attack, they point out, is no accident but rather the result of significant investments of time, money, and expertise. Nuclear weapons and other sensitive military systems enjoy the most basic form of Internet security. They are "air-gapped," meaning that they are not physically connected to the Internet and are therefore inaccessible to outside hackers. The Defense Department has been particularly vigilant in protecting key systems by isolating them from the Internet and even from the Pentagon's internal computer network. All new software must be submitted to the National Security Agency for security testing.

The 9/11 hijackings understandably led to an outcry that airliners are particularly susceptible to cyberterrorist attacks. In 2002, for instance, Senator Charles Schumer (D-N.Y.) described "the absolute havoc and devastation that would result if cyberterrorists suddenly shut down our air traffic control system, with thousands of planes in mid-flight." In fact, cybersecurity experts give some of their highest marks to the Federal Aviation Authority, which separates its administrative and air traffic control systems. And there is a reason the 9/11 hijackers used box-cutters instead of keyboards: it is impossible to hijack a plane remotely, which eliminates the possibility of a high-tech 9/11 scenario in which planes are used as weapons. Another source of concern is terrorist infiltration of the intelligence agencies. But here, too, the risk is described by Internet experts as slim. The CIA's classified computers are also air-gapped, as is the FBI's entire computer system.

That leaves less-well-protected secondary targets such as power grids, oil pipelines, and dams that do not present opportunities as nightmarish as do nuclear weapons systems but that nonetheless might be used to inflict other forms of mass destruction. Because most of these systems are in the private sector, they tend to be less secure than government systems. In addition, as noted above, companies increasingly use the Internet to manage SCADA systems that control such processes as regulating the flow of oil in pipelines and the level of water in dams. To illustrate the supposed ease with which terrorists could seize control of a dam, a story in the *Washington Post* in June 2003 on al Qaeda cyberterrorism related an anecdote about a twelve-year-old who hacked into the SCADA system at Arizona's Theodore Roosevelt Dam in 1998 and was, according to the article, within mere keystrokes of unleashing millions of gallons of water upon helpless downstream communities. However, a subsequent investigation by the tech-news site CNet.com revealed the tale to be largely apocryphal; investigators concluded that the hacker could not have gained control of the dam and that no lives or property were ever at risk.

To assess the potential threat of cyberterrorism, experts such as Denning suggest that two questions be asked: Are there targets that are vulnerable to cyberattacks? And are there actors with the capability and motivation to carry out such attacks? The answer to the first question is yes: critical infrastructure systems are complex and therefore bound to contain weaknesses that might be exploited, and even systems that seem "hardened" to outside manipulation might be accessed by insiders, acting alone or in concert with terrorists, to cause considerable harm. But what of the second question?

Few people besides a company's own employees possess the specific technical know-how required to run a specialized SCADA system. The most commonly cited example of SCADA exploitation bears this out. In April 2002, an Australian man used an Internet connection to release a million gallons of raw sewage along Queensland's Sunshine Coast after being turned down for a government job. When police arrested him, they discovered that he had worked for the company that designed the sewage treatment plant's control software.

It is possible, of course, that such disgruntled employees might be recruited by terrorist groups, but even if the terrorists did enlist inside help, the degree of damage they could cause would still be limited. As Joshua Green argues in "The Myth of Cyberterrorism" (which appeared in the *Washington Monthly* in November 2002), the employees of companies that handle power grids, oil and gas utilities, and communications are well rehearsed in dealing with the fallout from hurricanes, floods, tornadoes, and other natural disasters. They are also equally adept at containing and remedying problems that stem from human action.

In August 1999, the Center for the Study of Terrorism and Irregular Warfare at the Naval Postgraduate School (NPS) in Monterey, California, issued a report titled *Cyber-terror: Prospects and Implications.*

The report concluded that terrorists generally lack the wherewithal and human capital needed to mount attacks that involve more than annoying but relatively harmless hacks. The study examined five types of terrorist groups: religious, New Age, ethnonationalist separatist, revolutionary, and far-right extremists. Of these, only the religious groups were adjudged likely to seek the capacity to inflict massive damage. Hacker groups, the study determined, are psychologically and organizationally ill suited to cyberterrorism, and any massive disruption of the information infrastructure would run counter to their self-interest.

In October 2000, the NPS group issued a second report, this one examining the decision-making process by which substate groups engaged in armed resistance develop new operational methods, including cyberterrorism. The report concluded that while substate groups may find cyberterror attractive as a nonlethal weapon, terrorists have not yet integrated information technology into their strategy and tactics and that significant barriers between hackers and terrorists may prevent their integration into one group.

Another illustration of the limited likelihood of terrorists launching a highly damaging cyberattack comes from a simulation sponsored by the U.S. Naval War College. The college contracted with a research group to simulate a massive cyberattack on the nation's information infrastructure. Government hackers and security analysts gathered in July 2002 in Newport, R.I., for a war game dubbed "Digital Pearl Harbor." The results were far from devastating: the hackers failed to crash the Internet, although they did cause serious sporadic damage. According to a CNet.com report on the exercise published in August 2002, officials concluded that terrorists hoping to stage such an attack "would require a syndicate with significant resources, including $200 million, country-level intelligence and five years of preparation time."

## CYBERTERRORISM TODAY AND TOMORROW

It seems fair to say that the current threat posed by cyberterrorism has been exaggerated. No single instance of cyberterrorism has yet been recorded; U.S. defense and intelligence computer systems are air-gapped and thus isolated from the Internet; the systems run by private companies are more vulnerable to attack but also more resilient than is often supposed; the vast majority of cyberattacks are launched by hackers with few, if any, political goals and no desire to cause the mayhem and carnage of which terrorists dream. So, then, why has so much concern been expressed over a relatively minor threat?

The reasons are many. First, as Denning has observed, "cyberterrorism and cyberattacks are sexy right now. . . . [Cyberterrorism is] novel, original, it captures people's imagination." Second, the mass media frequently fail to distinguish between hacking and cyberterrorism and exaggerate the threat of the latter by reasoning from false analogies such as the following: "If a sixteen-year-old could do this, then what could a well-funded terrorist group do?" Ignorance is a third factor. Green argues that cyberterrorism merges two spheres—terrorism and technology—that many people, including most lawmakers and senior administration officials, do not fully understand and therefore tend to fear. Moreover, some groups are eager to exploit this ignorance. Numerous technology companies, still reeling from the collapse of the high-tech bubble, have sought to attract federal research grants by recasting themselves as innovators in computer security and thus vital contributors to national security. Law enforcement and security consultants are likewise highly motivated to have us believe that the threat to our nation's security is severe. A fourth reason is that some politicians, whether out of genuine conviction or out of a desire to stoke public anxiety about terrorism in order to advance their own agendas, have played the role of prophets of doom. And a fifth factor is ambiguity about the very meaning of "cyberterrorism," which has confused the public and given rise to countless myths.

Verton argues that "al Qaeda [has] shown itself to have an incessant appetite for modern technology" and provides numerous citations from bin Laden and other al Qaeda leaders to show their recognition of this new cyberweapon. In the wake of the 9/11 attacks, bin Laden reportedly gave a statement to an editor of an Arab newspaper claiming that "hundreds of Muslim scientists were with him who would use their knowledge . . . ranging from computers to electronics against the infidels." Sheikh Omar Bakri Muhammad, a supporter of bin Laden and often the conduit for his messages to the Western world, declared in an interview with Verton, "I would advise those who doubt al Qaeda's interest in cyber-weapons to take Osama bin Laden very seriously. The third letter from Osama bin Laden . . . was clearly addressing using the technology in order to destroy the economy of the capitalist states."

"While bin Laden may have his finger on the trigger, his grandchildren may have their fingers on the computer mouse," remarked Frank Cilluffo of the Office of Homeland Security in a statement that has been widely cited. Future terrorists may indeed see greater potential for cyberterrorism than do the terrorists of today. Furthermore, as Denning argues, the next generation of terrorists is now growing up in a digital world, one in which hacking tools are sure to become more powerful, simpler to use, and easier to access. Cyberterrorism may also become more attractive as the real and virtual worlds become more closely coupled. For instance, a terrorist group might simultaneously explode a bomb at a train station and launch a cyberattack on the communications infrastructure, thus magnifying the impact of the event. Unless these systems are carefully secured, conducting an online operation that physically harms someone may be as easy tomorrow as penetrating a website is today.

Paradoxically, success in the "war on terror" is likely to make terrorists turn increasingly to unconventional weapons such as cyberterrorism. The challenge before us is to assess what needs to be done to address this ambiguous but potential threat of cyberterrorism—but to do so without inflating its real significance and manipulating the fear it inspires. Denning and other terrorism experts conclude that, at least for now, hijacked vehicles, truck bombs, and biological weapons seem to pose a greater threat than does cyberterrorism. However, just as the events of 9/11 caught the world by surprise, so could a major cyberassault. The threat of cyberterrorism may be exaggerated and manipulated, but we can neither deny it nor dare to ignore it.

# 4

# The Grip and Reach of Cyber Terrorism

The FBI defines terrorism as the unlawful use of force or violence against persons or property to intimidate or coerce a government, the civilian population, or any segment thereof, in furtherance of political or social objectives.

Cyber-terrorism could thus be defined as the use of computing resources to intimidate or coerce others. An example of cyber-terrorism could be hacking into a hospital computer system and changing someone's medicine prescription to a lethal dosage as an act of revenge. It sounds far fetched, but these things can and do happen.

## *Why do we care?*

The idea of this site is to both illustrate the importance of understanding the dangers of cyber-terrorism, and provide information that can aid in that understanding.

Computing professionals all over the world need to be aware of possible areas of weakness to such terrorism, in order to better protect their computer systems and possibly help put an end to terrorist activity. An important part of any profession is promoting the good name of that profession, but cyber-terrorist continue to give the computing profession a bad reputation. Thus, it is important for computing professionals to understand cyber-terrorism for the benefit of themselves, their profession, and society as a whole.

## *What is being done?*

In response to heightened awareness of the potential for cyber-terrorism President Clinton, in 1996, created the Commission of Critical Infrastructure Protection. The board found that the combination of electricity, communications and computers are necessary to the survival of the U.S., all of which can be threatened by cyber-warfare. The resources to launch a cyber attack are commonplace in the world; a computer and a connection to the Internet are all that is really needed to wreak havoc. Adding to the problem is that the public and private sectors are relatively ignorant of just how much their lives depend on computers as well as the vulnerability of those computers. Another problem with cyber crime is that the crime must be solved, (i.e. who were the perpetrators and where were they when they attacked you) before it can be decided who has the actual authority to investigate the crime. The board recommends that critical systems should be isolated from outside connection or protected by adequate firewalls, use best practices for password control and protection, and use protected action logs.

Most other government organizations have also formed some type of group to deal with cyber-terrorists. The CIA created its own group, the Information Warfare Center, staffed with 1,000 people and a 24-hour response team. The FBI investigates hackers and similar cases. The Secret Service pursues banking, fraud and wiretapping cases. The Air Force created its own group, Electronic Security Engineering Teams, ESETs. Teams of two to three members go to random Air Force sites and try to gain control of their computers. The teams have had a success rate of 30% in gaining complete control of the systems.

## *How can I protect myself?*

Currently there are no foolproof ways to protect a system. The completely secure system can never be accessed by anyone. Most of the militaries classified information is kept on machines with no outside connection, as a form of prevention of cyber terrorism. Apart from such isolation, the most common method of protection is encryption. The wide spread use of encryption is inhibited by the governments ban on its exportation, so intercontinental communication is left relatively insecure. The Clinton administration and the FBI oppose the export of encryption in favor of a system where by the government can gain the key to an encrypted system after gaining a court order to do so. The director of the FBI's stance is that the Internet was not intended to go unpoliced and that the police need to protect people's privacy and public-safety rights there. Encryption's draw back is that it does not protect the entire system, an attack designed to cripple the whole system, such as a virus, is unaffected by encryption.

Others promote the use of firewalls to screen all communications to a system, including e-mail messages, which may carry logic bombs. Firewall is a relatively generic term for methods of filtering access to a network. They may come in the form of a computer, router other communications device or in the form of a network configuration. Firewalls serve to define the services and access that are permitted to each user. One method is to screen user requests to check if they come from a previously defined domain or Internet Protocol (IP) address. Another method is to prohibit Telnet access into the system.

Here are few key things to remember to pretect yourself from cyber-terrorism:

1. All accounts should have passwords and the passwords should be unusual, difficult to guess.
2. Change the network configuration when defects become know.
3. Check with venders for upgrades and patches.
4. Audit systems and check logs to help in detecting and tracing an intruder.
5. If you are ever unsure about the safety of a site, or receive suspicious email from an unkown address, don't access it. It could be trouble.

Some relavent ethical issues: The ethical issues involved in cyber-terrorism are manifold. Any sort of crime or ethical violation can occur using a computer. Extortion of banks takes money from the banks, as well as their customers. The bank's, on the other hand, which many times refuse to admit to their inadequate defenses violate the public trust that the bank will be secure. The illegal altering medical records is unethical, as it can quickly and easily cause harm to another. Spreading disinformation is unethical in its lack of regard for the truth, as well as for the safety of and consequences on others who believe the misinformation. Altering, destroying, or stealing others data is a violation of their privacy. The ordinary hacker is guilty of lack of regard for the privacy of the peoples systems that he or she would enter. Hacking-for-hire is additionally illicit because they openly sell their services to break into others systems.

## EXAMPLES OF CYBER-TERRORISM

Why would a terrorist decide to use the Internet, rather than using the usual methods of assassination, hostage taking and guerrilla warfare? Part of the problem is that terrorist may come to realize that removing one official from office only causes another to take the officials place, which may not cause the result the terrorist wished to achieve. By using the internet the terrorist can affect much wider damage or change to a country than one could by killing some people. From disabling a countries military defenses to shutting off the power in a large area, the terrorist can affect more people at less risk to him or herself, than through other means.

Cyber terrorism takes many forms. One of the more popular is to threaten a large bank. The terrorists hack into the system and then leave an encrypted message for senior directors, which threatens the bank. In essence, the message says that if they do not pay a set amount of money, then the terrorists will use anything from logic bombs to electromagnetic pulses and high-emission radio frequency guns to destroy the banks files.

What adds to the difficulty to catch the criminals is that the criminals may be in another country. A second difficulty is that most banks would rather pay the money than have the public know how vulnerable they are. Here are some examples of cyber-terroism in its many forms:

**Case 1:** Cyber-terrorists often commit acts of terrorism simply for personal gain. Such a group, known as the Chaos Computer Club, was discovered in 1997. They had created an Active X Control for the Internet that can trick the Quicken accounting program into removing money from a user's bank account. This could easily be used to steal money from users all over the world that have the Quicken software installed on their computer. This type of file is only one of thousands of types of viruses that can do everything from simply annoy users, to disable large networks, which can have disastrous, even life and death, results.

**Case 2:** Cyber-terrorist are many times interested in gaining publicity in any possible way. For example, information warfare techniques like Trojan horse viruses and network worms are often used to not only do damage to computing resources, but also as a way for the designer of the viruses to "show off." This is a serious ethical issue because many people are affected by these cases. For one, the viruses can consume system resources until networks become useless, costing companies lots of time and money. Also, depending on the type of work done on the affected computers, the damage to the beneficiaries of that work could be lethal. Even if the person never meant to harm someone with their virus, it could have unpredictable effects that could have terrible results.

**Case 3:** In one of its more unusual forms, cyber-terrorism can be used for an assassination. In one case, a mob boss was shot but survived the shooting. That night while he was in the hospital, the assassins hacked into the hospital computer and changed his medication so that he would be given a lethal injection. He was dead a few hours later.

They then changed the medication order back to its correct form, after it had been incorrectly administered, to cover their tracks so that the nurse would be blamed for the "accident". There are many ethical issues involved in a case like this. Most obviously, a man was killed by the hackers' actions. Also, the life of the nurse was probably ruined, along with the reputation of the hospital and all its employees. Thus, there are often more stakeholders in a terrorist situation that the immediate recipient of the terrorism.

**Case 4:** Terrorism can also come in the form of disinformation. Terrorists can many times say what they please without fear of reprisal from authorities or of accountability for what they say. In a recent incident, the rumor that a group of people were stealing people's kidneys for sale was spread via the Internet. The rumor panicked thousands of people. This is an ethical issue similar to screaming 'Fire' in a crowded theater. In case like this, the number of people affected is unlimited. Thousands of people were scared by this and could have suffered emotionally.

**Case 5:** Minor attacks come in the form of "data diddling", where information in the computer is changed. This may involve changing medical or financial records or stealing of passwords. Hackers may even prevent users who should have access from gaining access to the machine. Ethical issues in this case include things like invasion of privacy and ownership conflicts. It could be even more serious if, for instance, the person who needed access to the machine was trying to save someone's life in a hospital and couldn't access the machine. The patient could die waiting for help because the computer wouldn't allow the necessary access for the doctor to save his or her life.

## STATISTICS ON CYBER-TERRORISM

### *Who is at risk of an attack?*

Most feel that military installations, power plants, air traffic control centers, banks and telecommunication networks themselves are the most likely targets. Other targets include police, medical, fire and rescue systems, which could be hurt, along with Wall Street, water systems, etc.

### *Who are the terrorists?*

Cyber terrorism does not have to come from the average hacker or even online terrorists. The Govt. carried out a series of its own attacks on itself, in order to test its own defenses against online-based attacks. The Defense Information Security Agency (DISA) found that 88% of the 3000 defense computer systems that were attacked were "easily penetrable". Of the systems that were illegally entered, 96% of the entries were not detected. Of the 4% that were detected, only 5% of them were reported or investigated.

## *How common is unauthorized system entry?*

A survey conducted by the Science Applications International Corp. in 1996 found that 40 major corporations reported losing over $800 million to computer break-ins. An FBI survey of 428 government, corporate and university sites found that over 40% reported having been broken into at least once in the last year. One third said that they had been broken into over the Internet. Another survey found that the Pentagon's systems that contain sensitive, but unclassified information, had been accessed via networks illegally 250,000 times and only 150 of the intrusions were detected. The FBI estimates that U.S. businesses loose $138 million every year to hackers. According to the CIA in the past three years government systems have been illegally entered 250,000.

## Costs of cyber-terrorism

According to a source in Great Britain, terrorists have gained at least up to 400 million pounds from 1993 to 1995 by threatening institutions. Over the three years, there were 40 reported threats made to banks in the U.S. and Britain. In January of 1993, three separate incidents took place in London. During the sixth, a brokerage house paid out 10 million pounds after receiving a threat and one of their machines crashed. On the fourteenth incident, a blue-chip bank paid blackmailers 12.5 million pounds after receiving threats. Another brokerage house paid out 10 million pounds on the twenty-ninth incident. Some terrorists just take money, rather than resorting to blackmail. A Russian hacker, for example, tapped into Citibank's funds transfer system and took $10 million.

# 5

# Cyberterrorism—Fact or Fancy?

## INTRODUCTION

"We are at risk. Increasingly, America depends on computers. They control power delivery, communications, aviation, and financial services. They are used to store vital information, from medical records to business plans to criminal records. Although we trust them, they are vulnerable - to the effects of poor design and insufficient quality control, to accident, and perhaps most alarmingly, to deliberate attack. The modern thief can steal more with a computer than with a gun. Tomorrow's terrorist may be able to do more damage with a keyboard than with a bomb."(1)

Thus began the opening chapter of one of the foundation books in the computer security field. This book, commissioned by the National Academy of sciences, was the product of twenty-one experts in their field and was a proposed blueprint for future computer security in the United States. In the six years since this was written, computers and information technology has exploded. But most people, including those in the computer field, believe the above statement to still be true.

The combination of two of the great fears of the late twentieth century are combined in the term "cyberterrorism". The fear of random, violent victimization segues well with the distrust and outright fear of computer technology. Both capitalize on the fear of the unknown. It is easy to distrust that which one is not able to control.

Terrorism, with it's roots in the periphery of mainstream society, is feared. It is perceived as being random, incomprehensible and uncontrollable. Groups with obscure names and origins impact catastrophically on the innocent. It is, in fact, designed to be feared. That is its real power. Technology is feared from two perspectives. First, it is by definition arcane. It is complex, abstract and indirect in its impact on individuals. Because computers do things that used to be done by humans, there is a natural fear related to a loss of control. People believe, that technology has the ability to become the master, and humanity the servant. The popular press has further fueled the fires by "hyping" the concept of convergence. According to the press, one is lead to believe that all of the functions controlled by individual computers will all converge into a singular system. Further support for this scenario is the increase in "connectivity". Many people conclude that the entire world will soon be controlled by a single computer system. Ironically, these same people subjectively understand that since computers are products of, and operated by, human beings, they are not reliable in either a mechanical or logical sense. Certainly, there can be no doubt as to immense benefits from computer technology. With any technology, be it telephones or automobiles, there are risks. Most risks can be managed. It is the "unmanageable" risks that we fear. This paper will address what the risks and possibilities are of combining terrorism and computers.

## Definitions

Before we can discuss the possibilities of "cyberterrorism, we must have some working definitions. The word "cyberterrorism" refers to two elements: cyberspace and terrorism.

Another word for cyberspace is the "virtual world". Barry Collin defines the virtual world as "symbolic - true, false, binary, metaphoric representations of information - that place in which computer programs function and data moves."

Terrorism is a much used term, with many definitions. For the purposes of this presentation, we will use the United States Department of State definition: "The term 'terrorism' means premeditated, politically motivated violence perpetrated against noncombatant targets by sub national groups or clandestine agents." If we combine these definitions, we construct a working definition such as the following: "Cyberterrorism is the premeditated, politically motivated attack against information, computer systems, computer programs, and data which result in violence against noncombatant targets by sub national groups or clandestine agents." This definition is necessarily narrow. For the term "cyberterrorism" to have any meaning, we must be able to differentiate it from other kinds of computer abuse such as computer crime, economic espionage, or information warfare. I would suggest that the latter is a offensive and defensive function of governments.

## *What is it that computers do?*

In their essential elements computers do three things: they store information, they process information and they communicate. All of the myriad things that we associate with computers are really combinations of these three actions. An even simpler analogy is that a computer is like a box. You can put something into the box. You can take something out of the box (but not something that wasn't already there) and you can manipulate the things in the box. What is surprising to most people is that the computer does not "control". Computers, in and of themselves, do not act. They act either through humans or through devices attached to the computer. This point is important. In order to discuss the role of computers with respect to terrorism, we must understand their limits. Short of electrocuting one's self with the power supply or being so unfortunate as to walk under a falling machine, computers cannot, directly, kill or injure. That is not to say that there are not indirect risks of physical harm, nor direct risks of economic injury. Computers may communicate to other devices that do have physical actions which can cause death or injury. The direct risks of economic injury are perhaps the most significant of all the risks. While computers may be referred to as "weapons", they act indirectly.

## Risks to computer systems

There are several typologies concerning the risks to computer systems. These can be categorized as outcome based or method focused. The latter focuses on the methodologies used to attack systems. The method focused is very useful for evaluating specific targets. It cannot successfully anticipate all technologies and is therefore not very useful for strategic planning. We will apply the outcome based methodology.

Several writers have suggested typologies for outcome-based risk assessment. While they differ in structure, they identify three key risk factors. These can be summarized as: access, integrity, and confidentiality. We shall take a moment to discuss the significance of each of these issues.

Access is the ability of authorized parties to obtain information or cause actions to be taken as specified. That ability to operate the computer or obtain information can be limited or eliminated in several fashions. The information (data), programs (instructions) or the physical device can be destroyed. The computer system can also be interfered with to the extent that the system becomes so unreliable that it is useless. This interference can occur within the computer system's storage and/or processing or with respect to its' communications pathways.

Clifford Stoll, author of the "Cuckoo's Egg", once told this author that the worst thing that could happen to him, as a astro-physicist, was for someone to alter the fifth decimal place of the constant Pi. He reasoned that all of his calculations would be flawed and all of his work would then be useless. This reasoning highlights the reliance that we place on computerized data. If it is not correct, it may be worse than its' destruction. The mantra of the late 20th century is that information is power. This has become a reality. The possession of accurate, timely information is the key to competitive advantage. This is true regardless if you are a superpower government or a small business person. Computers have created new risks (and rewards) concerning the discovery of information which it originator wished to remain confidential. There is an inevitable trade-off between availability and privacy.

I have outlined the risks in the context of information. But, these same risks apply to computers designed for the control of processes. In effect, anything that can happen to information, can happen to processes controlled by computers.

Are these risks being currently being exploited? The answer is an unequivocal yes. Do these exploitation's directly impact the public? Indirectly yes. However, the impact is rarely serious or fatal. Why? The human being has not been taken out of the loop.

## TERRORIST APPLICATIONS FOR COMPUTER SECURITY RISKS

Could these vulnerabilities be utilized by terrorist elements? Certainly. These risks are independent of motive or perpetrator. These risks are structural to the use of computers. Let's examine some commonly presented scenarios.

Collin suggests a number of scenarios. I will discuss several of them. One that he proposes is for a "hacker" to take over the process control computers on a cereal manufacturing line. The subject then alters the amount of iron supplement added to a fatal dose. Boxed cereal then sickens and kills a nation of children.

There are a number of fallacies concerning this script. The quantity of an additive providing nutritional benefit is minimal. The quantity necessary to change s nutritious additive to become toxic is greater by a substantial amount, if it is even possible! Presumably, when the usual quantities of additive run out on the production line, someone will notice the increased consumption. Most food manufacturers conduct routine product testing for just such eventualities. It is a business necessity in this litigious world. It is also likely that the taste of the altered product will be changed, and not for the better. I submit that this may be possible, but the likelihood of success is minimal.

Another commonly offered scenario involves the air traffic system. The world's air traffic control system is highly computerized. The "terrorist" either obtains control of the system or alters the system in such a fashion that airplanes are flown into each other, resulting in mass death.

This scenario requires that the entire human element and the structure of the rules involving the control of aircraft are ignored(9).

The computers used in the air traffic control system do not control anything. They merely provide an aid to the human controller. Even if he/she were deceived by the computer, there is other human beings in the loop. A basic tenant in pilot training is "situational awareness". From the first day of training, pilots are taught to be aware of not only their location, direction and altitude, but those of all other aircraft. Pilots routinely catch errors committed by air traffic controllers. It is the spectacular human failures that result in aircraft collisions. Further, the "rules of the road" for aircraft operations anticipate the complete failure of the air traffic control system. In fact, the rules are designed to work where there is no air traffic control at all! Thousands of flights are conducted each day in bad weather, around the world without the benefit of an ATC system at all!

A similar scenario is proposed concerning the operation of a subway or train system. Brief reflection will show that failures of the electronic and mechanical controls are anticipated. That is why few of these systems are not "manned". It should also be noted that mechanical failures are much more common and catastrophic in nature and affect.

## CONCLUSION

The current state of cyberspace is such that information is seriously at risk. The impact of this risk to the physical health of mankind is, at present, indirect. Computers do not, at present, control sufficient physical processes, without human intervention, to pose a significant risk of terrorism in the classic sense. Therein rest two lessons.

The definition of terrorism needs to address the fundamental infrastructure upon which civilization is increasingly dependent. A proactive approach to protecting information infrastructure is necessary to prevent its becoming a more serious vulnerability.

As we build more and more technology into our civilization, we must ensure that there is sufficient human oversight and intervention to safeguard those whom the technology serves.

# 6

# Cyberterrorism

In 1996, a computer hacker allegedly associated with the White Supremacist movement temporarily disabled a Massachusetts Internet Service Provider and damaged part of the ISP=s record keeping system. The ISP had attempted to stop the hacker from sending out worldwide racist messages under the ISP=s name. The hacker signed off with the threat, "you have yet to see true electronic terrorism. This is a promise."

The hacker apparently never made good on his promise, but the threat of a cyberterrorist attack has many people worried. The highly acclaimed *Computers at Risk* report (1991) from the National Research Council concludes "Tomorrow's terrorist may be able to do more with a keyboard than with a bomb." And *Cybercrime, Cyberterrorims, and Cyberwarfare* (1998) from the Global Organized Crime Project of the Center for Strategic and International Studies in Washington, DC says "Cyberterrorists, acting for rogue states or groups that have declared holy war against the United States, are known to be plotting America's demise as a superpower."

## WHAT IS CYBERTERRORISM?

Cyberterrorism is the convergence of cyberspace and terrorism. It refers to unlawful attacks and threats of attack against computers, networks, and the information stored therein when done to intimidate or coerce a government or its people in furtherance of political or social objectives. Further, to qualify as cyberterrorism, an attack should result in violence against persons or property, or at least cause enough harm to generate fear. Attacks that lead to death or bodily injury, explosions, or severe economic loss would be examples. Serious attacks against critical infrastructures could be acts of cyberterrorism, depending on their impact. Attacks that disrupt nonessential services or that are mainly a costly nuisance would not.

Numerous scenarios have been suggested. In one, a cyberterrorist attacks the computer systems that control a large regional power grid. Power is lost for a sustained period of time and people die. In another, the cyberterrorist breaks into an air traffic control system and tampers with the system. Two large civilian aircraft collide. In a third, the cyberterrorist disrupts banks, international financial transactions, and stock exchanges. Economic systems grind to a halt, the public loses confidence, and destabilization is achieved. While none of these or similar scenarios has played out, many believe it is not a question of "if" but "when."

## TERRORISTS IN CYBERSPACE

Terrorists have moved into cyberspace to facilitate traditional forms of terrorism such as bombings. They use the Internet to communicate, coordinate events, and advance their agenda. While such activity does not constitute cyberterrorism in the strict sense, it does show that terrorists have some competency using the new information technologies.

By 1996, the headquarters of terrorist financier Osama bin Laden in Afghanistan was equipped with computers and communications equipment. Egyptian "Afghan" computer experts were said to have helped devise a communication network that used the Web, e-mail, and electronic bulletin boards. Hamas activists have been said to use chat rooms and e-mail to plan operations and coordinate activities, making it difficult for Israeli security officials to trace their messages and decode their contents. The Revolutionary Armed Forces of Columbia (FARC) uses e-mail to field inquiries from the press.

The Web is especially popular as a medium for reaching a global audience. For example, after the Peruvian terrorist group Tupac Amaru stormed the Japanese Ambassador's residence in Lima on

December 17, 1996 and took 400 diplomatic, political, and military officials as hostage, sympathizers in the United States and Canada put up solidarity Web sites. One site included detailed drawings of the residence and planned assault.

In February 1998, Hizbullah was operating three Web sites: one for the central press office (www.hizbollah.org), another to describe its attacks on Israeli targets (www.moqawama.org), and the third for news and information (www.almanar.com.lb). That month, Clark Staten, executive director of the Emergency Response & Research Institute (ERRI) in Chicago, testified before a U.S. Senate subcommittee that "even small terrorist groups are now using the Internet to broadcast their message and misdirect/misinform the general population in multiple nations simultaneously." He gave the subcommittee copies of both domestic and international messages containing anti-American and anti-Israeli propaganda and threats, including a widely distributed extremist call for "jihad" (holy war) against America and Great Britain.

In June 1998, *U.S. News & World Report* noted that 12 of the 30 groups on the U.S. State Department=s list of terrorist organizations are on the Web. Now, it appears that virtually every terrorist group is on the Web. Forcing them off the Web is impossible, because they can set up their sites in countries with free-speech laws. The government of Sri Lanka, for example, banned the separatist Liberation Tigers of Tamil Eelam, but they have not even attempted to take down their London-based Web site.

Even in democracies, however, there are limits to what terrorists can post on the Net. After a group of anti-abortionists put up a Web site terrorizing doctors who performed abortions, a federal jury ordered the pages be taken down and damages of more than $100 million paid. The Nuremberg Files site had listed the names of about 200 abortion providers under the heading of "baby butchers." Readers were invited to send in such personal details as the doctors' home addresses, license plate numbers, and the names of their children. Three doctors whose names appeared on the list were killed, and after each, the doctor's name was promptly crossed out. Doctors named on the site testified that they lived in constant fear and used disguises, bodyguards, and bulletproof vests. In ordering the site down, the federal jury said the site and "wanted" posters amounted to death threats against the doctors.

Many terrorists are using encryption to conceal their communications and stored files, compounding the difficulties of providing effective counter-terrorism. Hamas, for example, reportedly has used encrypted Internet communications to transmit maps, pictures, and other details pertaining to terrorist attacks. Ramsey Yousef, a member of the international terrorist group responsible for bombing the World Trade Center in 1994 and a Manila Air airliner in late 1995, encrypted files on his laptop computer. The files, which U.S. government officials decrypted, contained information pertaining to further plans to blow up eleven U.S.-owned commercial airliners in the Far East. The Aum Shinrikyo cult, which gassed the Tokyo subway in March 1995, killing 12 people and injuring 6,000 more, also used encryption to protect their computerized records, which included plans and intentions to deploy weapons of mass destruction in Japan and the United States.

## Cyberspace Attacks

Cyberspace is constantly under assault. Cyber spies, thieves, saboteurs, and thrill seekers break into computer systems, steal personal data and trade secrets, vandalize Web sites, disrupt service, sabotage data and systems, launch computer viruses and worms, conduct fraudulent transactions, and harass individuals and companies. These attacks are facilitated with increasingly powerful and easy-to-use software tools, which are readily available for free from thousands of Web sites on the Internet.

Many of the attacks are serious and costly. The ILOVEYOU virus and variants, for example, was estimated to have hit tens of millions of users worldwide and cost billions of dollars in damage. Denial-of-service attacks against Yahoo, CNN, eBay, and other e-commerce Web sites were estimated to have caused over a billion in losses. They also shook the confidence of business and individuals in e-commerce. Governments are particularly concerned with terrorist and state-sponsored attacks against the critical infrastructures that constitute their national life support systems. The Clinton Administration defined eight: telecommunications, banking and finance, electrical power, oil and gas distribution and storage, water supply, transportation, emergency services, and government services.

There have been numerous attacks against these infrastructures. Hackers have invaded the public phone networks, compromising nearly every category of activity, including switching and operations, administration, maintenance, and provisioning (OAM&P). They have crashed or disrupted signal transfer points, traffic switches, OAM&P systems, and other network elements. They have planted "time bomb" programs designed to shut down major switching hubs, disrupted emergency 911 services throughout the eastern seaboard, and boasted that they have the capability to bring down all switches in Manhattan. They have installed wiretaps, rerouted phone calls, changed the greetings on voice mail systems, taken over voice mailboxes, and made free long-distance calls at their victims= expense — sticking some victims with phone bills in the hundreds of thousands of dollars. When they can=t crack the technology, they use "social engineering" to con employees into giving them access.

In March 1997, one teenage hacker penetrated and disabled a telephone company computer that serviced the Worcester Airport in Massachusetts. As a result, telephone service to the Federal Aviation Administration control tower, the airport fire department, airport security, the weather service, and various private airfreight companies was cut off for six hours. Later in the day, the juvenile disabled another telephone company computer, this time causing an outage in the Rutland area. The lost service caused financial damages and threatened public health and public safety. On a separate occasion, the hacker allegedly broke into a pharmacist=s computer and accessed files containing prescriptions.

Banks and financial systems are a popular target of cyber criminals. The usual motive is money, and perpetrators have stolen or attempted to steal tens of millions of dollars. In one case of sabotage, a computer operator at Reuters in Hong Kong tampered with the dealing room systems of five of the company=s bank clients. In November 1996, he programmed the systems to delete key operating system files after a delay long enough to allow him to leave the building. When the "time bombs" exploded, the systems crashed. They were partially restored by the next morning, but it took another day before they were fully operational. However, the banks said the tampering did not significantly affect trading and that neither they nor their clients experienced losses.

In another act of sabotage against a critical infrastructure, a fired employee of Chevron's emergency alert network disabled the firm=s alert system by hacking into computers in New York and San Jose, California, and reconfiguring them so they=d crash. The vandalism was not discovered until an emergency arose at the Chevron refinery in Richmond, California, and the system could not be used to notify the adjacent community of a noxious release. During the 10-hour period in 1992 when the system was down, thousands of people in 22 states and 6 unspecified areas of Canada were put at risk.

An overflow of raw sewage on the Sunshine Coast of Australia in June was linked to a 49-year-old Brisbane man, who allegedly penetrated the Maroochy Shire Council's computer system and used radio transmissions to create the overflows. The man faced 370 charges that included stealing, computer hacking, and use radio communications equipment without authority.

Government computers, particularly Department of Defense computers, are a regular target of attack. Detected attacks against unclassified DoD computers rose from 780 in 1997 to 5,844 in 1998 and 22,144 in 1999.

The most damaging and costly attacks have been conducted for reasons other than the pursuit of terrorism. As the above cases illustrate, they have been motivated by greed, thrills, ego, revenge, and a variety of other non-ideological factors. They are properly classifified as cybercrimes, but not cyberterrorism

## Politically and Socially Motivated Cyberattacks

Terrorism is normally associated with attacks conducted in furtherance of political and social objectives. Numerous cyberattacks have been so motivated. For example, in 1998, ethnic Tamil guerrillas swamped Sri Lankan embassies with 800 e-mails a day over a two-week period. The messages read "We are the Internet Black Tigers and we=re doing this to disrupt your communications." Intelligence authorities characterized it as the first known attack by terrorists against a country=s computer systems.

Also in 1998, Spanish protestors bombarded the Institute for Global Communications (IGC) with thousands of bogus e-mail messages. E-mail was tied up and undeliverable to the San Francisco based ISP=s users, and support lines were tied up with people who couldn=t get their mail. The protestors also spammed IGC staff and member accounts, clogged their Web page with bogus credit card orders, and threatened to employ the same tactics against organizations using IGC services. They demanded that IGC stop hosting the Webs site for the *Euskal Herria Journal*, a New York-based publication supporting Basque independence. Protestors said IGC supported terrorism because a section on the Web pages contained materials on the terrorist group Fatherland and Liberty, or ETA, which claimed responsibility for assassinations of Spanish political and security officials, and attacks on military installations. IGC finally relented and pulled the site because of the "mail bombings."

During the Kosovo conflict in 1999, NATO computers were blasted with e-mail bombs and hit with denial-of-service attacks by hacktivists protesting the NATO bombings. In addition, businesses, public organizations, and academic institutes received highly politicized virus-laden e-mails from a range of Eastern European countries, according to reports. Web defacements were also common. After the Chinese Embassy was accidentally bombed in Belgrade, Chinese hacktivists posted messages such as "We won=t stop attacking until the war stops!" on U.S. government Web sites.

Since December 1997, the Electronic Disturbance Theater (EDT), a New York City based activist group, has been conducting Web sit-ins against various sites in support of the Mexican Zapatistas. At a designated time, thousands of protestors point their browsers to a target site using software that floods the target with rapid and repeated download requests. EDT=s software has also been used by animal rights groups against organizations said to abuse animals. Electrohippies, another group of hacktivists, conducted Web sit-ins against the WTO when they met in Seattle in late 1999. These sit-ins all require mass participation to have much effect, and thus are more suited to use by activists than by relatively small groups of terrorists operating in secrecy.

While the above incidents were motivated by political and social reasons, whether they were sufficiently harmful or frightening to be classified as cyberterrorism is a judgement call. To the best of my knowledge, no attack so far has led to violence or injury to persons, although some may have intimidated their victims. Both EDT and the Electrohippies view their operations as acts of civil disobedience, analogous to street protests and physical sit-ins, not as acts of violence or terrorism. This is an important distinction. Most activists, whether participating in a street march or Web sit-in, are not terrorists.

However, there are a few indications that some terrorist groups are pursuing cyberterrorism, either alone or in conjunction with acts of physical violence. In February 1998, Clark Staten told the Senate Judiciary Committee Subcommittee on Technology, Terrorism, and Government Information that it was believed that "members of some Islamic extremist organizations have been attempting to develop a 'hacker network' to support their computer activities and even engage in offensive information warfare attacks in the future."

In November 1998, the *Detroit News* reported that Khalid Ibrahim, who claimed to be a member of the militant Indian separatist group Harkat-ul-Ansar, had tried to buy military software from hackers who had stolen it from Department of Defense computers they had penetrated. The attempted purchase was discovered when an 18-year-old hacker calling himself Chameleon attempted to cash a $1,000 check from Ibrahim. Chameleon said he did not have the software and did not give it to Ibrahim, but Ibrahim may have obtained it or other sensitive information from one of the many other hackers he approached. Harkat-ul-Ansar declared war on the United States following the August cruise-missile attack on a suspected terrorist training camp in Afghanistan run by bin Laden, which allegedly killed nine of their members.

The Provisional Irish Republican Army employed the services of contract hackers to penetrate computers in order to acquire home addresses of law enforcement and intelligence officers, but the data was used to draw up plans to kill the officers in a single "night of the long knives" if the British government did not meet terms for a new cease-fire. As this case illustrates, terrorists may use hacking as a way of acquiring intelligence in support of physical violence, even if they do not use it to wreak havoc in cyberspace.

Terrorists might also engage in computer network attacks as a way of financing physical operations. For example, they could penetrate an e-commerce Web site and steal credit card numbers, conduct fraudulent transactions against an Internet bank, or extort money from victims by threatening electronic sabotage.

## Potential Threat

To understand the potential threat of cyberterrorism, two factors must be considered: first, whether there are targets that are vulnerable to attack that could lead to violence or severe harm, and second, whether there are actors with the capability and motivation to carry them out.

Looking first at vulnerabilities, several studies have shown that critical infrastructures are potentially vulnerable to cyberterrorist attack. Eligible Receiver, a Ano notice@ exercise conducted by the Department of Defense in 1997 with support from National Security Agency penetration testing teams, found the power grid and emergency 911 systems had weaknesses that could be exploited by an adversary using only publicly available tools on the Internet. Although neither of these systems were actually attacked, study members concluded that service on these systems could be disrupted. Also in 1997, the President=s Commission on Critical Infrastructure Protection issued its report warning that through mutual dependencies and interconnectedness, critical infrastructures could be vulnerable in new ways, and that vulnerabilities were steadily increasing, while the costs of attack were decreasing.

Although many of the weaknesses in computerized systems can be corrected, it is effectively impossible to eliminate all of them.

Even if the technology itself offers good security, it is frequently configured or used in ways that make it open to attack. In addition, there is always the possibility of insiders, acting alone or in concert with other terrorists, misusing their access capabilities. According to Russia=s Interior Ministry Col. Konstantin Machabeli, the state-run gas monopoly, Gazprom, was hit by hackers in 1999 who collaborated with a Gazprom insider. The hackers were said to have used a Trojan horse to gain control of the central switchboard which controls gas flows in pipelines, although Gazprom, the world=s largest natural gas producer and the largest gas supplier to Western Europe, refuted the report.

Consultants and contractors are frequently in a position where they could cause grave harm. This past March, Japan=s Metropolitan Police Department reported that a software system they had procured to track 150 police vehicles, including unmarked cars, had been developed by the Aum Shinryko cult. At the time of the discovery, the cult had received classified tracking data on 115 vehicles. Further, the cult had developed software for at least 80 Japanese firms and 10 government agencies.

They had worked as subcontractors to other firms, making it almost impossible for the organizations to know who was developing the software. As subcontractors, the cult could have installed Trojan horses to launch or facilitate cyberterrorist attacks at a later date. Fearing a Trojan horse of their own, last February, the U.S. State Department sent an urgent cable to about 170 embassies asking them to remove software, which they belatedly realized had been written by citizens of the former Soviet Union.

If we take as given that critical infrastructures are vulnerable to a cyberterrorist attack, then the question becomes whether there are actors with the capability and motivation to carry out such an operation. While many hackers have the knowledge, skills, and tools to attack computer systems, they generally lack the motivation to cause violence or severe economic or social harm. Conversely, terrorists who are motivated to cause violence seem to lack the capability or motivation to cause that degree of damage in cyberspace.

## Future Prospects

In August 1999, the Center for the Study of Terrorism and Irregular Warfare at the Naval Postgraduate School in Monterey, California, issued a report titled "Cyberterror: Prospects and Implications." Their objective was to articulate the demand side of terrorism. Specifically, they assessed the prospects of terrorist organizations pursuing cyberterrorism. They concluded that the barrier to entry for anything beyond annoying hacks is quite high, and that terrorists generally lack the wherewithal and human capital needed to mount a meaningful operation. Cyberterrorism, they argued, was a thing of the future, although it might be pursued as an ancillary tool.

The Monterey team defined three levels of cyberterror capability. First is simple-unstructured: the capability to conduct basic hacks against individual systems using tools created by someone else. The organization possesses little target analysis, command and control, or learning capability.

Second is advanced-structured: the capability to conduct more sophisticated attacks against multiple systems or networks and possibly, to modify or create basic hacking tools. The organization possesses an elementary target analysis, command and control, and learning capability.

Third is complex-coordinated: the capability for a coordinated attacks capable of causing mass-disruption against integrated, heterogeneous defenses (including cryptography). The organization has the ability to create sophisticated hacking tools. They possess a highly capable target analysis, command and control, and organization learning capability.

The Monterey team estimated that it would take a group starting from scratch 2-4 years to reach the advanced-structured level and 6-10 years to reach the complex-coordinated level, although some groups might get there in just a few years or turn to outsourcing or sponsorship to extend their capability.

The study examined five terrorist group types: religious, New Age, ethno-nationalist separatist, revolutionary, and far-right extremists. They determined that only the religious groups are likely to seek the most damaging capability level, as it is consistent with their indiscriminate application of violence. New Age or single issue terrorists, such as the Animal Liberation Front, pose the most immediate threat, however, such groups are likely to accept disruption as a substitute for destruction. Both the revolutionary and ethno-nationalist separatists are likely to seek an advanced-structured capability. The far-right extremists are likely to settle for a simple-unstructured capability, as cyberterror offers neither the intimacy nor cathartic effects that are central to the psychology of far-right terror. The study also determined that hacker groups are psychologically and organizationally ill-suited to cyberterrorism, and that it would be against their interests to cause mass disruption of the information infrastructure.

Thus, at this time, cyberterrorism does not seem to pose an imminent threat. This could change. For a terrorist, it would have some advantages over physical methods. It could be conducted remotely and anonymously, and it would not require the handling of explosives or a suicide mission. It would likely garner extensive media coverage, as journalists and the public alike are fascinated by practically any kind of computer attack. Indeed cyberterrorism could be immensely appealing precisely because of the tremendous attention given to it by the government and media.

Cyberterrorism also has its drawbacks. Systems are complex, so it may be harder to control an attack and achieve a desired level of damage than using physical weapons. Unless people are injured, there is also less drama and emotional appeal. Further, terrorists may be disinclined to try new methods unless they see their old ones as inadequate, particularly when the new methods require considerable knowledge and skill to use effectively.

Terrorists generally stick with tired and true methods. Novelty and sophistication of attack may be much less important than assurance that a mission will be operationally successful. Indeed, the risk of operational failure could be a deterrent to terrorists. For now, the truck bomb poses a much greater threat than the logic bomb.

The next generation of terrorists will grow up in a digital world, with ever more powerful and easy-to-use hacking tools at their disposal. They might see greater potential for cyberterrorism than the terrorists of today, and their level of knowledge and skill relating to hacking will be greater. Hackers and insiders might be recruited by terrorists or become self-recruiting cyberterrorists, the Timothy McVeigh=s of cyberspace. Some might be moved to action by cyber policy issues, making cyberspace an attractive venue for carrying out an attack. Cyberterrorism could also become more attractive as the real and virtual worlds become more closely coupled, with a greater number of physical devices attached to the Internet. Some of these may be remotely controlled. Terrorists, for example, might target robots used in telesurgery. Unless these systems are carefully secured, conducting an operation that physically harms someone may be easy as penetrating a Web site is today.

Although the violent pursuit of political goals using exclusively electronic methods is likely to be at least a few years into the future, the more general threat of cybercrime is very much a part of the digital landscape today. In addition to cyberattacks against digital data and systems, many people are being terrorized on the Internet today with threats of physical violence. On-line stalking, death threats, and hate messages are abundant. These crimes are serious and must be addressed. In so doing, we will be in a better position to prevent and respond to cyberterrorism if and when the threat becomes more serious.

## CYBER TERRORISM: MASS DESTRUCTION OR MASS DISRUPTION?

Just days after the September 11 terrorist attacks the U.S. Federal Bureau of Investigation began warning the public that the potential for future attacks exist, and among the threats was that of cyber terrorism. The concept is not a new one, such attacks have been taking place between Palestinian and Israeli groups, and between U.S. and Chinese sources, in response to political conflicts. And now, in light of new terrorism and cyber exclusions in insurance policies, commercial insurance buyers are wondering how to protect themselves from the potential threat of today's "hacktivists" becoming tomorrow's cyber terrorists, and weapons of mass disruption turning into weapons of mass destruction.

February 2002 - Al-Qaida, (the notorious terrorist group formed by Osama bin Laden, has not engaged in computer-based attacks in the past. However, in the wake of the World Trade Center (WTC) attacks, bin Laden has suggested that Al-Qaida has the expertise to use computer technology as a weapon, reports Canada's Office of Critical Infrastructure Protection and Emergency Preparedness (OCIPEP).

In response to reports from the FBI about the potential threat of cyber attacks in the wake of September 11, OCIPEP began issuing such advisories, and notes that "retaliatory cyber attacks" against coalition countries, primarily in the form of website defacements had already begun. In late November, the Canadian government helped draft the Council of Europe's Convention on Cybercrime, an international effort to deal with issues of terrorist financing, money laundering and cyber terrorism.

The September 11 terrorist attacks changed perceptions of the world's security infrastructure, and the insurance industry's understanding of risk. What had once been inconceivable was now reality and so began the process of imagining the unimaginable in terms of catastrophic risks. Cyber terrorism, a heretofore unconsidered threat, was suddenly put on the world stage amongst a host of new potential threats.

## Digital Pearl Harbor

When the U.S. government's new cyber terrorism expert, Richard Clarke, suggested the possibility of a "digital Pearl Harbor", he was greeted with skepticism. The concept of one, large-scale attack on the Internet seems far-reaching, despite the claims of Al Qaida and other Muslim extremist groups who claim to, or are known to, use the Internet as a tool. *That said, there is ample evidence that politically motivated hack attacks are on the rise, notes DK Matai, chairman and CEO of the mi2g intelligence unit, which deals in cyber security.*

Tensions between the U.S. and China following the accidental bombing of the Chinese Embassy in Belgrade led to a cyber conflict.

In the U.S., key government sites, including the Energy Department, the Interior Department and even the White House were targeted. The Chinese domain, ".cn", and that of Taiwan, ".tw", became the two most defaced domains behind ".com" last year. India (.in) and Pakistan (.pk) saw similar increases in the number of web site defacements due to political tensions (see Charts 1 and 2).

Following NATO air attacks on Serbia in 1999, hackers began to tap into U.S. defense computers and those of other defense related businesses. And, since September 11, several high profile U.S. government sites have been defaced, some bearing the Saudi flag and threatening messages aimed at the U.S. The groups involved, sometimes called "cyber mujihadeens", have hit sites including the U.S. Army Waterways Experiment Station and the National Institute of Health's Human Genome Project.

***Striking at .ca:*** Canada is not immune to the cyber threat, experts say. *Matai points out that the ".ca" domain experienced a similar increase in defacements last year, with 215 hits, up from 59 in 2000 and 52 in 1999. He notes that many Canadian sites bear the ".com" domain, as well as ".org" and ".net", also popular targets. Hits are similarly not aimed solely at government sites, he adds. "Admittedly there is some bias of attacks towards high profile sites such as whitehouse.gov or fbi.gov, however more and more attacks are on commercial web sites."*

"The 11 September attack had an even deeper ripple effect: the temporary disruption of the entire U.S. financial and transportation infrastructure," notes the OCIPEP report. "If the terrorists did not fully anticipate these aftershocks, they can see them clearly now. This raises the possibility that those responsible may shift their sights away from primarily symbolic targets, such as heavily populated buildings or sports stadiums, toward critical infrastructures."

*There are about 10,000 "serious grade crackers" using original code attack systems, as opposed to what Matai calls "script-kiddies", or hackers who rely on ready-made tools. "In terms of defacement attacks on large corporations, attackers penetrate the systems as multi-level attacks using subterfuge and social engineering," he explains.* Criticisms of lax electronic security are still being heard, despite the growing awareness created by large-scale attacks such as the "I Love You" and "Melissa" viruses, and worms like "Nimda" and "Code Red". Criticisms of lax electronic security are still being heard, despite the growing awareness created by large-scale attacks such as the "I Love You" and "Melissa" viruses, and worms like "Nimda" and "Code Red".

"My own opinion is that the potential is there [for cyber terrorists to attack], everyone's networks are so poorly protected, but no one has taken advantage of it," says Chuck Wilmink, director of the Canadian Center for Information Technology Security (CCITS).

A study by the U.S.-based Computer Security Institute reports that 85% of companies admit to having their networks breached in 2000, and 64% acknowledge significant financial losses due to those breaches. A recent report by the U.S. Congress gave two-thirds of American's federal agencies failing grades in cyber security, including the departments of Defense, Justice, Energy and Treasury.

Similarly, in Canada, a 1999 Senate report pointed to the potential for a major cyber attack in Canada, and admitted that the FBI has characterized Canada as a "hacker haven". Perhaps fortunately, Canada is more often a base for hackers to attack other countries, rather than a target itself. "Canadian hackers have traditionally tended to attack outside of Canada as opposed to within," says Matai. He notes that Canada's quieter political demeanor means that it is less often viewed as a target. ".ca Canadian sites are less vulnerable than .com or .uk because Canada is not seen to be so aggressive on the world stage."

"I really don't think we've ever considered Canada to be at the same threat level (as the U.S.)," says Max London, manager of public affairs for OCIPEP. However, OCIPEP has issued the FBI warnings post-September 11, giving companies advance warning in the event of a cyber attack. Ultimately, London explains, corporations are responsible for their own security systems.

He notes that OCIPEP is aware of "hacktivist" activity in Canada, specifically "around some of the larger meetings", such as the G-8 Summit or World Trade Organization meetings. However, these are a far cry from the threat by a foreign government or terrorist organization that might harm Canada's critical infrastructure, including systems that support communications, transportation and services such as health care and finance. With the "increasing dependence and increasing interconnectivity" of such systems comes a greater risk, however. In the past, OCIPEP has been involved in public awareness campaigns around threats including the "Code Red" worm, which was viewed as "a very real threat to the Internet", and has worked with the U.S. National Infrastructure Protection Center (NIPC), an FBI operation, to disseminate infornation. The NPIC issued warnings in mid-October of a potential cyber threat aimed at the U.S. power grid, and yet another aimed at online financial sites.

## Insurer Reaction

Canada's insurers have been jumping into the terrorism risk fray since September 11, trying to understand what exposures they might face in the future. Just as no one predicted the events that represent the largest insurance loss in history, there is fear of what other unforeseen risks may lie ahead.

As insurers met through the Insurance Bureau of Canada's (IBC) terrorism task force to discuss the new risk horizon, cyber threats were one possibility on the table, says Anne MacKenzie, assistant vice president, claims technical, at the Dominion of Canada General Insurance Company and a member of the task force. She adds, however, that they did not top the list of concerns for several reasons, including the notion that terrorists generally tend towards visible, high profile acts. "It's usually physical acts of terrorism," she says. "Terrorists like to put the population at fear." OCIPEP also notes that terrorists have traditionally relied on "bombs over bytes" as the weapon of choice.

Cyber terrorism has not dominated discussion of electronic risks, adds Jennifer Soper, assistant vice president, technology, at St. Paul Canada. Most of the talk seems centered around the major viruses that have plagued companies. This is partly because many companies do not see themselves as targets for such acts. "When you're not in the Fortune 500 or brand name companies, you can get an 'it can't happen to me', almost false sense of security."

She adds that companies often do not discuss the nature of attacks, and still have a "keep it in the closet" attitude about cyber security breaches. The benefit is that this policy of silence denies attackers the desired result of publicity. However, terrorists may soon find that cyber attacks will gain them the same kind of notoriety as physical attacks, MacKenzie adds. "Nothing would scare people more than to learn that terrorists had hacked into government sites".

## Exclusions, Exclusions

Commercial insurance buyers are no doubt facing a tough market in the post-September 11 era, although the situation was already beginning to grow bleak prior to the terrorist attacks. Reinsurers had already stated their intention to introduce cyber exclusions into their treaties, leaving insurers to follow suit.

However, insurers assert that cyber or "data" coverage was never really part of commercial general liability (CGL) policies. In light of the potential for differing interpretations (such as the U.S. case of Ingram v. Micro, where it was found that business interruption due to computer failure should be included in CGL policies), more specific wording was added to most policies. "The data exclusion was just a clarification to make sure consumers knew what they were buying, there never was coverage for data," explains MacKenzie. This clarification is apparent in most policies as of yearend 2001, adds Dominion president George Cooke. "Our view is that the wordings don't do anything the old wordings didn't do, they're just clearer."

However, the wordings have left many companies scrambling for coverage, Soper says. "What is available is not widely available." Companies will either have to negotiate coverage as a limited buy-back option in existing policies, or hunt it down as a separate policy from another carrier. "In terms of coverage, if there is anything going on it is on a customer-by-customer level. It has to be." Given the difficulty in quantifying cyber risks, there is no "one size fits all" policy.

Cooke says he is concerned with the lack of cyber coverage available, but acknowledges that insurers simply are not in a position to offer it. "It's a situation that troubles me. But we can't buy coverage [in the reinsurance market], so it's impossible for us to offer it."

September 11 did not help the situation either. He predicts that notwithstanding the terrorist attacks, cyber coverage would have been a top issue for insurers, but given the shift in priorities, insurers were unable to come up with private market capital solutions in advance of yearend commercial policy renewals. "September 11 kind of eclipsed concerns over whether we should be developing new products to deal with cyber risks," says MacKenzie. However, she adds, "we will want to revisit it" in the future.

## Overriding Concern

Regardless of new cyber covers, with the current terrorism exclusions being written, any act deemed as "cyber terrorism" would not be covered, as the terrorism exclusion would be overriding. In the wake of September 11, with reinsurers refusing to cover terrorism in their treaties, insurers were forced to either introduce similar exclusions in their policies or to negotiate a deal with the government, which would act as excess of loss reinsurer through a "terrorism pool" arrangement.

By yearend, no such pool had been devised, despite lengthy discussions between IBC representatives and the government. "The nature of the discussions evolved as the market evolved," says Cooke, who is also chair of the IBC. "The decision was taken to wait. It was probably a smart decision."

The U.S. government's inability to come to a solution prior to breaking at the end of the year was among the contributing factors. Cooke recognizes that it was "politically difficult" for the Canadian government to come forward with a solution before the U.S., given the fact that the situation was not of the same scale here. This situation may change as the U.S. House reconvenes in late January. "People have said that the government wasn't prepared to act, but I don't buy that," he adds. "Minister Peterson and the staff in Finance were seriously engaged in discussions and are prepared to act if the need arises."

The need for a solution may not be quite as pressing as originally thought, with renewals moving along despite the lack of a solution, and the fact that many commercial policies on target risks have not yet reached renewal.

However, Cooke still feels a solution is needed. The government has consulted with other associations, most notably the Canadian Bankers Association (CBA), who claim that there is no need for the coverage. "I think they're wrong," Cooke says, but their resistance makes it difficult for insurers to press for a solution. He is most displeased with the view that insurers are looking for a "bail out". "We are not doing an 'Air Canada' here. We're more than prepared to take our pains for our past sins." But without reinsurance coverage in place, it is not economically feasible for insurers to offer the coverage.

The terrorism task force was "driven by the sudden recognition that there was now infinite risk and infinite exposure and that wasn't economically sustainable," says MacKenzie. "It [terrorism coverage] isn't anything we could write even if we wanted to."

With no cap on the exposure, insurers would be leaving themselves open to unquantifiable risks, a situation that extends into the domain of cyber terrorism.

"Putting a box around the exposure" or quantifying the risk is especially difficult with cyber risks, says Soper.. "The 'net is worldwide. It is difficult to know where it (an attack) is going to come from, and how it's going to come."

She adds, "It's hard when you're an industry that likes to put dollars and cents to things. There's just no history. You can't go into the archives and pluck out something and say 'this is going to work for me today'." September 11 was a "humbling" experience for the industry, says MacKenzie, and as the industry learns more about that event, "we realize we don't know about all the risks". Prior to September 11 "there was a sense that we could talk about 100-year events and worst case scenarios...everyone's trying to come up with scenarios, however, the end of the conversation always comes to the same conclusion, we just can't imagine."

*Web Site Defacements, 2001 (increase over 2000)*

| Location | Domain | Number Incidents | Percentage Increase |
|---|---|---|---|
| Canada | .ca | 215 | 265 |
| China | .cn | 1298 | 1326 |
| Taiwan | .tw | 1355 | 1178 |
| Israel | .il | 413 | 220 |
| India | .in | 250 | 205 |
| pakistan | .pk | 72 | 300 |
| UK government | .gov.uk | 43 | 378 |
| UK organisations | .org.uk | 25 | 400 |
| UK companies | .co.uk | 385 | 181 |
| US government | .gov.com | 248 | 37 |
| US military | .mil.com | n/a | 128 |

# 7

# The Future of Cyberterrorism: Where the Physical and Virtual Worlds Converge

## TERRORISM TO CYBERTERRORISM

The definition of "terrorism" has been well studied, defined, and documented. There is also a degree of understanding of the meanings of *CyberTerrorism*, either from the popular media, other secondary sources, or personal experience. This paper examines the future of CyberTerrorism - a term the author coined a decade ago, as the indicia of technological dependence and frailty were forming in our New World disOrder. Indeed, that future has come to fruition, today.

The face of terrorism is changing. While the motivations remain the same, we are now facing new and unfamiliar weapons. The intelligence systems, tactics, security procedures and equipment that were once expected to protect people, systems, and nations, are powerless against this new, and very devastating weapon. Moreover, the methods of counter-terrorism that our world's specialists have honed over the years are ineffectual against this enemy. Because, this enemy does not attack us with truckloads of explosives, nor with briefcases of Sarin gas, nor with dynamite strapped to the bodies of fanatics. This enemy attacks us with one's and zero's, at a place we are most vulnerable: the point at which the *physical* and *virtual* worlds converge. Let us first define theses two domains.

## The Physical World

The physical world is matter and energy - light, dark, hot and cold, all physical matter - that place in which we live and function.

## The Virtual World

The virtual world is symbolic - true, false, binary, metaphoric representations of information - that place in which computer programs function and data moves.

The physical and virtual worlds are inherently disparate worlds. It is now the intersection, the convergence, of these two worlds that forms the vehicle of CyberTerrorism, the new weapon that we face.

## Reliance and Dependence

This convergence of the physical and virtual worlds, this lattice, is growing larger and more complex as we venture further into technological dependence. Each day, we move ahead with blinding speed into the computerization of every task and process that we face. We are becoming ever more inextricably reliant and dependent on the convergence of these two worlds.

## Points of Convergence

What are some of the more obvious points of convergence?

- A garage door opener.
- A heart pacemaker.
- The computer chip in a late model car.
- A microwave oven.

These are all things taken for granted. Yet, as we progress into a far more technological world, what other points of convergence are taken for granted?

- Food processing plants
- Pharmaceutical processing plants
- Electric and natural gas utilities
- Train crossings and traffic control systems
- Next generation air traffic control systems
- Virtually all modern military equipment

- Military and public safety communications
- Civilian communications

## Convergence Drivers

What is driving the convergence of these two worlds? There are three goals:

1. Access: the goal of universal, ubiquitous interface;
2. Control: the goal of remote administration; and
3. Mining: the goal of knowledge acquisition.

## Convergence Vehicles

To achieve these goals, there are four vehicles:

- Transmission: longer lines across land and through space;
- Connections: more links to more points;
- Aggregation: more information centralized, and disconnected information linked; and
- Retrieval: more ways of retrieving information, and more importantly, knowledge.

## Achieving CyberTerrorist Goals

So how does a CyberTerrorist achieve his mission? Like any terrorist, a CyberTerrorist actively exploits the goals of the target population in areas in which they take for granted. There are three potential acts in CyberTerrorism at the point of convergence:

1.Destruction;

2.Alteration; and

3.Acquisition and retransmission (these are a unit).

As we will see, these three types of acts are most heinous at the point where the physical and virtual worlds converge.

To achieve a true terrorist goal, as we know, we must have *scale* and *publicity*. So how does the CyberTerrorist approach a new age - an age of convergence of the physical and virtual worlds? An age where, thanks to our goals, he can perform his CyberTerrorist act's from his living room, undetected, from 8,000 kilometers away?

## Cracker or CyberTerrorist?

A great deal of "cracks" are committed for the purposes of anarchy, humor, or as often stated by the perpetrators, "to be annoying." However, is this the mindset of a CyberTerrorist? Does the CyberTerrorist make a garage door go up and down? Does he change an Internet web site to say a country's government is evil? Does he hack into a major corporation's voice mail system to make long distance calls? No - that is not the domain of the CyberTerrorist - that is the domain of the amateur cracker community that exists worldwide.

A CyberTerrorist's mindset is quite different. A CyberTerrorist would not alter a voice mail, or even abuse credit cards.

## Potential CyberTerrorist Acts

Let us examine some example CyberTerrorist acts. Based on the definitions of terrorism, a determination can be made if they in fact constitute terrorism:

- A CyberTerrorist will remotely access the processing control systems of a cereal manufacturer, change the levels of iron supplement, and sicken and kill the children of a nation enjoying their food. That CyberTerrorist will then perform similar remote alterations at a processor of infant formula. The key: the CyberTerrorist does not have to be at the factory to execute these acts.
- A CyberTerrorist will place a number of computerized bombs around a city, all simultaneously transmitting unique numeric patterns, each bomb receiving each other's pattern. If bomb one stops transmitting, all the bombs detonate simultaneously. The keys: 1) the CyberTerrorist does not have to be strapped to any of these bombs; 2) no large truck is required; 3) the number of bombs and urban dispersion are extensive; 4) the encrypted patterns cannot be predicted and matched through alternate transmission; and 5) the number of bombs prevents disarming them all simultaneously. The bombs *will* detonate.
- A CyberTerrorist will disrupt the banks, the international financial transactions, the stock exchanges. The key: the

people of a country will lose all confidence in the economic system. Would a CyberTerrorist attempt to gain entry to the Federal Reserve building or equivalent? Unlikely, since arrest would be immediate. Furthermore, a large truck pulling along side the building would be noticed. However, in the case of the CyberTerrorist, the perpetrator is sitting on another continent while a nation's economic systems grind to a halt. Destabilization *will* be achieved.

- A CyberTerrorist will attack the next generation of air traffic control systems, and collide two large civilian aircraft. This is a realistic scenario, since the CyberTerrorist will also crack the aircraft's in-cockpit sensors. Much of the same can be done to the rail lines.
- A CyberTerrorist will remotely alter the formulas of medication at pharmaceutical manufacturers. The potential loss of life is unfathomable.
- The CyberTerrorist may then decide to remotely change the pressure in the gas lines, causing a valve failure, and a block of a sleepy suburb detonates and burns. Likewise, the electrical grid is becoming steadily more vulnerable.

In effect, the CyberTerrorist will make certain that the population of a nation will not be able to eat, to drink, to move, or to live. In addition, the people charged with the protection of their nation will not have warning, and will not be able to shut down the terrorist, since that CyberTerrorist is most likely on the other side of the world.

Sadly, these examples are not science fiction. All of these scenarios can be executed today. As you may know, some of these incidents already have occurred in various nations. More of such acts will take place tomorrow. Are you prepared?

## CyberTerrorists: Who, Where, and Why?

The purpose of this paper is to help you understand the threats that exist, and hopefully, to help you prevent these types of atrocities. But know this - there are people out there with very different goals, who are our real threats, and who are, or will be, attacking us. Make no mistake, *the threats are real, today.* Who are the CyberTerrorists? There a great many poor movies and too many works of fiction about the hacker and cracker communities. In the popular media, there recently was the Kevin Mitnick incident, where one cracker broke into another cracker's systems. This spawned endless press and at least two best selling books. While this incident received much attention, the events amounted to meaningless children's games.

By and large, the cracker community, based primarily in the United States, Europe, the Middle East, Asia, and in the nations of the former Soviet Union, is composed of individuals who see the cracking process merely as a challenge, a brain teaser, a puzzle. They view themselves as not only being innocent of any crime, but perhaps even doing something righteous, something to counter the dark monoliths of the corporate and government worlds. They believe they are being persecuted. These individuals believe that what they are doing is not doing any true damage. At its least harmful, these crackers just look at information. However, privacy issues and military secrecy can render such infiltrations acts of terror.

Sometimes crackers make minor changes, just for fun, to be annoying, or to make a statement. The potential for damage here is enormous.

## Crackers as Facilitators

Individuals with a background in intelligence are aware that a frequent element of case execution is enlisting the indigenous, sometimes called "facilitators," to assist in a campaign. At the convergence of the physical and virtual worlds, the indigenous are the crackers. There is the incorrect assumption in the cracking community that they, the crackers, are so sophisticated or so knowledgeable as to know when they are being approached for a truly illicit reason (e.g., to be enlisted as a facilitator to commit an act of terrorism). However, despite cracker arrogance, these individuals are easy targets for enlistment.

What about those crackers who actively *wish* to cross the line, or more basically, need money? To a teenager, a $1,000 U.S. can purchase a good many compact disks, a new modem, and a great deal of libation. Beyond youths, there are professionals in this arena as well.

Historically, individuals engaged in the practice of terror tended not to be people working upon a computer 20 hours per day. Terrorists have not been in the business of tracking the latest holes found in UNIX or an obscure government telnet opportunity. There *are* people, however, who are in that business - for illicit as well as good cause. As stated, just as indigenous people may be turned into soldiers, so can crackers be turned into CyberTerrorists. Sometimes such a transition may be motivated by money or prestige. Usually, this transition will occur without the cracker's cognizance. The potential threat from such transitions is mind boggling, considering the damage even one mis-directed cracker can cause.

Further, as young, educated people are brought into the folds of terrorist groups, this new generation will have the talent to execute the acts of CyberTerrorism of which we have spoken.

We are going to see increasing levels of in-house expertise, and concomitant exponential increases CyberTerrorism. Unlike other methods of terrorism, CyberTerrorism is safe and profitable, and difficult to counter without the right expertise and understanding of the CyberTerrorist's mind. Combine our increasing vulnerability, with the explosive increases in the level of violence, and increasing expertise available inside terrorist organizations through new blood and outside through facilitators, and we can see that at the point where the physical and virtual worlds converge, the old models of managing terrorism are obsolete.

## Methods of Protection: No Easy Answers

We must consider the following elements when building a counter-CyberTerrorist program:

- We must accept that while the theories of terrorism stand true, the way in which we approach counter-terrorism, in this case, counter-CyberTerrorism, must change.
- We must cooperate and share intelligence in ways we have never have before.

- We must enlist the assistance of those individuals who understand the weapons we are facing and have experienced fighting these wars.
- We must learn the new rules, the new technologies, and the new players.

Unfortunately, one cannot learn how to fight this very unconventional warfare from someone who hasn't been there, nor from someone whose experience is in the old ways and old technologies. The old data processing, auditing, and computer security models in use today are obsolete. On this battlefield, against this weapon, the terrorist is already far ahead. The building of a counter-CyberTerrorist team *must* be real-time and dynamic, as the weapons will continually change, to morph, in an attempt to beat you, your systems, and your people. There is no re-machining, and unlike other terrorists, if the CyberTerrorist loses today, he does not die - he learns what did not work, and will use that information against you tomorrow.

## CONCLUSION

If a computer security advisor states that you, your organization, and your country are safe behind firewalls, behind a system put into place by people who have never fought cyberbattles, behind audit trails, passwords, and encryption, then a great and dangerous fallacy (or fantasy) is being perpetrated upon you. The only solution is the quick deployment of a counter-CyberTerrorist - someone who knows what you are up against today, someone who lives in the world of the people who are, and will be, attacking - someone who can train the people who must fight the battles.

## Ex Post Facto

An effective auditing system will only inform the target manager that they have taken a hit; perhaps a fatal hit. By that point, it is too late. *Now* is the time to take action. Unfortunately, due to this open nature of this document, specific counter-CyberTerrorism measures cannot be discussed. Those discussions must be reserved for secured facilities.

Counter-terrorists of all backgrounds are duty-bound to save property, and more importantly, save lives. However, we are not isolated. We are all increasingly connected, dependent, and vulnerable. The very basic things we take for granted (e.g., food, medicine, energy, air, freedom of movement, communications, freedom from violence) are being threatened by the new weapon of CyberTerrorism.

If we do not work together, *we* will be responsible for the outcome. If we fail to be ready when and where the virtual and physical worlds converge, then all that will be left is terror - in one's and zero's.

## ASSESSING THE RISKS OF CYBER TERRORISM, CYBER WAR AND OTHER CYBER THREATS

Cyber-warfare conjures up images of information warriors unleashing vicious attacks against an unsuspecting opponent's computer networks, wreaking havoc and paralyzing nations. This a frightening scenario, but how likely is it to occur? What would the effects of a cyber attack be on a potential opponent?

Cyber attacks, network security and information pose complex problems that reach into new areas for national security and public policy. This paper looks at one set of issues – those related to cyber-terrorism and cyber attacks on critical infrastructure and their implications for national security. Cyber-terrorism is "the use of computer network tools to shut down critical national infrastructures (such as energy, transportation, government operations) or to coerce or intimidate a government or civilian population." The premise of cyber terrorism is that as nations and critical infrastructure became more dependent on computer networks for their operation, new vulnerabilities are created – "a massive electronic Achilles' heel." A hostile nation or group could exploit these vulnerabilities to penetrate a poorly secured computer network and disrupt or even shut down critical functions.

Much of the literature on cyber-terrorism assumes that the vulnerability of computer networks and the vulnerability of critical infrastructures are the same, and that these vulnerabilities put national security at a significant risk. Given the newness of computer network technology and the rapidity with which it spread into economic activity, these assumptions are not surprising. A closer look at the relationships between computer networks and critical infrastructures, their vulnerability to attack, and the effect on national security, suggests that the assumption of vulnerability is wrong. A full reassessment is outside the scope of this paper, but a brief review suggests that while many computer networks remain very vulnerable to attack, few critical infrastructures are equally vulnerable.

A reassessment of the cyber threat has four elements. First, we need to put cyber-warfare and cyber-terrorism in the historical context of attacks against infrastructure. Strategies that emphasize attacks on critical civil infrastructures have discussed for more than eighty years. Second, we need to examine cyber attacks against a backdrop of routine infrastructure failures. There is extensive data on power outages, flight delays and communications disruptions that occur normally and the consequences of these routine failures can be used to gage the effect cyber-warfare and cyber-terrorism. Third, we need to measure the dependence of infrastructure on computer networks and the redundancy already present in these systems. Finally, for the case of cyber-terrorism, we must consider the use of cyber-weapons in the context of the political goals and motivations of terrorists, and whether cyber-weapons are likely to achieve these goals. A preliminary review of these factors suggests that computer network vulnerabilities are an increasingly serious business problem but that their threat to national security is overstated. Modern industrial societies are more robust than they appear at first glance. Critical infrastructures, especially in large market economies, are more distributed, diverse, redundant and self-healing than a cursory assessment may suggest, rendering them less vulnerable to attack. In all cases, cyber attacks are less effective and less disruptive than physical attacks. Their only advantage is that they are cheaper and easier to carry out than a physical attack.

## Infrastructure as Target

Cyber-terrorism is not the first time a new technology has been seized upon as creating a strategic vulnerability. While the match between theories of cyber-warfare and air power is not precise, a comparison of the two is useful. In reaction to the First World War, European strategists like Douhet and Trenchard argued that aerial bombing attacks against critical infrastructure well behind the front lines would disrupt and cripple an enemies' capacity to wage war. Their theories were put to the test by the U.S. Army and Royal Air Forces during World War II in strategic bombing campaigns aimed at destroying electrical power, transportation and manufacturing facilities. Much of the first tranche of literature on cyber attacks resembles in many ways (and owes an unspoken debt to) the early literature on strategic bombing.

A key document for understanding how attacks on infrastructure affect societies is the Strategic Bombing Survey conducted by the United State during and after World War II. During the war, Britain and America launched thousands of heavy bombers that dropped millions of tons of high explosives on Germany, seeking to cripple its infrastructure, destroy its industrial base and break the will of the population to continue the war. Early theorists of air warfare had predicted that such an onslaught would paralyze or cripple the target. What the survey found, however, is that industrial societies are impressively resilient. Industrial production actually increased for two years under the bombing and it was not until ground forces occupied Germany that resistance ceased:

> As the air offensive gained in tempo, the Germans were unable to prevent the decline and eventual collapse of their economy. Nevertheless, the recuperative and defensive powers of Germany were immense; the speed and ingenuity with which they rebuilt and maintained essential war industries in operation clearly surpassed Allied expectations. Germany resorted to almost every means an ingenious people could devise to avoid the attacks upon her economy and to minimize their effects….
>
> The mental reaction of the German people to air attack is significant. Under ruthless Nazi control, they showed surprising resistance to the terror and hardships of repeated air attack, to the destruction of their homes and belongings, and to the conditions under which they were reduced to live. Their morale, their belief in ultimate victory or satisfactory compromise, and their confidence

in their leaders declined, but they continued to work efficiently as long as the physical means of production remained.... The U.S. found similar results from aerial bombardment during the Vietnam War. Counter-intuitively, the effect of aerial attack was often to harden and increase popular support for continued resistance. The advent of nuclear weapons (and perhaps large precision-guided munitions) gave air power the ability to disrupt civil infrastructures needed to achieve the visions of Douhet, Trenchard or Mitchell, but cyber attacks do not pose the same level of lethality.

One of the Strategic Bombing Survey's conclusions was that "The German experience showed that, whatever the target system, no indispensable industry was permanently put out of commission by a single attack. Persistent re-attack was necessary." However, cyber attacks are likely to be single attacks. Once a hacker has gained access and the damage done, the target usually responds quickly to close off the vulnerability that allowed that line of attack and to bring systems back on line. Cyber attackers would continually need to exploit new vulnerabilities and new tactics to ensure sustained disruption. Cyber attacks also seldom if ever produce physical damage that requires time-consuming repairs.

## 'Routine' Failure versus Cyber Attack

Critical infrastructure protection creates a new set of problems for national security. Different actors are involved. The focus is on civilian and commercial systems and services. Military force is less important. The scope of these new problems depends on how we define national security and how we set thresholds for acceptable damage. From a legal or public safety perspective, no country will accept even a single attack on infrastructure or interruption of services. If the goal is to prevent cyber-attacks from costing a single day of electric power or water service, we have set a very high standard for security. However, from a strategic military perspective, attacks that do not degrade national capabilities are not significant. From this perspective, if a cyber-attack does not cause damage that rises above the threshold of the routine disruptions that every economy experiences, it does not pose an immediate or significant risk to national security.

It is particularly important to consider that in the larger context of economic activity, water system failures, power outages, air traffic disruptions and other cyber-terror scenarios are routine events that do not affect national security. On a national level, where dozens or even hundreds of different systems provide critical infrastructure services, failure is a routine occurrence at the system or regional level, with service denied to customers for hours or days. Cyber-terrorists would need to attack multiple targets simultaneously for long periods of time to create terror, achieve strategic goals or to have any noticeable effect. For most of the critical infrastructure, multiple sustained attacks are not a feasible scenario for hackers, terrorist groups or nation states (particularly for nation states, where the risk of discovery of what would be universally seen as an act of war far outweigh the limited advantages gained from cyber attacks on infrastructure).

## Weapons of Mass Annoyance

A detailed examination of some of the scenarios for attacks on critical infrastructures helps place cyber-attacks more accurately in a strategic or national security context. For example, dams used for water storage and for power generation are often cited as a likely target for cyber attack. The Washington Post recently wrote that unnamed "U.S. analysts" believe that "by disabling or taking command of the floodgates in a dam, for example, or of substations handling 300,000 volts of electric power, an intruder could use virtual tools to destroy real-world lives and property."

In the United States, the water supply infrastructure would be an elusive target for cyber attack. There are 54,064 separate water systems in the U.S. Of these, 3,769 water systems serve eighty one percent of the population and 353 systems served forty-four percent of the population. However, the uneven spread of diverse network technologies complicates the terrorists' task. Many of these water supply systems in the U.S., even in large cities, continue to rely on technologies not easily disrupted by network attacks. There have been cases in the U.S. when a community's water supply has been knocked out for days at a time (usually as a result of flooding), but these have produced neither terror nor paralysis. A cyber terrorist or cyber warrior would need to carry out a sustained attack that would simultaneously disrupt several hundred of these systems to gain any strategic benefit.

Assuming that a terrorist could find a vulnerability in a water supply system that would allow him to shut down one city's water for a brief period, this vulnerability could be exploited to increase the damage of a physical attack (by denying fire fighters access to water). In general, a cyber attack that alone might pass unnoticed in the normal clutter of daily life could have useful multiplier effects if undertaken simultaneously with a physical attack. This sort of simultaneous combination of physical and cyber attacks might be the only way in which cyber weapons could be attractive to terrorists. The American Waterworks Association assessment of the terrorist threat to water supplies placed "physical destruction of the system's components to disrupt the supply of water" as the most likely source of infrastructure attack.

Comparing aerial and cyber attacks on hydroelectric dams helps provide a measure for cyber-threats. Early in World War II, the Royal Air Force mounted a daring attack on dams in the Ruhr, a chief source of electrical power for German industry. The raid was a success, the dams breached by bombs and, for a period of time, the electrical supply in the region was disrupted.

A comparable cyber attack occurred when a young hacker reportedly gained access to the computer controls for a dam in the U.S. Southwest, but did not disrupt service or cause physical damage.

In neither attack was the damage or the reduction in electrical power paralyzing. Of the two, the cyber attack was less effective in that it caused no physical damage and could be classed more as an annoyance than a threat. The aerial attack resulted in physical damage that needed to be repaired. The only advantage of a cyber attack is that it is less expensive - a teen-ager and a desktop computer rather than valuable aircrews and expensive aircraft.

Many analyses have cyber-terrorists shutting down the electrical power system. One of the better cyber security surveys found that power companies are a primary target for cyber attacks and that seventy percent of these companies had "suffered a severe attack" in the first six months of 2002. The U.S. electrical power grid is a desirable target, but it is a network of multiple, redundant systems that are used to routine system failure and disruption. The national electrical grid is a highly interconnected system of over 3,000 public and private utilities and cooperatives. These 3,000 electrical power providers use a variety of different information technologies to operate their controls for power generation and transmission. A hacker or even a large group of hackers would need to find vulnerabilities in multiple systems to significantly disrupt the power supply and even then, an attack might only disrupt service for a few hours.

The North American Electric Reliability Council, an industry group formed after the 1965 New York blackout, has been working with the Federal government since the 1980s to improve the security of the electrical system and to develop rapid responses to large outages. In Congressional testimony, NERC officials have said that in the last few years, neither viruses nor Distributed Denial of Service attacks against the U.S. electrical system have interrupted service. While industry sources can paint an over-optimistic picture at times, it remains true that falling trees have caused many electric system disruptions while cyber attacks have caused none. A risk assessment by the Information Assurance Task Force of the National Security Telecommunications Advisory Committee concluded "Physical destruction is still the greatest threat facing the electric power infrastructure. Compared to this, electronic intrusion represents an emerging, but still relatively minor, threat." The U.S. has already run a large-scale experiment on the effects of disrupting electrical power supplies, thanks to California's experience with 'deregulation' last year. California's efforts to de-regulate the electrical power market resulted in months of blackouts and rolling brownouts across the state. Deregulation was a more powerful 'attack' on the electrical infrastructure than anything a cyber-terrorist could mount. There was clearly economic cost to the California regulatory event, but it was not crippling nor did it strike terror into the hearts of Americans. Similarly, power outages across the country in 1999 affected millions of people and cost electrical power customers millions of dollars in lost business and productivity. These outages were the result of increased electricity use prompted by sustained high summer temperatures. In contrast to California's State government or hot weather, the number of blackouts in U.S. caused by hackers or cyber-terrorists remains zero.

Interference with national air traffic systems to disrupt flights, shut down air transport and endanger passenger and crews is another frequently cited cyber-threat. We are not yet at a stage where computer networks operate aircraft remotely, so it is not possible for a cyber-attacker to take over an aircraft. Aircraft still carry pilots who are trained to operate the plane in an emergency. Similarly, the Federal Aviation Authority does not depend solely on computer networks to manage air traffic, nor are its communications dependent on the Internet. The high level of human involvement in the control and decision making process for air traffic reduces the risk of any cyber attack. In a normal month storms, electrical failures and programming glitches all ensure a consistently high level of disruption in air traffic. Pilots and air traffic controllers are accustomed to unexpected disruptions and have adapted their practices to minimize the effect. Airlines and travelers are also accustomed to and expect a high degree of disruption in the system. In the United States, it is normal for 15,000 to 20,000 flights to be delayed or cancelled every month. A cyber attack that degraded the air traffic system would create delays and annoyance, but it would not pose a risk to national security.

The FAA has 90 major computer systems and nine different communications networks. These networks rely on elderly equipment and use proprietary software that make them difficult for outsiders to hack. This may explain why the few reported attacks have not affected air traffic. In one reported incident, a young hacker interrupting local phone service in a New England, cutting off a regional airport's control tower and the ability to turn on runway lights. Although the interruption lasted six hours, there were no accidents at the airport. In other cases, FAA headquarters computer networks have been penetrated, allowing hackers to make public unpublished information on airport passenger screening activities, and in another case, a hacker was able to enter an FAA mail server. None of these cases resulted in any disruption to flight. Ironically, modernization could actually increase FAA vulnerability if greater attention is not given to security.

A recent attack on the Internet illustrates the nature of vulnerabilities from cyber attack. For a one-hour period in October 2002, unknown parties launched a Distributed Denial of Service attack on the thirteen 'root servers' that form the basis of the domain names system that governs Internet addresses. Eight of the thirteen servers were forced off-line because of the attacks. The attack itself was invisible and without effect on Internet users. The attack on the DNS system did not noticeably degrade Internet performance. Most DNS data needed for the daily operation of the Internet is stored locally and updated daily. Very few requests require assistance from the root servers. Additionally, the presence of thirteen servers (of which five were not affected by the attack) gives a degree of redundancy that suggests that if there are vulnerabilities to the Internet, the DNS servers are not one of them. In contrast to the DNS attack, shortly after it occurred thousands of Internet customers in the western United States experienced serious delays when their service provider had routing problems due to programming errors. Unlike the attack, this DNS failure actually disrupted service, but it had no effect on national security.

While the Internet may have a few points of failure that offer the possibility for system-wide disruption, it was designed to be a robust, distributed communications network capable of continuing operations after a strategic nuclear exchange. Packet switching and Internet protocols were developed to allow communications to be maintained even when some nodes in the network were eliminated and the Internet itself was designed to automatically route around damage to allow for continued communications. Additionally, computer networks rely on a backbone of high capacity telecommunications systems that are relatively secure from cyber-attack. The introduction of new communications technologies also enhances survivability. Wireless and satellite communications also provide some redundancy for landline systems. Most industrial countries now have access to three or four different modes of communications, making the system considerably more robust than it was a decade ago. Increased use of ultra wideband and mesh radio networks will also increase redundancy and survivability against cyber attack in communications networks.

The 911 emergency response system, a specialized communications network that relies on local telephone service, is also a favorite target for theorists of cyber-terrorism, but like other infrastructures, it is a robust target. The U.S. for example, does not use a single 911 system in but instead has several thousand local systems using different technologies and procedures. No 911 system in a major city has been hacked. It might be possible to send a flood of email messages instructing people to call 911 for important information and thus overload the system (this was the technique used in the 1997 U.S. cyber exercise "Eligible Receiver"). This sort of technique usually works only once - but made in conjunction with a bombing or other physical attack they could act as a 'force multiplier' for a terrorist event.

Manufacturing and economic activity are increasingly dependent on computer networks, and cyber crime and industrial espionage are new dangers for economic activity. However, the evidence is mixed as to the vulnerability of manufacturing to cyber attack. A virus in 2000 infected 1,000 computers at Ford Motor Company. Ford received 140,000 contaminated e-mail messages in three hours before it shut down its network. E-mail service was disrupted for almost a week within the company. Yet, Ford reported, "the rogue program appears to have caused only limited permanent damage. None of its 114 factories stopped, according to the automaker. Computerized engineering blueprints and other technical data were unaffected. Ford was still able to post information for dealers and auto parts suppliers on Web sites that it uses for that purpose." Companies now report that the defensive measures they have taken meant that viruses that were exceptionally damaging when they first appeared are now only "nuisances."

Cyber attacks are often presented as a threat to military forces and the Internet has major implications for espionage and warfare.

Information warfare covers a range of activities of which cyber attacks may be the least important. While information operations and information superiority have become critical elements in successful military operations, no nation has placed its military forces in a position where they are dependent on computer networks that are vulnerable to outside attack. This greatly limits the effectiveness of cyber weapons (code sent over computer networks). The many reports of military computer networks being hacked usually do not explain whether these networks are used for critical military functions. It is indicative, however, that despite regular reports of tens of thousands of network attacks every year on the Department of Defense, there has been no degradation of U.S. military capabilities.

For example, while there were many attack against U.S. military computer networks during operations in Kosovo, these attacks did not result in sorties being cancelled or in a single casualty. Similarly, a foreign power that used cyber-weapons to try to prevent a carrier battle group from leaving the U.S. would be unlikely to succeed. A recent attack by a British hacker neither compromised classified information nor disrupted military operations. A Rand study conducted for the U.S. Air Force on military operations and information vulnerabilities noted "while most of the current topical interests has focused on the newer, trendier threats to information systems, particularly computer hacking and associated disruption and manipulation…our analysis showed that some of the "old-fashioned" threats pose a greater danger…."

## HACKING AND TERROR

Much of the early work on the 'cyber threat' depicted hackers, terrorists, foreign spies and criminal gangs who, by typing a few commands into a computer, can take over or disrupt the critical infrastructure of entire nations. This frightening scenario is not supported by any evidence. Terrorist groups like Al Qaeda do make significant use of the Internet, but as a tool for intra-group communications, fund-raising and public relations. Cyber terrorist could also take advantage of the Internet to steal credit card numbers or valuable data to provide financial support for their operations.

Cyber-terrorism has attracted considerable attention, but to date, it has meant little more than propaganda, intelligence collection or the digital equivalent of graffiti, with groups defacing each other's websites. No critical infrastructures have been shut down by cyber attacks.

Terrorists seek to make a political statement and to inflict psychological and physical damage on their targets. If terrorism is an act of violence to achieve political objects, how useful will terrorists find an economic weapon whose effects are gradual and cumulative? One of Al Qaeda's training manuals, "Military Studies in the Jihad Against the Tyrants" notes that explosives are the preferred weapon of terrorist because "explosives strike the enemy with sheer terror and fright." Explosions are dramatic, strike fear into the hearts of opponents and do lasting damage. Cyber attacks would not have the same dramatic and political effect that terrorists seek. A cyber attack, which might not even be noticed by its victims, or attributed to routine delays or outages, will not be their preferred weapon. If terrorism is an act of violence to create shock and achieve political objects, how useful will terrorists find an economic tool whose effects are at best gradual and cumulative?

An analysis of the risk of cyber terrorism is also complicated by the tendency to initially attribute cyber events to military or terrorist efforts when their actual source is civilian recreational hackers. When DOD computer networks were penetrated in an attack that occurred in the late 1990s, the U.S. was quick to suspect potential opponents, particularly Iraq or China, as the culprit. U.S. officials debated the merits of an active defense and whether this was an act of war, justifying a counter-attack. As tension mounted, the U.S. discovered that far from being a hostile power, the source of the attack was two high school students in southern California. It is difficult, especially in the early stages of an incident, to determine if the attacker is a, terrorist, group, foreign state, criminals, or a teenager in California. However, a quick survey of incidents over the last four years suggests that criminals and bored teenagers are the most likely sources of attack. To this day, the vast majority of hacking incidents result from the actions of recreational hackers.

While the press has reported that government officials are concerned over Al Qaeda plans to use the Internet to wage cyber-terrorism, these stories often recycle the same hypothetical scenarios previously attributed to foreign governments' cyber-warfare efforts. The risk remains hypothetical but the antagonist has changed from hostile states to groups like Al Qaeda. The only new element attributed to Al Qaeda is that the group might use cyber attacks to disrupt emergency services in order to reinforce and multiply the effect of a physical attack. If cyber-attacks were feasible, the greatest risk they might pose to national security is as corollaries to more traditional modes of attacks.

Espionage opportunities created by a greater reliance on internet-accessible computer networks will create greater risk for national security than cyber attacks. Terrorist groups are likely to use the Internet to collect information on potential targets, and intelligence services can not only benefit from information openly available on the web but, more importantly, can benefit from the ability to clandestinely penetrate computer networks and collect information that is not publicly available. This is very different from hacking, in that in the event of a successful penetration of a hostile network, a terrorist group or an intelligence service will want to be as unobtrusive as possible. A sophisticated opponent might hack into a system and sit there, collecting intelligence and working to remain unnoticed. It will not disrupt essential services or leave embarrassing messages on websites, but remain quietly in the background collecting information. Collection techniques for the Internet differ significantly from earlier signals and communications intercept techniques, and while different kinds of data will be collected, the overall effect may be to make some espionage activities much more rewarding. This topic, the implications for espionage of the greater use of computer networks and Internet protocols, deserves further study.

## CYBER CRIME AND THE ECONOMY

Cyber attacks do pose a very real risk in their potential for crime and for imposing economic costs far out of proportion to the price of launching the attack. Hurricane Andrew, the most expensive natural disaster in U.S. history, caused $25 billion dollars in damage and the average annual cost from tornadoes, hurricanes, and flood damage in the U.S. is estimated to be $11 billion. In contrast, the Love Bug virus is estimated to have cost computer users around the world somewhere between $3 billion and $15 billion. Putting aside for the moment the question of how the estimates of the Love Bug's cost were calculated (these figures are probably over-estimates), the ability of a single university student in the Philippines to produce this level of damage using inexpensive equipment shows the potential risk from cyber crime to the global economy.

The financial costs to economies from cyber attack include the loss of intellectual property, financial fraud, damage to reputation, lower productivity, and third party liability. Opportunity cost (lost sales, lower productivity, etc) make up a large proportion of the reported cost of cyber attacks and viruses. However, opportunity costs do not translate directly into costs to the national economy. For example, if a Distributed Denial of Service attack prevents customers from reaching one online bookseller, they may instead go to another to purchase their books. The aggregate national sale of books could remain the same although the first bookseller's market share would decline. A small number of customers may choose not to bother going to another site if their first choice is unavailable, but some of these lost sales may well be recouped by later return to the sight by the customer.

Businesses face greater damage from financial fraud and theft of intellectual property over the Internet, crimes that continue to grow in number. Emphasizing the transnational nature of cyber security issues, the last few years have seen the emergence of highly sophisticated criminal gangs capable of exploiting vulnerabilities in business networks. Their aim is not terror, but fraud or the collection of economically valuable information. Theft of proprietary information remains the source of the most serious losses, according to surveys of large corporations and computer crime. These crimes must be differentiated from the denial of service attacks and the launching of viruses. Denial of services or viruses, while potentially damaging to business operations, do not pose the same level of risk.

Cyber crime is a serious and growing threat, but the risk to a nation-state in deploying cyber-weapons against a potential opponent's economy are probably too great for any country to contemplate these measures. For example, writers in some of China's military journals speculated that cyber attacks could disable American financial markets. The dilemma for this kind of attack is that China is as dependent on the same financial markets as the United States, and could suffer even more from disruption. With other critical infrastructures, the amount of damage that can be done is, from a strategic viewpoint, trivial, while the costs of discovery for a nation state could be very great. These constraints, however, do not apply to non-state actors like Al Qaeda. Cyber attacks could potentially be a useful tool (albeit not a fatal or determinative tool) for non-state actors who reject the global market economy.

## CONCLUSION

The Internet is a new thing, and new things can appear more frightening than they really are. Much of the early analysis of cyber-threats and cyber security appears to have "The Sky is Falling" as its theme. The sky is not falling, and cyber weapons seem to be of limited value in attacking national power or intimidating citizens. The examples presented in this paper suggest that nations are more robust and resilient than the early theories of cyber terror assumed. To understand the vulnerability of critical infrastructures to cyber attack, we would need for each target infrastructure a much more detailed assessment of redundancy, normal rates of failure and response, the degree to which critical functions are accessible from public networks and the level of human control, monitoring and intervention in critical operations.

This initial assessment suggests that infrastructures in large industrial countries are resistant to cyber attack. Terrorists or foreign militaries may well launch cyber attacks, but they are likely to be disappointed in the effect. Nations are more robust than the early analysts of cyber-terrorism and cyber-warfare give them credit for, and cyber attacks are less damaging than physical attacks. Digital Pearl Harbors are unlikely. Infrastructure systems, because they have to deal with failure on a routine basis, are also more flexible and responsive in restoring service than early analysts realized. Cyber attacks, unless accompanied by a simultaneous physical attack that achieves physical damage, are short lived and ineffective. However, if the risks of cyber-terrorism and cyber-war are overstated, the risk of espionage and cyber crime may be not be fully appreciated by many observers.

This is not a static situation, and the vulnerability of critical infrastructure to cyber attack could change if three things occur. Vulnerability could increase as societies move to a ubiquitous computing environment  when more daily activities have become automated and rely on remote computer networks. The second is that vulnerability could increase as more industrial and infrastructure applications, especially those used for SCADA (Supervisory Control and Data Acquisition), move from relying on dedicated, proprietary networks to using the Internet and Internet protocols for their operations. This move to greater reliance on networks seems guaranteed given the cost advantage of Internet communications protocols (Transmission Control Protocol/Internet Protocol), but it also creates new avenues of access. These changes will lead to increased vulnerabilities if countries do not balance the move to become more networked and more dependent on Internet protocols with efforts to improve network security, make law enforcement more effective, and ensure that critical infrastructures are robust and resilient.

From a broader security perspective, nations now face a range of amorphous threats to their safety that are difficult for the traditional tools of national security to reach. The lines between domestic and foreign, private and public, or police and military are blurring, and the nature and requirements of national security are changing rapidly. The most important implications of these changes for cyber security may well be that national policies must adjust to growing interdependence among economies and emphasize the need for cooperation among nations to defeat cyber threats.

# 8

# Cyberterror: Clear and Present Danger

Is cyberterrorism a real threat or just a distraction from the day-to-day job of maintaining network security?

"Our enemies will use our technology against us...the fact that they may be from a Third World country should not in any way suggest to us that they will not understand how to use our technology. They will see the places where we did not think we needed to build in security and they will take advantage of those seams."

This extract from a speech made by Richard Clarke, former special advisor for Cyberspace Security to the US president, in the December following the events of September 11th, describes a scenario that probably seemed entirely plausible and inevitable to the audience of the Global Tech Summit given recent events. But two years on and despite the numerous terror attacks in Bali, Turkey and Iraq, the consensus among security experts is that there has never been a recorded act of cyberterrorism pre- or post-September 11th.

Despite no precedence to support the idea of an "electronic Pearl Harbour", governments continue to warn and even legislate around the issue. Just last month Singapore beefed up its Computer Misuse Act, giving police and other security agencies sweeping powers to "foil cyberterrorists before they attack." The controversial Act, which has been criticised by opposition MPs as an "an instrument of oppression itself" allows for pre-emptive action. Anyone who hacks or defaces a Web site may be jailed for up to three years or fined up to $10,000.

"Instead of a backpack of explosives, a terrorist can create just as much devastation by sending a carefully engineered packet of data into the computer systems which control the network for essential services, for example the power stations," said Ho Peng Kee, Singapore's senior minister of state for law and home affairs.

## THE UK APPROACH

The UK is taking a less alarmist approach to the potential of an electronic attack but remains concerned. Responding to a parliamentary question recently, the home secretary, David Blunkett, said the threat from computer-related attacks by terrorists or their supporters is kept under continuous review, as are measures to counter it. "The risk is assessed to be low, but growing. It could change rapidly at any time and our response will need to adjust to remain proportionate. I will keep closely under review the level of funding needed for this work," he said.

There are numerous UK government departments with responsibility for responding to an act of cyberterrorism, including GCHQ, CESG, and the Cabinet Office. The main body charged with monitoring attacks against the critical national infrastructure, the network of essential services both private and publicly owned, is the National Infrastructure Security Co-ordination Centre (NISCC).

According to a Home Office spokesperson, although there have been no known cyberterror attempts against the UK so far: "The NISCC has assessed that the threat of electronic attack is increasing. The threat of the sort of attack that could disable a critical service is low but less serious and damaging attacks that might deface a Web site or deny service from a Web site are more likely."

## CYBERTERROR OR JUST CYBERCRIME?

Although there has never actually been an act of cyberterrorism, there have been plenty of instances of politically motivated hacking incidents that sit outside the realm of simple cybercrime. A report published by the US Institute for Security and Technology Studies at Dartmouth College, in the weeks following September 11th, Cyber Attacks During The War on Terrorism, warned that US retaliation following September 11th was likely to result in "cyberattacks by terrorist groups themselves or by targeted nation states."

The report cited four case studies as evidence of the growing menace of cyberterrorism. The first example, although not a terrorist incident per se, followed the mid-air collision between a US spy plane and a Chinese fighter on 1 April, 2001. The reports author, Michael Vatis, a director at the institute, claims that as a direct result of the incident approximately 1,200 US sites, including the White House, the US Air Force, and the Department of Energy were subject to DDoS attacks or defaced by pro-Chinese images.

"Chinese hacker groups, such as the Honker Union of China and the Chinese Red Guest Network Security Technology Alliance, organised a massive and sustained week-long campaign of cyberattacks against American targets," the report states.

Although Vatis accepts that it is unclear if the Chinese government sanctioned these attacks, he pointed out that the activities were "highly visible and no arrests were made by Chinese officials, it can be assumed that they were at least tolerated, if not directly supported by Chinese authorities."

Another example cited in the report is the sustained "cyberbattle" running in parallel to the ongoing conflict between Israel and Palestine. In one instance, responding to the kidnapping of three Israeli soldiers in October 2000, pro-Israeli hackers launched a "sustained DDoS attacks against sites of the Palestinian Authority. Pro-Palestinian hackers apparently retaliated by taking down sites belonging to the Israeli Parliament, the Israeli Defence Forces, and the Tel Aviv Stock Exchange, the report claims.

While these kinds of events may be regarded as politically motivated hacking, they fall short of being acts of cyberterrorism, according to security experts. The consensus seems to be that a cyberattack only becomes cyberterrorism when there is serious damage to property, loss of life — or it causes "terror" or fear in the target community. "Despite the heightened sense of civilian unease and government vigilance in developed countries since 11 September, there hasn't been a validated case of 'cyberterrorism' worldwide. Although terrorists undoubtedly are using the Internet to communicate among themselves and as a research tool, their use of the Internet as a delivery vehicle for a significant, digital terrorist attack is a nightmare scenario not grounded in reality. There have been no losses of life or property because of a digital attack," says Gartner analyst Richard Mogull.

Gartner defines cyberterrorism as a "terrorism attack using a digital channel." The FBI defines terrorism as "unlawful or threatened use of force or violence...against persons or property to intimidate or force a government or civilian population to further political or social objectives." Mogull says that although terrorists are using the Internet to communicate among themselves, their use of the Internet as a "delivery vehicle for a significant, digital terrorist attack is a nightmare scenario not grounded in reality." There have been no losses of life or property because of a digital attack, he adds.

## Don't believe the Hype

Speaking at the CeBit technology fair earlier this year, Bruce Schneier, security expert and chief technology officer of network-monitoring company Counterpane Internet Security, said the threat posed by cyberterrorism had been overestimated. "The hype is coming from the US government and I don't know why. If they want to attack they will do it with bombs like they always have," he said.

He added that rather than fostering a climate of fear, disrupting the Net and other communications networks would probably just annoy people. Schneier, like Mogull, claims that companies and consumers should concentrate on "real" threats from criminals, viruses, worms and Trojans. Responding to Schneier's comments, a statement from the UK NISCC agreed that currently terrorists are more likely to mount physical than electronic attacks and generic warnings around cyberterrorism could be less than helpful.

"Each company, industry, user will face different threats and have different vulnerabilities. It is for each to identify where the greatest threat is likely to come from and to protect against it," the memo stated.

According to Gatner's Mogull, there are real security issues that the IT industry has to face up to before worrying about cyberterrorism, which is still only a potential threat. "We are not doing ourselves any favours in the security industry by focusing on it; there are plenty of other issues we need to face and we have enough vulnerabilities to manage in protecting our critical national infrastructure as it is."

## ACTIVISM, HACKTIVISM, AND CYBERTERRORISM: THE INTERNET AS A TOOL FOR INFLUENCING FOREIGN POLICY

The conflict over Kosovo has been characterized as the first war on the Internet. Government and non-government actors alike used the Net to disseminate information, spread propaganda, demonize opponents, and solicit support for their positions.

Hackers used it to voice their objections to both Yugoslav and NATO aggression by disrupting service on government computers and taking over their Web sites. Individuals used it to tell their stories of fear and horror inside the conflict zone, while activists exploited it to amplify their voices and reach a wide, international audience. And people everywhere used it to discuss the issues and share text, images, and video clips that were not available through other media. In April, the Los Angeles Times wrote that the Kosovo conflict was "turning cyberspace into an ethereal war zone where the battle for the hearts and minds is being waged through the use of electronic images, online discussion group postings, and hacking attacks."

Anthony Pratkanis, professor of psychology at the University of California, Santa Cruz, and author of Age of Propaganda: The Everyday Use and Abuse of Persuasion, observed, "What you're seeing now is just the first round of what will become an important, highly sophisticated tool in the age-old tradition of wartime propaganda.... The war strategists should be worried about it, if they aren't yet."

Just how much impact did the Internet have on foreign policy decisions relating the war? It clearly had a part in the political discoursetaking place, and it was exploited by activists seeking to alter foreign policy decisions. It also impacted military decisions. While NATO targeted Serb media outlets carrying Milosovic's propaganda, it intentionally did not bomb Internet service providers or shut down the satellite links bringing the Internet to Yugoslavia. Policy instead was to keep the Internet open. James P. Rubin, spokesman for the U.S. State Department, said "Full and open access to the Internet can only help the Serbian people know the ugly truth about the atrocities and crimes against humanity being perpetrated in Kosovo by the Milosevic regime." Indirectly, the Internet may have also affected public support for the war, which in turn might have affected policy decisions made during the course of the conflict.

The purpose of this paper is to explore how the Internet is altering the landscape of political discourse and advocacy, with particular emphasis on how it is used by those wishing to influence foreign policy. Emphasis is on actions taken by nonstate actors, including both individuals and organizations, but state actions are discussed where they reflect foreign policy decisions triggered by the Internet. The primary sources used in the analysis are news reports of incidents and events. These are augmented with interviews and survey data where available. A more scientific study would be useful.

The paper is organized around three broad classes of activity: activism, hacktivism, and cyberterrorism. The first category, activism, refers to normal, non-disruptive use of the Internet in support of an agenda or cause. Operations in this area includes browsing the Web for information, constructing Web sites and posting materials on them, transmitting electronic publications and letters through e-mail, and using the Net to discuss issues, form coalitions, and plan and coordinate activities. The second category, hacktivism, refers to the marriage of hacking and activism. It covers operations that use hacking techniques against a targets Internet site with the intent of disrupting normal operations but not causing serious damage. Examples are Web sit-ins and virtual blockades, automated e-mail bombs, Web hacks, computer break-ins, and computer viruses and worms. The final category, cyberterrorism, refers to the convergence of cyberspace and terrorism. It covers politically motivated hacking operations intended to cause grave harm such as loss of life or severe economic damage. An example would be penetrating an air traffic control system and causing two planes to collide. There is a general progression toward greater damage and disruption from the first to the third category, although that does not imply an increase of political effectiveness. An electronic petition with a million signatures may influence policy more than an attack that disrupts emergency 911 services.

Although the three categories of activity are treated separately, the boundaries between them are somewhat fuzzy. For example, an e-mail bomb may be considered hacktivism by some and cyberterrorism by others. Also, any given actor may conduct operations across the spectrum. For example, a terrorist might launch viruses as part of a larger campaign of cyberterrorism, all the while using the Internet to collect information about targets, coordinate action with fellow conspirators, and publish propaganda on Web sites. Thus, while the paper distinguishes activists, hacktivists, and terrorists, an individual can play all three roles.

The following sections discuss and give examples of activity in each of these three areas. The examples are drawn from the Kosovo conflict, cryptography policy, human rights in China, support for the Mexican Zapatistas, and other areas of conflict. The examples are by no means exhaustive of all activity in any of these areas, but intended only to be illustrative. Nevertheless, they represent a wide range of players, targets, and geographical regions.

The main conclusion of the paper is that the Internet can be an effective tool for activism, especially when it is combined with other communications media, including broadcast and print media and face-to-face meetings with policy makers. It can benefit individuals and small groups with few resources as well as organizations and coalitions that are large or well-funded. It facilitates activities such as educating the public and media, raising money, forming coalitions across geographical boundaries, distributing petitions and action alerts, and planning and coordinating events on a regional or international level. It allows activists in politically repressive states to evade government censors and monitors.

With respect to hacktivism and cyberterrorism, those who engage in such activity are less likely to accomplish their foreign policy objectives than those who do not employ disruptive and destructive techniques. They may feel a sense of empowerment, because they can control government computers and get media attention, but that does not mean they will succeed in changing policy. The main effect is likely to be a strengthening of cyberdefense policies, both nationally and internationally, rather than accommodation to the demands of the actors.

## Activism

The Internet offers a powerful tool for communicating and coordinating action. It is inexpensive to use and increasingly pervasive, with an estimated 201 million on-line as of September 1999. Groups of any size, from two to millions, can reach each other and use the Net to promote an agenda. Their members and followers can come from any geographical region on the Net, and they can attempt to influence foreign policy anywhere in the world. This section describes five modes of using the Internet: collection, publication, dialogue, coordination of action, and direct lobbying of decision makers. While treated separately, the modes are frequently used together and many of the examples described here illustrate multiple modes.

## Collection

One way of viewing the Internet is as a vast digital library. The World Wide Web alone offers about a billion pages of information, and much of the information is free. Activists may be able to locate legislative documents, official policy statements, analyses and discussions about issues, and other items related to their mission. They may be able to find names and contact information for key decision makers inside the government or governments they ultimately hope to influence. They may be able to identify other groups and individuals with similar interests, and gather contact information for potential supporters and collaborators. There are numerous tools that help with collection, including search engines, e-mail distribution lists, and chat and discussion groups. Many Web sites offer their own search tools for extracting information from databases on their sites.

One advantage of the Internet over other media is that it tends to break down barriers erected by government censors. For example, after Jordanian officials removed an article from 40 print copies of the Economist on sale in Jordan, a subscriber found a copy on-line, made photocopies, and faxed it to 1,000 Jordanians. According to Daoud Kuttab, head of the Arabic Media Internal Network (AMIA), the government would have been better off leaving the print version intact. "We found this very exciting," he said. "For the first time the traditional censorship that exists within national borders was bypassed." Kuttab said AMIA opened Jordanian journalists to the non-Arab world and use of the Web as a research tool. "In the Jordanian media, we have been able to detect a much more open outlook to the world as well as to Arab issues," he said.

The Internet itself is not free of government censorship. According to Reporters Sans Frontiers, 45 countries restrict their citizens' access to the Internet, typically by forcing them to subscribe to a state-run Internet service provider, which may filter out objectionable sites.5 Authoritarian regimes recognize the benefits of the Internet to economic growth, but at the same time feel threatened by the unprecedented degree of freedom of speech.

Chinese authorities block access to Web sites that are considered subversive to government objectives. This has been only partially effective, however, and Chinese activists have found ways of slipping information past the controls. For example, the editors of VIP Reference, a Washington-based electronic magazine with articles and essays about democratic and economic evolution inside China, e-mails their electronic newsletter directly to addresses inside mainland China. The e-mail is sent from a different address every day to get past e-mail blocks. It is also delivered to random addresses, compiled from commercial and public lists, so that recipients can deny having deliberately subscribed. As of January, about 250,000 people received the pro-democracy publication, including people inside the government who did not want it. Chinese officials were not, however, complacent. When 30-year-old Shanghai software entrepreneur Lin Hai sold 30,000 e-mail addresses to VIP Reference, he was arrested and later sentenced to two years in prison. In addition, authorities fined him 10,000 yuan (HK$9,300) and confiscated his computer equipment and telephone. Lin was said to be the first person convicted in China for subversive use of the Internet. He claimed he was only trying to drum up business and was not politically active.

During the Kosovo conflict, people in Yugoslavia had full access to the Internet, including Western news sites. The Washington Post reported that according to U.S. and British officials, the government controlled all four Internet access providers in Yugoslavia and kept them open for the purpose of spreading disinformation and propaganda. The Post also said that Belgrade, with a population of 1.5 million, had about 100,000 Internet connections in mid-April. Individuals without their own connections could get access at Internet cafes.

Even though Serbs had access to Western news reports, both through the Internet and through satellite and cable television, many did not believe what they saw and heard from Western media. They considered coverage on Western television stations such as CNN and Sky News to be as biased as that on the Yugoslav state-run station, citing instances when Western reports of Serbian atrocities turned out to be wrong. Alex Todorovic, a Serbian-American who spent time in Belgrade during the conflict observed, "By and large, Serbs mistrust the rest of the world=s media. CNN, for example, is considered the official voice of Washington." Some Yugoslav surfers did not even bother looking at Western news sites on the Internet. When asked if she visited Web sites of Western news stations, one 22-year-old student replied, "No, I don=t believe in their information, so why should I upset myself?"9 Thus, it is not clear that the decision on the part of either Milosovic or NATO to keep the Internet open in Yugoslavia undermined Milosovics objectives. Further, given that people living in Yugoslavia personally witnessed and felt the effects of the NATO bombing and either disbelieved reports or heard little about Serb atrocities against the ethnic Albanians in Kosovo, it is not surprising that an anti-NATO discourse ran throughout Belgrade. As one pharmacist observed, "I have two children. The people who are bombing my kids are my only enemy right now."

In addition to information relating to a particular policy issue, the Web offers cyberactivists various information that can help them use the Net effectively. For example, NetAction offers a training guide for the virtual activist. The guide provides information on the use of e-mail for outreach, organizing, and advocacy; Web-based outreach and advocacy tools; membership and fundraising; netiquette and policy issues; and various resources.

## Publication

The Internet offers several channels whereby advocacy groups and individuals can publish information (and disinformation) to further policy objectives. They can send it through e-mail and post it to newsgroups. They can create their own electronic publications or contribute articles and essays to those of others. They can put up Web pages with documents, images, audio and video clips, and other types of information. The Web sites can serve as a gathering place and source of information for supporters, potential supporters, and onlookers.

One reason the Internet is popular among activists is its cost advantage over traditional mass media. It is easier and cheaper to post a message to a public forum or put up a Web site than it is to operate a radio or television station or print a newspaper. Practically anyone can afford to be a publisher. In addition, the reach of the Internet is global. A message can potentially reach millions of people at no additional cost to the originator. Further, activists can control their presentation to the world. They decide what is said and how. They do not have to rely on the mass media to take notice and tell their story "right."

During the Kosovo conflict, organizations and individuals throughout the world used their Web sites to publish information related to the conflict and, in some cases, to solicit support. Non-government organizations with Kosovo-related Web pages included the press, human rights groups, humanitarian relief organizations, churches, and womens groups. Government Web sites on Kosovo tended to feature propaganda and materials that supported their official policies. An exception was the U.S. Information Agency Web site, which presented a survey of news stories from around the world, some of which were critical of NATO actions. Jonathan Spalter, USIA Chief Information Officer, commented that "The measure of our success is the extent to which we are perceived not as propaganda but anti-propaganda."

The British government's Foreign Office used their Web site, in part, to counter Serb propaganda. Concerned that the Yugoslav public was getting a highly distorted view of the war, Foreign Secretary Robin Cook posted a message on their Web site intended for the Serbs. The message said that Britain has nothing against the Serbs, but was forced to act by the scale of Yugoslav President Slobodan Milosevic's brutality. British Defense Secretary George Robertson said the Ministry of Defence (MoD) had translated its Web site into Serbian to counter censorship by Belgrade of the news.

The Yugoslav media was controlled by the Serbian government and served to promote Milosevic's policies. Yugoslavia had an independent, pro-democracy radio station, B92, but it was raided by the police in the early days of the Kosovo conflict and turned over to a government-appointed station manager. B92 had had a run-in with the government earlier in late 1996 when government jammers tried to keep it from airing news broadcasts. At that time, however, B92 prevailed, in part by encoding their news bulletins in RealAudio format and posting them on a Web site in Amsterdam. Radio Free Europe acquired tapes of the news programs and rebroadcasted them back to the Serbs, circumventing the jammers, who then gave up.

But when the government took over B92's facility in 1999, B92's then-managers ceded to the government and also discontinued posting materials on their Web site, which had offered viewers a reliable source of information about the conflict. This was considered a great loss to Yugoslavia's pro-democracy movement and general public, which had rallied behind Belgrade's top-rated news station.

A few individuals inside Yugoslavia posted to the Internet first-hand accounts of events as they were being witnessed or shortly thereafter. Their stories told of fear and devastation, the latter caused not only by the Serb military, but also by NATO bombs. By all accounts, the situation inside Yugoslavia was horrible for citizens everywhere, whether Serbian or ethnic Albanian. The stories may have inspired activists and influenced public opinion, but it is not clear what if any impact they had on government decision making.

New-media artists used to the Web to voice their opinions on the Balkans conflict. In late March, artist and high-school teacher Reiner Strasser put up a site called Weak Blood, which featured works of visual poetry, kinetic imagery, and interactive art, all making an anti-violence statement. Strasser vowed to add one or two pieces a day "as long as bombs are falling and humans are massacred" in the region.

Some Serbs with Internet access sent e-mails to American news organizations calling for an end to the NATO bombing. Many of the messages contained heated rhetoric that was anti-NATO and anti-U.S. One letter directed to the Associated Press ended, "To be a Serb now is to be helpless ... to listen to the euphemistic and hypocritic phrases as 'peace-making mission,' moral imperative." Other messages contained human stories about how their lives were affected. Tom Reid, London correspondent to the Washington Post, said he received 30-50 messages a day from professors at universities and activists all over Yugoslavia.

The general tenor of the messages was all the same, "'Please remember there are human beings under your bombs,'" he said. The Serbs used e-mail distribution lists to reach tens of thousands of users, mostly in the United States, with messages attacking the NATO bombing campaign.

One message read AIn the last nine days, NATO barbarians have bombed our schools, hospitals, bridges, killed our people but that was not enough for them now they have started to destroy our culture monuments which represents the core of existence of our nation. Most recipients were annoyed by this unwanted "spam," which the Wall Street Journal dubbed AYugospam.

Dennis Longley, a professor in the Information Security Research Centre at Australia's Queensland University of Technology, said they received a suspicious e-mail from Serbia. The message had two paragraphs. The first was the usual friendly greetings, while the second was a rant about NATO that read like pure propaganda, characterizing NATO as a "terrorist organization" that "brought nothing but a gigantic humanitarian disaster to Kosovo," while attributing the cause of the problem to "albanian terrorist and separatist actions, not the repression by the government security forces." The second paragraph exhibited a style unlike the first and a standard of English well below that of the sender, leading them to speculate that Serb authorities had modified the e-mail. If that is so, one is left wondering how much other anti-NATO talk hitting the Net was the work of the government.

Of course, not all of the messages coming out of the Balkans were anti-NATO. Shortly after the Kosovo conflict began, I found myself on a list called "kcc-news," operated by the Kosova [sic] Crisis Center from the Internet domain "alb-net.com." The messages included Human Rights Flashes from Human Rights Watch, Action Alerts from the Kosova Task Force, and other appeals for support in the war against the Serbs. One message contained a flier calling for "sustained air strikes until total Serb withdrawal" and "ground troops to STOP GENOCIDE now." The flier included links to Web pages that documented Serb atrocities and aggression.

Even though the Yugoslav government did not prohibit Internet activity, fear of government reprisals led some to post their messages through anonymous remailers so they could not be identified. This allowed for a freer discourse on Internet discussion groups and contributed to the spread of information about the situation inside Belgrade and Kosovo. Microsoft Corp. initiated a section called "Secret Dispatches from Belgrade" on the Web site of their online magazine Slate. An anonymous correspondent gives daily reports of both alleged Serb atrocities and civilian suffering inflicted by NATO bombs.

After human rights organizations expressed concern that the Yugoslav government might be monitoring Internet activity and cracking down on anyone expressing dissenting views, Anonymizer Inc., a provider of anonymous Web browsing and e-mail services, launched the Kosovo Privacy Project Web site. The site, which went on-line in April, offered surfers anonymous e-mail and instant, anonymous access to Voice of America, Radio Free Europe, and about 20 other Web sites. According to Federal Computer Week, Anonymizer planned to add NATO and other Western government information sites to the Kosovo list, and to launch similar projects for human rights situations in other parts of the world, for example, China. However, the effectiveness of the Kosovo project was never established. In August, USA Today reported that activists said the project was little noticed inside Kosovo, where traditional media seemed unaware while the fighting knocked out Internet trunk lines in short order.

The Internet has raised numerous policy issues in such areas as privacy, encryption, censorship, electronic commerce, international trade, intellectual property protection, taxation, Internet governance, cybercrime, and information warfare, all of which have a foreign policy dimension. As the issues surfaced and took on some urgency, existing industry and public-interest groups began to address them. In addition, both national and international advocacy groups sprung up specifically devoted to Internet issues. They all operate Web sites, where they publish policy papers and information about issues, events, and membership. Many also send out e-mail newsletters and alerts.

In the area of encryption policy, for example, the major players include Americans for Computer Privacy (ACP), the Center for Democracy and Technology (CDT), Cyber-Rights & Cyber Liberties, the Electronic Frontier Foundation (EFF), the Electronic Privacy Information Center (EPIC), the Global Internet Liberty Campaign (GILC), and the Internet Privacy Coalition. The ACP has perhaps the largest group of constituents, being composed of 40 trade associations, over 100 companies, and more than 3,000 individual members. GILC is one of the most global, with member organizations from Europe, North America, Australia, and Asia. In July 1999, nine leading U.S.-based Internet companies joined forces to become the voice of the Internet on issues such as privacy, consumer protection, and international trade. The industry group, called NetCoalition.com, includes America Online, Amazon.com, eBay, Lycos, Yahoo!, DoubleClick, Excite@Home, Inktomi, and Theglobe.com. The companies represent 7 of the top 10 Internet sites and more than 90% of the world=s Internet users visit one of the sites at least once a month. The group plans to focus on 150 Internet-related bills that were introduced in Congress.

The Internet is used extensively as a publication medium by hackers (including hacktivists) and terrorists. Hackers publish electronic magazines and put up Web sites with software tools and information about hacking, including details about vulnerabilities in popular systems (e.g., Microsoft Windows) and how they can be exploited, programs for cracking passwords, software packages for writing computer viruses, and scripts for disabling or breaking into computer networks and Web sites. In March 1997, an article in the New York Times reported that there were an estimated 1,900 Web sites purveying hacking tips and tools, and 30 hacker publications.

Terrorist groups use the Internet to spread propaganda. Back in February 1998, Hizbullah was operating three Web sites: one for the central press office (www.hizbollah.org), another to describe its attacks on Israeli targets (www.moqawama.org), and the third for news and information (www.almanar.com.lb). That month, Clark Staten, executive director of the Emergency Response & Research Institute (ERRI) in Chicago, testified before a U.S. Senate subcommittee that "even small terrorist groups are now using the Internet to broadcast their message and misdirect/misinform the general population in multiple nations simultaneously." He gave the subcommittee copies of both domestic and international messages containing anti-American and anti-Israeli propaganda and threats, including a widely distributed extremist call for A jihad (holy war) against America and Great Britain. In June 1998, U.S. News & World Report noted that 12 of the 30 groups on the U.S. State Department=s list of terrorist organizations are on the Web. As of August 1999, it appears that virtually every terrorist group is on the Web, along with a mishmash of freedom fighters, crusaders, propagandists, and mercenaries. Forcing them off the Web is impossible, because they can set up their sites in countries with free-speech laws. The government of Sri Lanka, for example, banned the sepaiatist Liberation Tigers of Tamil Eelam, but they have not even attempted to take down their London-based Web site.

## Dialogue

The Internet offers several venues for dialogue and debate on policy issues. These include e-mail, newsgroups, Web forums, and chat. Discussions can be confined to closed groups, for example through e-mail, as well as open to the public. Some media sites offer Web surfers the opportunity to comment on the latest stories and current issues and events. Government officials and domain experts may be brought in to serve as catalysts for discussion, debate issues, or answer questions. Discussion can even take place on Web sites that themselves lack such facilities. Using Gooey software from the Israeli company Hypernix, for example, visitors to a Web site can chat with other Gooey users currently at the site.

Internet discussion forums are frequently used to debate, blast, and maybe even attempt to influence government policies. Encryption policy, for example, is discussed on the e-mail lists "cypherpunks" and "ukcrypto" and on several newsgroups, including alt.privacy and sci.crypt.

The ukcrypto list created was created in early 1996 by two academics, Ross Anderson (Cambridge) and Paul Leyland (Oxford), and one person then in government, Brian Gladman (NATO SHAPE), who was acting outside his official capacity. Motivated by a concern that a lack of public discussion and debate in the United Kingdom on cryptography issues was allowing the government to set policies that they believed were not in interests of the United Kingdom and its citizens, they formed the list with the objective of impacting cryptography policy. They were concerned both with domestic policy, particularly proposals to restrict the use of cryptography by U.K. citizens, and on foreign policy, particularly export controls. As of May 1999, the list has 300 subscribers, including government officials responsible for U.K.policy and persons in other countries, including the United States. Many of the key contributors held influential positions in other policy making fora. Focus is on U.K. policy issues, but items of international interest are also discussed, including export controls adopted under the Wassenaar Arrangement (31 countries participate); policy changes adopted by France, the United States, and other countries; policy statements from the European Union and other organizations; and some technical issues.

Gladman believes the list has made four contributions:

(1) educating many about the policy issues and encouraging journalists and writers to write about them;

(2) bringing individual and industry views closer together and allowing U.K. industry to see more clearly that agreeing with their government may not be a good thing if private citizens do not support government policy;

(3) encouraging the more progressive voices in government to speak out and argue from within government that their views represent those of the public; and

(4) bringing groups together that were previously campaigning separately. "The most significant contribution of ukcrypto is not direct," Gladman said. "It is the contribution that it has made in promoting an educated community of commentators and a forum for the review of what government is doing that is fully open."

On the downside, some postings on ukcrypto may alienate the very government officials the authors hope to influence. According to Gladman, Adiscussions on the list can become slinging matches that quickly put those in government on the defensive and hence inclined to discount what is being said. It would be more effective if we had a way of focusing on the issues and not the personalities. But Andrew Brown gave ukcrypto high marks, crediting it with most of the thought and co-ordination behind the successful campaign to keep strong cryptography legal and widely available. "There, for the past two years, the civil servants responsible for policy have actually been available, more or less, to the people who disagree with them," he wrote in New Statesman. "They have had to justify their actions, not to the public, but to a small group of geographically dispersed experts ... It's a kind of updated version of Lions v Christians."

Nigel Hickson, one of the principal players in the policy debates from the U.K. Department of Trade and Industry, agrees the Internet and ukcrypto in particular have played a role in shaping U.K. cryptography policy. But he was also critical of the list: "Whilst ukcyrpto has undoubtedly had an influence on the development of UK encryption policy, it has tended to polarise the debate into extremes. This may be because there tends to be a large silent majority on the list who do not directly contribute because o f commercial or policy reasons." Besides participating in ukcrypto, the DTI has published draft consultation documents on the Web for comment. Many of the comments they receive arrive through electronic mail. DTI has also met with industry groups and participated in non-Internet forums such as conferences and seminars. These have also helped shape policy decisions.

There are Usenet newsgroups and other interactive forums that focus on practically every conceivable topic relating to foreign (and domestic) policy. Whether these are effective or not in terms of influencing policy is another matter. After studying the impact of the Net on the American political system, Richard Davis, a political science professor at Brigham Young University and author of The Web of Politics, observed that "In Usenet political discussions, people talk past one another, when they are not verbally attacking each other. The emphasis is not problem solving, but discussion dominance." Davis also found interactivity on the Internet to be primarily an illusion: "Interest groups, party organizations, and legislators seek to use the Web for information dissemination, but they are rarely interested in allowing their sites to become forums for the opinions of others."

## Coordination of Action

Advocacy groups can use the Internet to coordinate action among members and with other organizations and individuals. Action plans can be distributed by e-mail or posted on Web sites. Services are cheaper than phone and fax (although these services can also be delivered through the Internet), and faster than physical delivery (assuming Internet services are operating properly, which is not always the case). The Internet lets people all over the world coordinate action without regard to constraints of geography or time. They can form partnerships and coalitions or operate independently.

One Web site was created to help activists worldwide coordinate and locate information about protests and meetings. According to statements on Protest.Net, the Web site serves "to help progressive activists by providing a central place where the times and locations of protests and meetings can be posted." The site=s creator said he hoped it would "help resolve logistical problems that activists face in organizing events with limited resources and access to mass media." The site features news as well as action alerts and information about events.

The power of the Internet to mobilize activists is illustrated by the arrest of Kurdish rebel leader Abdullah Ocalan. According to Michael Dartnell, a political science professor at Concordia University, when Turkish forces arrested Ocalan, Kurds around the world responded with demonstrations within a matter of hours. He attributed the swift action in part to the Internet and Web. "They responded more quickly than governments did to his arrest," he said. Dartnell contends the Internet and advanced communication tools were changing the way people around the world play politics. Anti-government groups are establishing alliances and coalitions that might not have existed before the technology was introduced.

The force of the Internet is further illustrated by the day of protest against business that took place on June 18, 1999. The protests, which were set up to coincide with a meeting of the G8 in Cologne, Germany, was coordinated by a group called J18 from a Web site inviting people to plan individual actions focusing on disrupting "financial centres, banking districts and multinational corporate power bases." Suggested activity included marches, rallies, and hacking. In London, up to 2,000 anti-capitalists coursed through the city shouting slogans and spray-painting buildings. According to the Sunday Times, teams of hackers from Indonesia, Israel, Germany, and Canada attacked the computers of at least 20 companies, including the Stock Exchange and Barclays. More than 10,000 attacks were launched over a 5-hour period.

During the Kosovo conflict, the Kosova Task Force used the Internet to distribute action plans to Muslims and supporters of Kosovo. A March 31 Action Alert, for example, asked people to organize rallies in solidarity with Kosovo at local federal buildings and city halls on April 3 at 11:00 AM; organize public funeral prayers; make and encourage others to make daily calls or send e-mail to the White House asking for Kosovo independence, sustained air strikes until total Serb withdrawal from Kosovo, and arming of ethnic Albanians in Kosovo; and make and encourage others to make calls to their Representatives and Senators. An April 18 alert asked every community in the U.S. to establish a Kosova Room for action and information. Each room was to be equipped with a bank of phones for making 1,000 calls to the White House and Congress in support of resolution #HCR 9, calling for independence of Kosovo.

The International Campaign to Ban Landmines (ICBL), a loose coalition of over 1,300 groups from more than 75 countries, has made extensive use of the Internet in their efforts to stop the use, production, stockpiling, and transfer of antipersonnel landmines, and to increase international resources for humanitarian mine clearance and victim assistance. According to ICBL=s Liz Bernstein, the Net has been the dominant form of communication since 1996. It has been used to coordinate events and committee functions, distribute petitions and action alerts, raise money, and educate the public and media. Although most direct lobbying is done through face-to-face meetings and letters, e-mail has facilitated communications with government policy makers. Bernstein said the Net Ahas helped the nature of the campaign as a loose coalition, each campaign setting their own agenda yet with common information and communication. Ken Rutherford, co-founder of Land Mine Survivors Network, noted that the Internet also helped establish bridges from North America and Europe to Asia and Africa, and helped enable quick adoption of the 1997 landmine treaty. It became international law on March 1, 1999 and, as of September 16,1999, has been signed by 135 countries and ratified by 86. In 1997, the Nobel Peach Prize was awarded to the ICBL and its then coordinator, Jody Williams.

Human rights workers increasingly use the Internet to coordinate their actions against repressive governments. One tool that has become important in their battles is encryption, as it allows activists to protect communications and stored information from government interception. Human rights activists in Guatemala, for example, credited their use of Pretty Good Privacy (PGP) with saving the lives of witnesses to military abuses. Encryption is not the ultimate solution, however, as governments can outlaw its use and arrest those who do not comply.

PGP was originally developed by a Colorado engineer and activist, Phil Zimmermann, who wanted to make strong encryption available to the public for privacy protection against government eavesdroppers. Although the software was export-controlled, someone (not Zimmermann) quickly posted it on a foreign Internet site where it could be downloaded by anyone, anywhere, despite export regulations. Since then, other encryption tools have been posted on Internet sites all over the world, and the argument is frequently made that the availability of such tools demonstrates the futility of export controls. This is one factor driving export policy towards increased liberalization, but other factors have also contributed, including the role of encryption in electronic commerce and a concern that export controls harm the competitiveness of industry. That drive is countered, however, by a concern that the widespread availability of encryption will make it harder for law enforcement and intelligence agencies to gather intelligence from communications intercepts.

Indeed, terrorists also use the Internet to communicate and coordinate their activities. Back in 1996, the headquarters of terrorist financier bin Laden in Afghanistan was equipped with computers and communications equipment. Egyptian "Afghan" computer experts were said to have helped devise a communication network that used the Web, e-mail, and electronic bulletin boards. Hamas activists have been said to use chat rooms and e-mail to plan operations and coordinate activities, making it difficult for Israeli security officials to trace their messages and decode their contents.

The U.S. government's program to establish an Advanced Encryption Standard (AES) illustrates how government can use the Internet to invite and coordinate participation in a decision-making process of international significance. The Department of Commerce National Institute of Standards and Technology (NIST) set up a Web site with information about the AES program and AES conferences, a schedule of events, candidate encryption algorithms (more than half from outside the United States), documentation and test values, and links to public analysis efforts all over the world. The site contains an electronic discussion forum and Federal Register call for comments. Public comments are posted on the site and NIST representatives contribute to the on-line discussions and answer questions. Because the AES will offer a foundation for secure electronic commerce and privacy internationally, involving the international community from the beginning will help ensure its success and widespread adoption. Cryptographers from all over in the world have been participating.

NIST's use of the Internet to aid a decision process seems to be unusual. While most government sites provide an e-mail address for making contact, they do not support discussion forums or even actively solicit comments on specific pending policy decisions. However, to the extent that government agencies invite or welcome e-mail messages and input through electronic discussion groups, the Internet can serve the democratic process. Because it is easier to post or send a message on the Internet than to send a written letter, professionals and others with busy schedules may be more inclined to participate in a public consultation process or attempt to influence policy when policy makers are readily accessible through the Internet.

## Lobbying Decision Makers

Whether or not government agencies solicit their input, activists can use the Internet to lobby decision makers. One of the methods suggested by the Kosova Task Force for contacting the White

House, for example, was e-mail. Similarly, a Canadian Web site with the headline "Stop the NATO Bombing of Yugoslavia Now!" urged Canadians and others interested in stopping the war to send e-mails and/or faxes to the Canadian Prime Minister, Jean Chretien, and all members of the Canadian Parliament. A sample letter was included. The letter concluded with an appeal to Astop aggression against Yugoslavia and seek a peaceful means to resolve the Kosovo problem.

E-mail has been credited with halting a U.S. banking plan aimed to combat money laundering. Under the "Know Your Customer" policy, banks would have been required to monitor customer's banking patterns and report inconsistencies to federal regulators. Recognizing the value of the Internet to its deliberations, the Federal Deposit Insurance Corporation (FDIC) put up a Web site, published an e-mail address for comments, and printed out and tabulated each message. By the time the proposal was withdrawn, they had received 257,000 comments, 205,000 (80%) of which arrived through e-mail. All but 50 of the letters opposed the plan. FDIC=s chair, Donna Tanoue, said it was the huge volume of e-mail that drove the decision to withdraw the proposal. "It was the nature and the volume [of the comments]," she said. "When consumers can get excited about an esoteric bank regulation, we have to pay attention."

Most of the e-mail was driven by an on-line advocacy campaign sponsored by the Libertarian Party. About 171,000 (83%) of the e-mail messages were sent through the party's Web site. The party advertised its advocacy campaign in talk radio interviews and by sending a notice to its e-mail membership list. One could argue that the results were due more to the efforts of a large non-government organization than to a grassroots response from the citizens.

Indeed, many e-mail campaigns have been driven by non-government organizations. The organizations send e-mail alerts on issues to electronic mailing lists, offer sample letters to send members of Congress and other decision making bodies, and, in some cases, set up e-mailboxes or Web sites to gather signatures for petitions. The petition process can be automated, making it possible to gather huge volumes of signatures across a wide geographic area with little effort and cost. One Web site, e-The People, offers hundreds of petitions to choose from and 170,000 e-mail addresses of government officials. Computer Professionals for Social Responsibility (CPSR) organized an Internet petition campaign in early 1994 to protest the U.S. government's proposal to adopt the Clipper encryption chip as a standard. The chip offered strong encryption, but would have given law enforcement agencies the capability to decrypt a subject's messages when conducting a court-ordered wiretap against the subject. Despite numerous safeguards to ensure government agencies could not violate the privacy of users of the chip, Clipper was strongly opposed for privacy (and other) reasons, and the general sentiment expressed on Internet newsgroups and e-mail discussion lists was strongly anti-Clipper. CPSR announced their petition through e-mail and set up an e-mail address whereby people could sign on. They collected tens of thousands of signatures, but it is not clear the petition had much impact. The government moved forward with the standard anyway.

Although Clipper was to be a U.S. standard, it was tied in with the government=s foreign encryption policy. Because of its back door, it was to be generally exportable, unlike other encryption products with comparable cryptographic strength. Also, the Administration urged other governments to adopt a similar approach. However, after extensive lobbying efforts by industry and civil liberties groups, Clipper met its death. The government moved instead toward a more flexible and liberal approach to encryption export controls.

Because of the low cost of operation, individuals can run their own advocacy campaigns. For example, during the heart of the impeachment process against President Clinton, Joan Blades and Wes Boyd, a husband and wife team in Berkeley, founded MoveOn.org and put up a Web site inviting citizens to sign a one-sentence petition: "The Congress must immediately censure President Clinton and move on to pressing issues facing the country." In just four months, the petition gathered a half-million signatures. Another petition that read "In the Year 2000 election, I will work to elect candidates who courageously address key national issues and who reject the politics of division and personal destruction" was sent to every member of the House and Senate. MoveOn.org received pledges of $13 million and more than 650,000 volunteer hours for congressional candidates in the 2000 election who supported their position. It is difficult to assess the impact of the site on the impeachment process, but it may have amplified public opinion polls, which showed the American public supported Clinton and wanted Congress to turn to other issues.

While activists can attempt to influence policy makers through e-mail, it is not clear most policy makers listen (the FDIC, which asked for comments, was an exception). Richard Davis found that "the Internet has not lived up to its promise as a forum for public expression to elected officials. In fact, while publicly encouraging e-mail, members are becoming increasingly disenchanted with it. If the most idealistic members originally envisioned e-mail as the impetus for intelligent communication with constituents, they have seen e-mail deteriorate into a mass mailing tool for political activists." Davis concluded that "members may even discount e-mail communication." According to the Wall Street Journal, Senator Charles Schumer's office gives first priority to old-fashioned letters. Persons sending an e-mail to his account get back an automatic response telling them to submit a letter if they want a personal reply. The most successful advocacy groups are likely to be those that use the Internet to augment traditional lobbying methods, including personal visits to decision makers and use of broadcast media to reach the public. These operations can be time consuming and expensive, favoring groups that are well-funded. They also require a network of long-term and trusted relationships with policy makers, sponsors, and voters. This supports Davis's conclusion that the promise of the Internet as a forum for participatory democracy is unlikely to be realized. Davis found that existing dominant players in American politics — the media, interest groups, candidates, and policy makers — are adapting to the Internet to retain preeminence; and that the Internet is not an adequate tool for public political movement.

## Hacktivism

Hacktivism is the convergence of hacking with activism, where "hacking" is used here to refer to operations that exploit computers in ways that are unusual and often illegal, typically with the help of special software ("hacking tools"). Hacktivism includes electronic civil disobedience, which brings methods of civil disobedience to cyberspace. This section explores four types of operations: virtual sit-ins and blockades; automated e-mail bombs; Web hacks and computer break-ins; and computer viruses and worms. Because hacking incidents are often reported in the media, operations in this category can generate considerable publicity for both the activists and their causes.

## Virtual Sit-Ins and Blockades

A virtual sit-in or blockade is the cyberspace rendition of a physical sit-in or blockade. The goal in both cases is to call attention to the protestors and their cause by disrupting normal operations and blocking access to facilities.

With a sit-in, activists visit a Web site and attempt to generate so much traffic against the site that other users cannot reach it. A group calling itself Strano Network conducted one of the first such demonstrations as a protest against French government policies on nuclear and social issues. On December 21, 1995, they launched a one-hour Net-Strike attack against the Web sites operated by various government agencies. At the appointed hour, participants from all over the world were instructed to point their browsers to the government Web sites. According to reports, at least some of the sites were effectively knocked out for the period.

In 1998, the Electronic Disturbance Theater (EDT) took the concept of electronic civil disobedience a step further. They organized a series of Web sit-ins, first against Mexican President Zedillo=s Web site and later against President Clinton=s White House Web site, the Pentagon, the School of the Americas, the Frankfurt Stock Exchange, and the Mexican Stock Exchange. The purpose was to demonstrate solidarity with the Mexican Zapatistas.65 According to EDT=s Brett Stalbaum, the Pentagon was chosen because Awe believe that the U.S. military trained the soldiers carrying out the human rights abuses.@ For a similar reason, the School of the America=s was selected.66 The Frankfurt Stock Exchange was targeted, Stalbaum said, "because it represented capitalism's role in globalization utilizing the techniques of genocide and ethinic cleansing, which is at the root of the Chiapas' problems. The people of Chiapas should play a key role in determining their own fate, instead of having it pushed on them through their forced relocation (at gunpoint), which is currently financed by western capital."

To facilitate the strikes, the organizers set up special Web sites with automated software. All participants had to do was visit one of the FloodNet sites. When they did, their browser would download the software (a Java Applet), which would access the target site every few seconds. In addition, the software let protesters leave a personal statement on the targeted server=s error log. For example, if they pointed their browsers to a non-existent fiie such as "human_rights" on the target server, the server would return and log the message "human_rights not found on this server." Stalbaum, who wrote the software, characterized FloodNet as "conceptual net art that empowers people through active/artistic expression."

EDT estimated that 10,000 people from all over the world participated in the sit-in on September 9 against the sites of President Zedillo, the Pentagon, and the Frankfurt Stock Exchange, delivering 600,000 hits per minute to each. The Pentagon, however, did not sit by idly. It struck back. When their server sensed an attack from the FloodNet servers, they launched a counter-offensive against the users= browsers, redirecting them to a page with an Applet program called "HostileApplet."

Once there, the Applet was downloaded to their browsers, where it endlessly tied up their machines trying to reload a document until the machines were rebooted. President Zedillo=s site did not strike back on this occasion, but at a June sit-in, they used software that caused the protestors= browsers to open window after window until their computers crashed.

The Frankfurt Stock Exchange reported that they were aware of the protest, but believed it had not affected their services. They said that they normally got about 6 million hits a day. Overall, EDT considered the attack a success. "Our interest is to help the people of Chiapas to keep receiving the international recognition that they need to keep them alive," said Stalbaum.

When asked about the impact of their Web strikes, EDT's Ricardo Dominguez responded, "Digital Zapatismo is and has been one of the most politically effective uses of the Internet that we know of since January 1, 1994. It has created a distribution network of information with about 100 or more autonomous nodes of support. This has enabled the EZLN (Zapatista National Liberation Army) to speak to the world without having to pass through any dominant media filter. The Zapatistas were chosen by Wired as one of the twenty-five most important people on-line in 1998. ... The Zapatista network has, also, held back a massive force of men and the latest Drug War technologies from annihilating the EZLN in a few days." Regarding FloodNet specifically, he said the main purpose of the Electronic Disturbance Theatre's Zapatista FloodNet performance "is to bring the situation in Chiapas to foreground as often as possible. The gesture has created enough ripples with the Pentagon and the Mexican government that they have had to respond using both on-line and off-line tactics. Thus, these virtual sit-ins have captured a large amount of traditional media attention. You would not be interviewing us if this gesture had not been effective in getting attention to the issues on a global scale."

EDT has used their FloodNet software against the White House Web site to express opposition to U.S. military strikes and economic sanctions against Iraq. In their "Call for FloodNet Action for Peace in the Middle East," EDT articulated their philosophy. "We do not believe that only nation-states have the legitimate authority to engage in war and aggression. And we see cyberspace as a means for non-state political actors to enter present and future arenas of conflict, and to do so across international borders." Animal rights activists have also used the FoodNet software to protest the treatment of animals. Over 800 protestors from more than 12 countries joined a January 1999 sit-in against Web sites in Sweden.72 And on June 18, FloodNet was one of the tools used in the anti-capitalist attack coordinated by J18.

Whether Web sit-ins are legal is not clear. Mark Rasch, former head of the Department of Justice=s computer crime unit, said that such attacks run the risk of violating federal laws, which make it a crime to distribute a program, software code, or command with the intent to cause damage to another's site. AIt may be an electronic sit-in, but people get arrested at sit-ins,@ he said. A related question is the legality of using a denial-of-service counter-offensive. In the case of the Pentagon, their response most likely would be considered lawful, as it is permissible for a nation to take "proportional" actions to defend against an attack that threatens its security.

There are a variety of methods whereby an individual, acting alone, can disrupt or disable Internet servers. These frequently involve using attack software that floods the server with network packets. During the Kosovo conflict, Belgrade hackers were credited with conducting such attacks against NATO servers. They bombarded NATO=s Web server with Aping@ commands, which test whether a server is running and connected to the Internet. The effect of the attacks was to cause line saturation of the targeted servers.

When large numbers of individuals simultaneously attack a designated site, such as with the ECD Web sit-ins, the operation is sometimes referred to as "swarming." Swarming can amplify other types of attack, for example, a ping attack or an e-mail bombing (discussed next).

## E-Mail Bombs

It is one thing to send one or two messages to government policy makers, even on a daily basis. But it is quite another to bombard them with thousands of messages at once, distributed with the aid of automated tools. The effect can be to completely jam a recipient=s incoming e-mail box, making it impossible for legitimate e-mail to get through. Thus, an e-mail bomb is also a form of virtual blockade. Although e-mail bombs are often used as a means of revenge or harassment, they have also been used to protest government policies.

In what some U.S. intelligence authorities characterized as the first known attack by terrorists against a country's computer systems, ethnic Tamil guerrillas were said to have swamped Sri Lankan embassies with thousands of electronic mail messages. The messages read "We are the Internet Black Tigers and we=re doing this to disrupt your communications." An offshoot of the Liberation Tigers of Tamil Eelam, which had been fighting for an independent homeland for minority Tamils, was credited with the 1998 incident.

The e-mail bombing consisted of about 800 e-mails a day for about two weeks. William Church, editor for the Centre for Infrastructural Warfare Studies (CIWARS), observed that "the Liberation Tigers of Tamil are desperate for publicity and they got exactly what they wanted ... considering the routinely deadly attacks committed by the Tigers, if this type of activity distracts them from bombing and killing then CIWARS would like to encourage them, in the name of peace, to do more of this type of "terrorist activity." The attack, however, was said to have had the desired effect of generating fear in the embassies.

During the Kosovo conflict, protestors on both sides e-mail bombed government sites. According to PA News, Nato spokesman Jamie Shea said their server had been saturated at the end of March by one individual who was sending them 2,000 messages a day. Fox News reported that when California resident Richard Clark heard of attacks against NATO=s Web site by Belgrade hackers, he retaliated by sending an e-mail bomb to the Yugoslav government=s site. Clark said that a few days and 500,000 e-mails into the siege, the site went down. He did not claim full responsibility, but said he "played a part." That part did not go unrecognized. His Internet service provider, Pacific Bell, cut off his service, saying his actions violated their spamming policy.

An e-mail bombing was conducted against the San Francisco-based Internet service provider Institute for Global Communications (IGC) in 1997 for hosting the Web pages of the Euskal Herria Journal, a controversial publication edited by a New York group supporting independence of the mountainous Basque provinces of northern Spain and southwestern France. Protestors claimed IGC "supports terrorism" because a section on the Web pages contained materials on the terrorist group Fatherland and Liberty, or ETA, which was responsible for killing over 800 during its nearly 30-year struggle for an independent Basque state. The attack against IGC began after members of the ETA assassinated a popular town councilor in northern Spain. The protestor's objective was censorship. They wanted the site pulled. To get their way, they bombarded IGC with thousands of bogus messages routed through hundreds of different mail relays. As a result, mail was tied up and undeliverable to IGC's e-mail users, and support lines were tied up with people who couldn't get their mail. The attackers also spammed IGC staff and member accounts, clogged their Web page with bogus credit card orders, and threatened to employ the same tactics against organizations using IGC services. The only way IGC could stop the attack was by blocking access from all of the relay servers.

IGC pulled the site on July 18, but not before archiving a copy so that others could put up mirrors. Within days of the shutdown, mirror sites appeared on half a dozen servers on three continents. Chris Ellison, a spokesman for the Internet Freedom Campaign, an English group that was hosting one of the mirrors, said they believe "the Net should prove an opportunity to read about and discuss controversial ideas." The New York-based journal maintained their objective was to publish "Ainformation often ignored by the international media, and to build communication bridges for a better understanding of the conflict." An article by Yves Eudes in the French newspaper Le Monde said the e-mail bomb attack against the IGC site represented an "unprecedented conflict@ that Ahas opened up a new era of censorship, imposed by direct action from anonymous hackers."

About a month after IGC threw the controversial Basque journal Euskal Herria Journal off its servers, Scotland Yard=s Anti-Terrorist Squad shut down Internet Freedom's U.K. Web site for hosting the journal. According to a press release from Internet Freedom, the squad claimed to be acting against terrorism. Internet Freedom said it would move its news operations to its U.S. site.

The case involving Euskal Herria Journal illustrates the power of hacktivists on the Internet. Despite IGC's desire to host the controversial site, they simply could not sustain the attack and remain in business. They could have ignored a few e-mail messages demanding that the site be pulled, but they could not ignore an e-mail bombing. The case also illustrates the power of the Internet as a tool for free speech. Because Internet venues for publication are rich and dispersed throughout the world, it is extremely difficult for governments and hacktivists alike to keep content completely off the Internet. It would require extensive international cooperation and, even then, a site could operate out of a safe haven that did not sign on to international agreements.

## Web Hacks and Computer Break-Ins

The media is filled with stories of hackers gaining access to Web sites and replacing some of the content with their own. Frequently, the messages are political, as when a group of Portuguese hackers modified the sites of 40 Indonesian servers in September 1998 to display the slogan "Free East Timor" in large black letters. According to the New York Times, the hackers also added links to Web sites describing Indonesian human rights abuses in the former Portuguese Colony. Then in August 1999, Jose Ramos Horta, the Sydney-based Nobel laureate who represents the East Timor independence movement outside Indonesia, warned that a global network of hackers planned to bring Indonesia to a standstill if Jakarta sabotaged the ballot on the future of East Timor. He told the Sydney Morning Herald that more than 100 hackers, mostly teenagers in Europe and the United States, had been preparing the plan.

In June 1998, a group of international hackers calling themselves Milw0rm hacked the Web site of India's Bhabha Atomic Research Center (BARC) and put up a spoofed Web page showing a mushroom cloud and the text "If a nuclear war does start, you will be the first to scream ...". The hackers were protesting India=s recent nuclear weapons tests, although they admitted they did it mostly for thrills. They said that they also downloaded several thousand pages of e-mail and research documents, including messages between India's nuclear scientists and Israeli government officials, and had erased data on two of BARC's servers. The six hackers, whose ages range from 15 to 18, hailed from the United States, England, the Netherlands, and New Zealand. Another way in which hacktivists alter what viewers see when they go to a Web site is by tampering with the Domain Name Service so that the site=s domain name resolves to the IP address of some other site. When users point their browsers to the target site, they are redirected to the alternative site.

In what might have been one of the largest mass home page takeovers, the antinuclear Milw0rm hackers were joined by Ashtray Lumberjacks hackers in an attack that affected more than 300 Web sites in July 1998. According to reports, the hackers broke into the British Internet service provider EasySpace, which hosted the sites. They altered the ISP=s database so that users attempting to access the sites were redirected to a Milw0rm site, where they were greeted with a message protesting the nuclear arms race. The message concluded with "... use your power to keep the world in a state of PEACE and put a stop to this nuclear bullshit." John Vranesevich, who runs the hacker news site AntiOnline, said, "They're the equivalent to the World Trade Center bombings; [they] want to get their story told and bring attention to themselves."

Several Web sites were hacked during the Kosovo conflict. According to Fox News, the Boston Globe reported that an American hacking group called Team Spl0it broke into government Web sites and posted statements such as "Tell your governments to stop the war." Fox also said that the Kosovo Hackers Group, a coalition of European and Albanian hackers, had replaced at least five sites with black and red "Free Kosovo" banners. The Bosnian Serb news agency SRNA reported that the Serb Black Hand hackers group had deleted all data on a U.S. Navy computer, according to the Belgrade newspaper Blic. Members of the Black Hand group and Serbian Angel planned daily actions that would block and disrupt military computer operated by NATO countries, Blic wrote. Black Hand had earlier claimed responsibility for crashing a Kosovo Albanian Web site. "We shall continue to remove (ethnic) Albanian lies from the Internet," a member of the group told Blic.

In the wake of NATO's accidental bombing of China=s Belgrade embassy in May, angry Chinese allegedly hacked several U.S. government sites. Newsbytes reported that the slogan Adown with barbarians@ was placed in Chinese on the home page of the U.S. Embassy in Beijing, while the Department of Interior Web site showed images of the three journalists killed during the bombing, crowds protesting the attack in Beijing, and a fluttering Chinese flag. According to the Washington Post, Interior spokesman Tim Ahearn said their computer experts had traced their hacker back to China. The newspaper also reported that the Department of Energy's home page read:

"Protest U.S.A.=s Nazi action! Protest NATO=s brutal action! We are Chinese hackers who take no cares about politics. But we can not stand by seeing our Chinese reporters been killed which you might have know. Whatever the purpose is, NATO led by U.S.A. must take absolute responsibility. You have owed Chinese people a bloody debt which you must pay for. We won=t stop attacking until the war stops!"

NATO did not, of course, declare an end to the war because of the hacking. The impact on foreign policy decisions, if any at all, likely paled in comparison to the bombing itself. Following the accident, China suspended high-level military contacts with the United States. Acting in the name of democracy and human rights, hackers have targeted Chinese government computers. One group, called the Hong Kong Blondes, allegedly infiltrated police and security networks in an effort to monitor China=s intelligence activities and warn political targets of imminent arrests. According to OXblood Ruffin, "foreign minister" of the Cult of the Dead Cow, the Blondes are an underground group of Chinese dissidents who aim to destabilize the Chinese government. They have threatened to attack both Chinese state-owned organizations and Western companies investing in the country.

The Los Angeles Times reported that a California computer science student who calls himself Bronc Buster and his partner Zyklon cracked the Chinese network, defacing a government-run Web site on human rights and interfering with censorship. The hacker said they came across about 20 firewall servers blocking everything from Playboy.com to Parents.com, and that they disabled the blocking on five of the servers. He said they did not destroy any data, but only moved files.

Bronc Buster belonged to a group of 24 hackers known as the Legion of the Underground (LoU). In a press conference on Internet

Relay Chat (IRC) in late December 1998, an LoU member declared cyberwar on the information infrastructures of China and Iraq. He cited civil rights abuses and said LoU called for the complete destruction of all computer systems in China and Iraq.

The declaration of cyberwar prompted a coalition of other hacking groups to lash out against the campaign. A letter co-signed by 2600, the Chaos Computer Club, the Cult of the Dead Cow (CDC), !Hispahak, L0pht Heavy Industries, Phrack, Pulhas, and several members of the Dutch hacking community denounced the cyberwar, saying "Declaring war against a country is the most irresponsible thing a hacker group could do. This has nothing to do with hacktivism or hacker ethics and is nothing a hacker could be proud of." Reid Fleming of the CDC said "One cannot legitimately hope to improve a nation=s free access to information by working to disable its data networks."

By the time the letter went out, LoU had already issued a statement saying that the declaration of war on IRC did not represent the position of the group. "The LoU does not support the damaging of other nations computers, networks or systems in any way, nor will the LoU use their skills, abilities or connections to take any actions against the systems, networks or computers in China or Iraq which may damage or hinder in any way their operations." Bronc Buster said the IRC declaration was issued by a member before he left and never came back.

In August 1999, a cyberwar erupted between hackers in China and Taiwan. Chinese hackers defaced several Taiwanese and government Web sites with pro-China messages saying Taiwan was and would always be an inseparable part of China. "Only one China exists and only one China is needed," read a message posted on the Web site of Taiwan=s highest watchdog agency. Taiwanese hackers retaliated and planted a red and blue Taiwanese national flag and an anti-Communist slogan: "Reconquer, Reconquer, Reconquer the Mainland," on a Chinese high-tech Internet site. The cyberwar followed an angry exchange by Chinese and Taiwanese in response to Taiwan's President Lee Teng-hui's statement that China must deal with Taiwan on a "state-to-state" basis.

One of the consequences of hacking is that victims might falsely attribute an assault to a foreign government rather than the small group of activists that actually conducted it. This could strain foreign relations or lead to a more serious conflict.

The Chinese government has been accused of attacking a U.S. Web site devoted to the Falun Gong meditation sect, which Chinese authorities outlawed in July 1999. Bob McWee, a sect practitioner in Middleton, Maryland, said his site had been under a persistent electronic assault. In addition to a continuous denial-of-service attack, someone had tried breaking into his server. He said he was able to trace the penetration attempt to the Internet Monitoring Bureau of China's Public Security Ministry. If the attack did indeed originate with the Chinese police, this would have major foreign policy implications. It would suggest that the Chinese government views Web sites operating on foreign soil as legitimate targets of aggression when those sites support activities prohibited on home soil.

Web hacks and computer break-ins are extremely common, and targets include commercial and educational computers as well as government ones. The results of the 1999 Information Security Industry Survey showed that the number of companies experiencing penetrations jumped from 12% in 1997 to 23% in 1998 (almost double). About 26% of respondents to the ERRI/EmergencyNet News Local/County/State Computer "Hacking" Survey said they thought they had been the victims of an unauthorized intrusion or attack on their computer systems. And 30% of respondents to the 1999 CSI/FBI Computer Crime and Security Survey reported intrusions from outsiders. Most of the attacks, however, were probably not motivated by politics (hacktivism), but rather thrills, curiosity, ego, revenge, or financial gain. In the area of Web hacks alone, Attrition.Org recorded more than 1,400 cases of vandalism by July 1999 for the year.

## Computer Viruses and Worms

Hacktivists have used computer viruses and worms to spread protest message and damage target computer systems. Both are forms of malicious code that infect computers and propagate over computer networks. The difference is that a worm is an autonomous piece of software that spreads on its own, whereas a virus attaches itself to other files and code segments and spreads through those elements, usually in response to actions taken by users (e.g., opening an e-mail attachment). The boundary between viruses and worms, however, is blurry and not important to the discussion here.

The first protest to use a worm occurred about a decade ago, when anti-nuclear hackers released a worm into the U.S. National Aeronautics and Space Administration SPAN network. On October 16, 1989, scientists logging into computers at NASA's Goddard Space Flight Center in Greenbelt, Maryland, were greeted with a banner from the WANK

You talk of times of peace for all, and then prepare for war.

At the time of the attack, antinuclear protestors were trying to stop the launch of the shuttle that carried the Galileo probe on its initial leg to Jupiter. Galileo's 32,500-pound booster system was fueled with radioactive plutonium. John McMahon, protocol manager with NASA's SPAN office, estimated that the worm cost them up to half a million dollars of wasted time and resources. It did not have its intended effect of stopping the launch. The source of the attack was never identified, but some evidence suggested that it might have come from hackers in Australia.

Computer viruses have been used to propagate political messages and, in some cases, cause serious damage. In February 1999, the London Sunday Telegraph reported that an Israeli teen had become a national hero after he claimed to have wiped out an Iraqi government Web site. "It contained lies about the United States, Britain and Israel, and many horrible statements against Jews," 14-year-old Nir Zigdon said. "I figured that if Israel is afraid of assassinating Saddam Hussein, at least I can try to destroy his site. With the help of some special software I tracked down the site=s server to one of the Gulf states." The Tel Aviv hacktivist then sent a computer virus in an e-mail attachment to the site. "In the e-mail message, I claimed I was a Palestinian admirer of Saddam who had produced a virus capable of wiping out Israeli websites," Zigdon said. "That persuaded them to open the message and click on the designated file. Within hours the site had been destroyed. Shortly afterwards I received an e-mail from the site manager, Fayiz, that told me to 'go to hell'."

During the Kosovo conflict, businesses, public organizations, and academic institutes received virus-laden e-mails from a range of Eastern European countries, according to mi2g, a London-based Internet software company. "The contents of the messages are normally highly politicised attacks on NATO's unfair aggression and defending Serbian rights using poor English language and propaganda cartoons," the press release said. It went on to say "The damage to the addressee is usually incorporated in several viruses contained within an attachment, which may be plain language or anti-NATO cartoon." In an earlier press release, mi2g warned that "The real threat of cyber warfare from Serbian hackers is to the economic infrastructure of NATO countries and not to their better prepared military command and control network."

It is extremely difficult, perhaps impossible, for an organization to prevent all viruses, as users unwittingly open e-mail attachments with viruses and spread documents with viruses to colleagues. Although anti-viral tools can detect and eradicate viruses, the tools must be kept up-to-date across the enterprise, which may have tens of thousands of machines, and they must be installed and used properly. While viruses bearing political messages may not seem to pose a serious problem, an organization hit by one may have to shut down services in order to eradicate it from its network.

The seriousness of viruses is underscored by two recent surveys. The 1999 Information Security Industry survey found that 77% of respondents had experienced a computer virus. This was up from 73% in 1998. More distressing, the ERRI/EmergencyNet News Local/County/State Computer "Hacking" Survey found that almost 83% of respondents had been the victim of a virus. Even a benign virus could significantly impact the ability of governments to provide essential services.

Viruses, especially those carrying destructive payloads, are a potentially potent tool in the hands of cyberterrorists. Other tools of hacktivism, including computer network attacks, could likewise be put to highly destructive ends. This is the topic discussed next.

## CYBERTERRORISM

In the 1980s, Barry Collin, a senior research fellow at the Institute for Security and Intelligence in California, coined the term "cyberterrorism" to refer to the convergence of cyberspace and terrorism. Mark Pollitt, special agent for the FBI, offers a working definition: "Cyberterrorism is the premeditated, politically motivated attack against information, computer systems, computer programs, and data which result in violence against noncombatant targets by subnational groups or clandestine agents." Politically motivated attacks that cause serious harm, such as severe economic hardship or sustained loss of power or water, might also be characterized as cyberterrorism.

This section discusses the extent to which cyberterrorism is a problem today and is likely to be a problem in the near future. It also covers domestic and international initiatives aimed as countering a wide variety of cyberthreats, including cyberterrorism, certain forms of hacktivism, and other non-politically motivated computer network attacks.

### The Threat

As discussed in the preceding sections, terrorist groups are using the Internet extensively to spread their message and to communicate and coordinate action. However, there have been few if any computer network attacks that meet the criteria for cyberterrorism. The 1998 e-mail bombing by the Internet Black Tigers against the SRI Lanken embassies was perhaps the closest thing to cyberterrorism that has occurred so far, but the damage cause by the flood of e-mail, for example, pales in comparison to the deaths of 240 people from the physical bombings of the U.S. embassies in Nairobi and Dar es Salaam in August of that year.

Is cyberterrorism the way of the future? For a terrorist, it would have some advantages over physical methods. It could be conducted remotely and anonymously, it would be cheap, and it would not require the handling of explosives or a suicide mission. It would likely garner extensive media coverage, as journalists and the public alike are fascinated by practically any kind of computer attack. One highly acclaimed study of the risks of computer systems began with a paragraph that concludes "Tomorrow's terrorist may be able to do more with a keyboard than with a bomb."

In a 1997 paper, Collin describes several possible scenarios. In one, a cyberterrorist hacks into the processing control system of a cereal manufacturer and changes the levels of iron supplement. A nation of children get sick and die. In another, a cyberterrorist attacks the next generation of air traffic control systems. Two large civilian aircraft collide. In a third, a cyberterrorist disrupts banks, international financial transactions, and stock exchanges. Economic systems grind to a halt, the public loses confidence, and destabilization is achieved.

Analyzing the plausibility of Collin's hypothetical attacks, Pollitt concludes that there is sufficient human involvement in the control processes used today that cyberterrorism does not B at present B pose a significant risk in the classical sense. In the cereal contamination scenario, for example, he argues that the quantity of iron (or any other nutritious substance) that would be required to become toxic is so large that assembly line workers would notice. They would run out of iron on the assembly line and the product would taste different and not good. In the air traffic control scenario, humans in the loop would notice the problems and take corrective action. Pilots, he says, are trained to be aware of the situation, to catch errors made by air traffic controllers, and to operate in the absence of any air traffic control at all. Pollitt does not imply by his analysis that computers are safe and free from vulnerability. To the contrary, his argument is that despite these vulnerabilities, because humans are in the loop, a cyberattack is unlikely to have such devastating consequences. He concludes that "As we build more and more technology into our civilization, we must ensure that there is sufficient human oversight and intervention to safeguard those whom technology serves."

In a 1997 article titled "How Many Terrorists Fit on a Computer Keyboard?" William Church presents a strong case that the United States does not yet face a compelling threat from terrorists using information warfare techniques to disrupt critical infrastructure.

They lack either the motivation, capabilities, or skills to pull off a cyberattack at this time. Church does not rule out a physical attack against the infrastructure, but such a threat is neither new nor matured by U.S. reliance on technology.

There are drawbacks to terrorists using cyber weapons over physical ones. Because systems are complex, it may be harder to control an attack and achieve a desired level of damage. Unless people are injured, there is also less drama and emotional appeal. Further, terrorists may be disinclined to try new methods unless they see their old ones as inadequate.

There is little concrete evidence of terrorists preparing to use the Internet as a venue for inflicting grave harm. However, in February 1998, Clark Staten, executive director of the Emergency Response & Research Institute in Chicago, testified that it was believed that "members of some Islamic extremist organizations have been attempting to develop a >hacker network= to support their computer activities and even engage in offensive information warfare attacks in the future." And in November, the Detroit News reported that Khalid Ibrahim, who claimed to be a member of the militant Indian separatist group Harkat-ul-Ansar, had tried to buy military software from hackers who had stolen it from U.S. Department of Defense computers they had penetrated. Harkat-ul-Ansar, one of the 30 terrorist organizations on the State Department list, declared war on the United States following the August cruise-missile attack on a suspected terrorist training camp in Afghanistan run by Osama bin Laden, which allegedly killed nine of their members. The attempted purchase was discovered when an 18-year-old hacker calling himself Chameleon attempted to cash a $1,000 check from Ibrahim. Chameleon said he did not have the software and did not give it to Ibrahim, but Ibrahim may have obtained it or other sensitive information from one of the many other hackers he approached.

Given that there are no instances of cyberterrorism, it is not possible to assess the impact of acts that have taken place. It is equally difficult to assess potential impact, in part because it is hard to predict how a major computer network attack, inflicted for the purpose of affecting national or international policy, would unfold. So far, damages from attacks committed for reasons other than terrorism, for example, to seek revenge against a former employer, have generally been confined to immediate targets. No lives have been lost.

## Cyberdefense

The main impact of cyberthreats on foreign and domestic policy relates to defending against such acts, particularly attacks against critical infrastructures. At the international level, several countries, including the U.S., have been addressing such issues as mutual legal assistance treaties, extradition, the sharing of intelligence, and the need for uniform computer crime laws so that cybercriminals can be successfully investigated and prosecuted even when their crimes cross international borders, as they so often do. This effort is not focused on either cyberterrorism or hacktivism, but rather addresses an array of actions that includes all forms of hacking and computer network attacks, computer and telecommunications fraud, child pornography on the Net, and electronic piracy (software, music, etc.). It also covers state-sponsored cyberwarfare operations that use hacking and computer network attacks as a military weapon.

At the initiative of the Russian Federation, the U.N. General Assembly adopted a resolution related to cybercrime, cyberterrorism, and cyberwarfare in December 1998. Resolution 53/70, Developments in the Field of Information and Telecommunications in the Context of International Security, invites member states to inform the Secretary-General of their views and assessments on (a) the issues of information security, (b) definition of basic notions related to information security, and 8 advisability of developing international principles that would enhance the global information and telecommunications systems and help combat information terrorism and criminality.

The U.S. has taken several steps to better protect its critical infrastructures. In July 1996, President Clinton announced the formation of the President=s Commission on Critical Infrastructure Protection (PCCIP) to study the critical infrastructures that constitute the life support systems of the nation, determine their vulnerabilities to a wide range of threats, and propose a strategy for protecting them in the future. Eight infrastructures were identified: telecommunications, banking and finance, electrical power, oil and gas distribution and storage, water supply, transportation, emergency services, and government services. In their final report, issued in October 1997, the commission reported that the threats to critical infrastructures were real and that, through mutual dependence and interconnectedness, they could be vulnerable in new ways. "Intentional exploitation of these new vulnerabilities could have severe consequences for our economy, security, and way of life."

The PCCIP noted that cyberthreats have changed the landscape. "In the past we have been protected from hostile attacks on the infrastructures by broad oceans and friendly neighbors. Today, the evolution of cyberthreats has changed the situation dramatically. In cyberspace, national borders are no longer relevant. Electrons don't stop to show passports. Potentially serious cyberattacks can be conceived and planned without detectable logistic preparation. They can be invisibly reconnoitered, clandestinely rehearsed, and then mounted in a matter of minutes or even seconds without revealing the identity and location of the attacker."

In assessing the threat from both physical and cyberattacks, the PCCIP concluded that "Physical means to exploit physical vulnerabilities probably remain the most worrisome threat to our infrastructures today. But almost every group we met voiced concerns about the new cyber vulnerabilities and threats. They emphasized the importance of developing approaches to protecting our infrastructures against cyberthreats before they materialize and produce major system damage." The recommendations of the PCCIP led to Presidential Decision Directive (PDD) 63, which established the National Infrastructure Protection Center (NIPC), the Critical Infrastructure Assurance Office (CIA), the National Infrastructure Assurance Council (NIAC), and private sector Information Sharing and Assessment Centers (ISACs).129 The Department of Defense also established a Joint Task Force - Computer Network Defense (JTF-CND).

That critical systems are potentially vulnerable to cyberattacks was underscored by a June 1997 exercise, code named Eligible Receiver, conducted by the National Security Agency (NSA). The objective was to determine the vulnerability of U.S. military computers and some civilian infrastructures to a cyberattack. According to reports, two-man teams targeted specific pieces of the military infrastructure, including the U.S. Pacific Command in Hawaii, which oversees 100,000 troops in Asia. One person played the role of the attacker, while another observed the activity to ensure that it was conducted as scripted. Using only readily available hacking tools that could easily be obtained from the Internet, the NSA hackers successfully gained privileged access on numerous systems. They concluded that the military infrastructure could be disrupted and possible troop deployments hindered. The exercise also included written scenarios against the power grid and emergency 911 system, with resulting service disruptions. For the latter, they postulated that by sending sufficient e-mails to Internet users telling them the 911 system had a problem, enough curious people would phone 911 at once to overload the system. No actual attacks were made against any civilian infrastructures.

The vulnerability of commercial systems to cyberattacks is repeatedly demonstrated by survey results such as those mentioned earlier. There is no evidence that non-government systems are any more or less vulnerable than government ones, or that the security posture of either group, as a whole, is generally improving — despite the availability and use of a growing supply of information security tools.

## Conclusions

The Internet is clearly changing the landscape of political discourse and advocacy. It offers new and inexpensive methods for collecting and publishing information, for communicating and coordinating action on a global scale, and for reaching out to policy makers. It supports both open and private communication. Advocacy groups and individuals worldwide are taking advantage of these features in their attempts to influence foreign policy.

Several case studies show that when the Internet is used in normal, non-disruptive ways, it can be an effective tool for activism, especially when it is combined with other media, including broadcast and print media and face-to-face meetings with policy makers. As a technology for empowerment, the Net benefits individuals and small groups with few resources as well as organizations that are large or well-funded. It facilitates activities such as educating the public and media, raising money, forming coalitions across geographical boundaries, distributing petitions and action alerts, and planning and coordinating events on a regional or international level. It allows activists in politically repressive states to evade government censors and monitors.

In the area of hacktivism, which involves the use of hacking tools and techniques of a disruptive nature, the Internet will serve mainly to draw attention to a cause, as such incidents are regularly reported by news media. Whether that attention has the desired effect of changing policy decisions related to the issue at hand is much less certain. Hacktivists may feel a sense of empowerment, because they can control government computers and get media attention, but that does not mean they will succeed in changing policy. So far, anecdotal evidence suggests that for the majority of cases, they will not.

With regards to cyberterrorism, that is, the use of hacking tools and techniques to inflict grave harm such as loss of life, few conclusions can be drawn about its potential impact on foreign policy, as there have been no reported incidents that meet the criteria. What can be said is that the threat of cyberterrorism, combined with hacking threats in general, is influencing policy decisions related to cyberdefense at both a national and international level. If one looks at terrorism in general for insights into the potential impact of cyberterrorism, one finds that the impact of terrorism on the foreign policy issues at hand is similarly difficult to assess, but here again, the threat of terrorism, particularly chem, bio, and nuclear terrorism, is having a significant impact on national defense policy.

# 9

# Putting Cyberterrorism into Context

With the growth of the Internet in both its size and functionality from the 1970s through to the present, we have seen a massive change in both the nature of the threats and the level of malicious attack activity directed against Internet-connected systems.

During the last decade, broad sections of government and industry have embraced the Internet as a generally reliable and cost-effective platform for business critical communication and services. During the same period, with increased exposure to and dependence on Internet connectivity and dependent services, government, media and the public have also increasingly given more attention to the potential threat of cyberterrorism to these Internet-connected systems, particularly for the critical information infrastructures of nation states. In this regard, Australia is no different from most affluent and technology dependent nations.

For sometime now (even dating back to the Gulf War in 1991) there has been a heightened level of interest in the potential threat of cyberterrorism coupled with an unhelpful amount of hype and misinformation surrounding the use of the term.

Part of the problem is one of definition - there are broadly different definitions as to what actually constitutes 'cyberterrorism'. There are a number of well-accepted definitions which share common similarities and are outlined below. But increasingly, there are a number of loose definitions which are promulgated to encourage the purchase of particular computer security products or services or to generate interest in a story by the media. If these definitions are not clearly articulated, an uninformed reader/viewer may rely on their own, possibly misinformed, understanding of the nature of the threat of cyberterrorism. As long as the term 'cyberterrorism' continues to be used loosely and inconsistently, misinformation and hype associated with the threat will remain.

The purpose of this article is to present a legitimate definition of 'cyberterrorism' and identify some common misuses of the term. Once we are clear about accepted uses of the term, we will then provide an assessment of the threat of cyberterrorism for Australian networks and compare this threat with other existing cyber threats.

## Definition

Before defining 'cyberterrorism' it is necessary to define and understand what we mean by 'terrorism' - afterall there should be similarities between the usage of the terms. The United States' State Department defines terrorism as politically motivated acts of violence against non-combatants.

In Australia, the recently enacted *Security Legislation Amendment (Terrorism) Act 2002* defines a terrorist act to mean:

*an action or threat of action where:*

(a) the action falls within subsection (2) and does not fall within subsection (2A); and

(b) the action is done or the threat is made with the intention of advancing a political, religious or ideological cause; and

(c) the action is done or the threat is made with the intention of:

(i) coercing, or influencing by intimidation, the government of the Commonwealth or a State, Territory or foreign country, or of part of a State, Territory or foreign country; or

(ii) intimidating the public or a section of the public.

(2) Action falls within this subsection if it:

(a) causes serious harm that is physical harm to a person; or

(b) causes serious damage to property; or

(c) causes a person's death; or

(d) endangers a person's life, other than the life of the person taking the action; or

(e) creates a serious risk to the health or safety of the public or a section of the public; or

*(f) seriously interferes with, seriously disrupts, or destroys, an electronic system including, but not limited to:*

(i) an information system; or

(ii) a telecommunications system; or

(iii) a financial system; or

(iv) a system used for the delivery of essential government services; or

(v) a system used for, or by, an essential public utility; or

*(vi) a system used for, or by, a transport system.*

(2A) Action falls within this subsection if it:

(a) is advocacy, protest, dissent or industrial action; and

*(b) is not intended:*

(i) to cause serious harm that is physical harm to a person; or

(ii) to cause a person's death; or

(iii) to endanger the life of a person, other than the person taking the action; or

*(iv) to create a serious risk to the health or safety of the public or a section of the public.*

In a study of 109 academic and official definitions of terrorism, three common elements were identified:

- the use of violence
- political objectives
- the purpose of sowing fear within a target population

For cyberterrorism to apply, these same elements should also exist as they do in the following definitions:

1. According to the US Federal Bureau of Investigation: Cyberterrorism is any premeditated, politically motivated attack against information, computer systems, computer

programs, and data which results in violence against non-combatant targets by sub-national groups or clandestine agents.

2. A definition of cyberterrorism proposed by the US National Infrastructure Protection Center is a criminal act perpetrated by the use of computers and telecommunications capabilities, resulting in violence, destruction and/or disruption of services to create fear by causing confusion and uncertainty within a given population, with the goal of influencing a government or population to conform to a particular political, social, or ideological agenda.
3. Dorothy Denning defines cyberterrorism as unlawful attacks and threats of attack against computers, networks, and the information stored therein when done to intimidate or coerce a government or its people in furtherance of political or social objectives. Further, to qualify as cyberterrorism, an attack should result in violence against persons or property, or at least cause enough harm to generate fear.
4. James A. Lewis, Centre for Strategic and International Studies (2002) defined cyberterrorism as the use of computer network tools to shut down critical national infrastructures (such as energy, transportation, government operations) or to coerce or intimidate a government or civilian population.

Interestingly, two of the definitions (2 and 4) specify that computer systems or telecommunication cababilities are used to conduct cyberterrorist attacks. The other two definitions (1 and 3) only specify that computer and information systems are the targets of cyberterrorist attacks. Arguably both elements should apply. While an information system can be attacked in any number of ways (eg, conventional methods involving bombing, arson, etc), for an act to be classed as *cyber*terrorism, the attacker must use information systems or other electronic means to launch the attack (as applies to the term 'bioterrorism', where the method of attack is a toxic biological agent).

Cyberterrorism is but one form of cyber attack. Too often the terms cyberterrorism and cyber attack are used interchangeably and may result in a misunderstanding of the cyber threat in general and the threat of cyberterrorism in particular. These definitions demonstrate that for cyberterrorism to be perpetrated there are at least three elements which must be satisfied in order to distingish a cyberterrorist attack from an ordinary cyber attack. Denning notes that politically motivated cyber attacks that lead to death or bodily injury, explosions, or severe economic loss would be examples of cyberterrorism. Serious attacks against critical infrastructures could be acts of cyberterrorism, depending on their impact. Attacks that disrupt non-essential services or that are mainly a costly nuisance would not. Most cyber attacks in Australia, even 'serious' ones, will be offences under the Commonwealth *Cybercrime Act 2001* or similar State legislation rather than offences under the *Security Legislation Amendment (Terrorism) Act 2002*.

To date, there is no known publicly reported incident of cyberterrorism in the world that meets the first three definitions outlined above. The fourth definition, has been met, but only in so far as there have been several serious cyber attacks against critical information infrastructures but these are not assessed to be politically motivated .

## What Cyberterrorism is Not

In contrast to the above definitions, cyberterrorism has been used improperly to refer to the use of:

- encryption technologies for secure electronic storage of data and communication by and between supporters/ members of known terrorist groups;
- various forms of electronic communications (web sites, email etc) for the purposes of recruiting supporters, organising and communicating the messages (propaganda) of known terrorist groups;
- the occasional use by known terrorist groups of cyber attack techniques which are incapable of causing bodily harm, fear or serious economic damage; and
- the occurrence of port scans from countries considered to sponsor terrorism or which harbour known terrorist groups.

## What is the Threat of Cyberterrorism?

Assessments of the threat of cyberterrorism require an assessment of the intent and capability of attackers to cause fear and/or physical harm through cyber attack techniques. Except perhaps for national security agencies which are tasked with collecting and analysing intelligence about terrorist threats, there are few who are able to comment authoritatively on the intent or capability of known terrorist groups to conduct acts of cyberterrorism.

Notwithstanding this, there are however, some factors which are relevant to an assessment of the threat.

1. Terrorists by and large are not innovators: Despite a relatively long history of terrorism, to date terrorists' modus operandi mostly has involved the threat of physical harm; actual maiming or killing of people; and damage to property. In the vast majority of cases, terrorists have used conventional methods which involve the use of affordable, accessible and volatile substances, eg improvised explosive devices or weaponry. Less often non-conventional methods have been used such as the Aum Shinrikyo sarin gas attack on the Tokyo subway in 1995. But through the use of a chemical weapon, Aum Shinrikyo still sought to cause physical harm to a large group of people - necessary for instilling fear within a target population.
2. Terrorist attacks on critical infrastructures have used conventional methods of attack: Terrorists have frequently targeted critical infrastructure and sometimes this has been to cause disruption only. For example, during the 1990s, some of the operations planned and conducted by the Provisional Irish Republican Army were assessed to have the primary goal of causing damage and disruption to critical infrastructures while minimising harm to people. Two examples include the October 1992 week-end bombing of the Square Mile financial district of London. and the planned bombing of six substations of the London power grid in 1997.

At other times terrorists have targed critical infrastructures, including critical information infrastructures to maximise disruption in addition to generating fear through deliberate attacks on human life (as occurred with the World Trade Center attacks). World-wide there have been numerous cases of conventional methods used to attack critical information and other infrastructures.

3. Cyber attack as a tool for terrorism has limitations and would not be regarded as the tool of choice by most terrorists

**Uncertainty of attack impact:** A computer network attack on a critical information system such as a Supervisory Control and Data Acquisition (SCADA) system that controls devices which provide essential services such as power or gas, may potentially cause a harmful and unwanted incident that could seriously damage property or endanger lives. This is the essential concern associated with a cyberterrorist attack. While this is a possibility, unless the attacker has an intimate knowledge of the system being targeted then the best an attacker can expect is that the impact will be unknown or unreliable. Add to this the ability of network operators to manually over ride critical systems in the event of a malfunction or fail safe mechanisms to be triggered, then it is more difficult for an attacker to be certain his actions will achieve the desired result. By contrast, the impact of a conventional attack, on a critical information system or other target, is immediate and unequivocal and would require significantly less knowledge of the inner workings of the system itself .

**Recovery from a cyber attack is likely to be quicker and easier:** A computer network or electronic attack on critical computer control systems, such as SCADA systems, requires the attacker to manipulate data within that system to affect the way the systems being controlled by the attacked system, function. Once a computer network attack has been detected and diagnosed, corrections can usually be made to prevent further damage and compromise to the system itself and to the systems it controls. Recovery from a computer network attack on a critical information system can occur more quickly than a conventional attack - perhaps requiring a reinstall of operating system or other critical applications, back-up files, or additonal network hardening etc. By contrast, a conventional attack will usually involve serious physical damage and require the rebuilding of complex pieces of equipment and facilities which is likely to take considerably more time and resources than would be to recover from the system changes due to a cyber attack. If recovery is able to occur quickly then from a terrorist perspective, the attack may be less effective as a means of instilling fear or causing serious damage .

**Plausible deniability:** "Plausible deniability" in the context of cyber attacks generally refers to the ability of an attacker to conceal the true source of the attack, ie plausibly deny they did it . But 'plausible deniability' may also extend to the attacked site. In the event a critical service disruption or malfunction occurs due to a cyber attack, without evidence of clear physical damage, operators may plausibly deny the cause of the disruption or malfunction was due to a cyber attack. The detection and correct diagnosis of a cyber attack relies on the examination and analysis of largely hidden computer forensic evidence (assuming it is collected and retained for examination). By contrast, conventional attacks exhibit clear observable physical evidence that an attack took place. Denying it would be more difficult, if not infeasible. Regardless of how successful a cyber attack may prove to be in causing serious disruption to critical services or serious economic damage, without the targeted population being aware that the disruption was the result of a terrorist operation, then the incident loses its ability to generate fear and be an effective tool of terror, and becomes indistinguishable from other prolonged disruptions to essential services that have occurred in Australia and elsewhere.

**Vulnerability of critical information systems to cyber attack:** Finally, an assessment of the threat of cyberterrorism depends on the extent to which critical information systems are vulnerable to cyber attack. The greater their perceived and actual vulnerability, the more likely a terrorist may consider or experiment with cyber attack and the easier an attack will be. In theory, if the systems are recognised as being critical then the owners and operators of these systems should seek to mitigate the risk by protecting against cyber attacks to these systems - not only from cyber terrorists, but from others who may hold greater intent and capability to conduct attacks, including disgruntled employees or contractors, competitors, or ordinary hackers (attackers), or possibly nation states with identified information warfare programs during times of war.

If critical information infrastructures are being protected to the extent required of a critical system, ie commensurate with the risk, then the opportunities for targeting these systems by terrorists or others *should* theoretically be low. (Admittedly, *"should be"* and *"will be"* are not the same and this assumption may not apply to all critical systems. There have been an increasing number of reports claiming that some SCADA and other critical information systems are vulnerable to cyber attack , but while relevant, is beyond the scope of this current paper).

**What is the threat of other forms of politically-motivated cyber attacks?** During recent international conflicts or events and particularly since the emergence of the world wide web in the early 90s, politically motivated cyber attack activity or 'hacktivism' has been used as a form of protest around the world. But in comparison to other cyber attacks, it occurs less often. Politically motivated cyber attacks were launched during the Balkans conflict, during globalisation talks and in response to the Bali bombings, to name just a few examples .

Politically motivated cyber attacks, as a form of protest, usually involve web site defacements (with a political message) or some types of denial of service (DoS) attack and are usually conducted by loosely organised hacker groups or individuals, with hacker skills, sympathetic to a particular cause or who align themselves with a particular side in a conflict. For example, the downing of a US spy plane in Chinese airspace, resulted in an increase in attacks from both Chinese and US hackers (mostly web site defacements) who were apparently displeased with 'the other side' . Another example occurred, in 1997 when a group aligned with the Liberation Tigers of Tamil Elam (LTTE) reportedly swamped Sri Lankan embassies with 800 e-mails a day over a two-week period. The messages read

"We are the Internet Black Tigers and we're doing this to disrupt your communications." While the cyber attack was politically motivated, from the outset the attack was incapable of harming people or property or instilling fear into the target population. Its impact was primarily designed to cause disruption to the Sri Lankan embassies' email operations but with alternative forms of electronic communications available to the embassies, in all likelihood, the attack did not have a serious impact on critical lines of communication.

While DoS attacks have been used as form of political protest, they are most effective when the attacker publicly advertises the reason for the attack, eg through virtual-sit-ins which invite participation from ordinary Internet users as a form of political protest . Such attacks are usually symbolic expressions of protest and while they may be illegal are not intended to, or are incapable of causing damage or disruption sufficient to endanger life or cause serious economic damage. Such attacks are likely to continue on an opportunistic basis in response to international and global conflict.

**What is the threat of common forms of cyber attack?** Any organisation with an Internet connection faces a significant threat of cyber attack. The rate of malicious scanning that occurs against networks, the rate of new information about serious computer vulnerabilities and the frequency of reports of serious computer attacks crime demonstrate that the opportunities for attack are numerous as are the number of attackers willing to launch such attacks. The motives for other forms of cyber attack also vary and may range from illicit financial gain, personal use of resources, competitor advantage or malicious damage. Additionally, many attacks are indiscriminate, as attackers are less concerned with who they are attacking rather than launching the attack itself.

## CONCLUSION

The threat of cyber attack for organisations with Internet connections is high. For the most part this threat has little to do with the occurrence of conventional terrorist attacks, increased international tensions or nation state conflicts. Certainly, these events may increase the threat of politically motivated web site defacements or other forms of politically motivated low impact cyber attack, but only slightly. These forms of attack still occur relatively infrequently, despite tumultous events over the last few years, and requires a system to be vulnerable in order for a compromise to succeed. Cyberterrorism, while possible, is assessed to be very unlikely - and indeed, as far as we and others are aware - there have been no reported cases of it which match the above definitions. At present, terrorists seem to prefer the mileage to be gained from conventional methods of attack.

Misuse of the term or a pre-occupation with cyberterrorism as the seeming greatest source of threat may divert attention from addressing other forms of cyber attack which are capable of causing serious harm to organisations and infrastructures and which have occurred far more often and will continue to do so. Our focus should be on preventing serious and harmful cyber attack regardless of who conducts them or what their motives may be. If organisations are taking steps to protect themselves from ordinary cyber attacks of the type that are reported in the media and the *2003 Australian Computer Crime and Security Survey*, then they will be well placed to protecting against all forms of cyber attack.

As a final footnote, the Canberra bushfires earlier this year illustrated how a natural disaster, assessed to be a one in a hundred year event, was able to disrupt and damage critical telecommunications, power, gas, water and sewerage infrastructures, for an extended period of time and affected individuals, businesses, government and organisations that depended on these services. Organisations and businesses should therefore ensure they focus on managing all threats - deliberate, accidental or natural - logical or physical - and implement appropriate security measures to manage that risk. This includes having in place sound disaster recovery or business continuity plans and computer incident response plans.

# 10

# Critical Information Infrastructure Protection

## INTRODUCTION

"Cyberspace" can be defined as "the union of all extensive information and communication technology networks". In other words, it is the set of all computer communications networks, of which the Internet is the largest and most relevant piece. There are some networks outside what is discussed here, and these too have security issues that have been addressed elsewhere.

Cyberspace is a major technology-enabled medium providing the means of passage and the locus of objects of value. Many "critical information infrastructures" (CIIs) in the United States, Europe, and increasingly elsewhere in the world, depend on computer-communications systems for direct control and other functions. You could say that "cyberspace" includes a significant amount of "control space". The infrastructures in question include major forms of transportation, banking and finance, energy distribution, emergency preparedness and response, and public health. In this paper I will outline aspects of Critical Information Infrastructure Protection (CIIP), first setting it in the context of how cyberspace has spread globally, and of Internet security. Secondly, we will consider the various threats to which cyberspace is exposed. It is the vehicle of, and the potential victim of, globalization. We will summarize the uses which terrorists have made of cyberspace. A range of measures are seen as essential for protecting critical infrastructure. Effective communication of R&D agendas will allow preventative steps to be taken, or attacks to be repelled as quickly as possible. Governments and the private sector should work to build cyber security capabilities, especially by forming CSIRTs (Cyber Security Incident Response Teams). A legal framework for this new technology must be developed in terms of national legislation and, in view of the worldwide character of the networks, international conventions.

## CYBERSPACE AT A GLANCE

For the most part, the Internet is built upon national and international telecommunications infrastructures, including the landlines of most public phone systems and wireless, and satellite communications. Beyond the Internet, these telecommunications infrastructures tend to be highly dependent on computing technology. Thus, by our definition, they are part of cyberspace. There are currently about 1.3 billion Internet users worldwide. The Internet now comes to ground in over 200 "countries" (Top-Level Domains, i.e. the letters which follow the dot after the domain name).

This enormous growth has been achieved since the early 90s. The only thing growing faster than the Internet is cellular telephony, with about three billion phones in use, to which 1.6 million users are added every day. The fact that soon cellular telephones will be a platform for the Internet means that at least a billion new users will have access to this resource, and this expansion will mostly be in developing countries.

### (In)Security (Internet Security) at a Glance

The architecture, design, and practice of the Internet emphasize *access* (ease of use, low cost, universality). It has almost never considered security as a primary or important factor. It is an unfortunate result of the history of the way the Internet was developed that the protocols used by the Internet today are derived from those that were established in the early days of the ARPANet, where there were only a few wellrespected researchers using the infrastructure, and they were trusted to do no harm. Consequently, security considerations were not built in to the Internet. All cybersecurity measures taken today to protect the Internet are add-on measures that do not remedy the underlying security deficiencies.

The situation we have as a result is that current technology asymmetrically favors the attackers; it provides them great "nonlinear leverage", and attackers get their innovations into practice more quickly and effectively than defenders. If we make a comparison between cyber attacks and modern warfare, we would say that it is an asymmetrical conflict. While the state, because of its capacity, has a huge technological advantage over terrorists, the problem is that the kinds of nonlinearities associated with what terrorists do in cyberspace give leverage to those with relatively little technical capability. What has always been thought of as one of the great advantages of the networks can also threaten them: They give a small number of relatively weak people extensive access to a lot of information, each other, potential recruits and sympathizers, and prospective targets. There is also a negative aspect of tightening access against terrorists or other malicious users more generally because it would compromise access and privacy for many, many more "good" users.

The functionality of the Internet ranges greatly. Of particular concern for those aware of the threat of terrorism is the fact that SCADA (Supervisory Control and Data Acquisition) systems now more commonly use the Internet to transmit data and control instructions, rather than the dedicated networks that had been used before. Additionally, very few of the "cyber" parts of the critical infrastructures were designed or implemented with security as much of a consideration, if it was considered at all. Most are riddled with vulnerabilities, which are defined as weaknesses that can be exploited through either hostile attacks or accidents. It would be almost impossible to create "patches" to protect programs from malicious people who seek to find and exploit these vulnerabilities.

Another problem to recognize is that Internet defense pushes the burden outward to the end user organizations; most of these find it difficult, and often increasingly difficult, to defend themselves.

In particular, most of the over two hundred connected countries have little or no national cybersecurity capabilities.

## International Threats Arising from Globalization

One area of concern that extends broadly across all of the stages of defense is that globalization creates new populations of "insiders"—people who have authorized access with the potential for abuse that can cause great harm. Insiders still probably account for a majority of successful penetrations for criminal purposes. The problem is complicated by changes in organizational relations and technical architectures that make "inside" and "outside" more difficult even to define. The possibility that a terrorist or a terrorist sympathizer might gain employment that would enable him or her to conduct a devastating attack or to provide critical information or access to others cannot be discounted or ignored.

The two most general ways of dealing with infiltration are through deep preemployment investigations, something that most non-government entities are neither capable of doing nor permitted to do in many countries, and through stronger forms of containment and compartmentalization of access within an organization. Globalization has meant that the Internet is now less secure, with vulnerabilities resulting from new systems "intimacies". Transfer of information now takes place in unprecedented transnational contexts.

A particular problem for those who want to control or police the Internet is the spread and ownership of, and access to, transnational transportation infrastructures. Much of the day to day running is outsourced, and offshoring (outsourcing to foreign entities) means that any attempts to control the Internet require international cooperation.

## Terrorists in Cyberspace

What do we know or anticipate that terrorists want to do in cyberspace? I believe the answers to this question fall into three categories:

1. Terrorists want to support their activities and infrastructure, but not directly through an attack, using the Internet.
2. They may want explicitly to attack parts of the cyber infrastructure.

3. They may use cyberspace as a means of attacking other targets. These might include compromising transportation or other supervisory control systems to cause disasters resulting in extensive consternation and costing many lives.

It is certain that terrorists and their supporters have been engaging in extensive activities under category 1, and that they will continue to do so. This would cover communications, including encrypted communications with each other; recruiting and "advertising" (for example, via Web sites); and financial transactions such as money transfers and laundering. Training manuals for terrorists, including information about bomb-making and avoiding detection, are freely available. Terrorists are also likely to be scouring cyberspace for information on potential targets and on weapons of mass destruction.

As far as we can tell, terrorists have not been responsible for any of the major attacks or accidents that have occurred in recent years under categories 2 or 3. So much has been written about such possibilities—and they have had some prominence in the media—that it is inconceivable that terrorists are not aware of them. So far, for reasons we can only speculate about, they do not seem to have chosen to pursue these possibilities with vigor and effect, or perhaps they have tried and failed.

## Systems and Networks at Risk

Should an attack be launched against systems and networks, the following would be at risk:

1. The Internet.
2. Embedded/real-time computing (e.g. avionics systems for air traffic control, SCADA systems used by the amenities, routing for shipping containers, and process control for toxic chemical production, switching of telecommunications, bank teller machines, floodgates).
3. Dedicated computing devices (e.g. desktop computers).

Each has a different role, and may be the subject of different kinds of attack. Terrorists might attack the Internet physically or "through the wires", the latter being potentially more destructive.

One type of attack that we see is directed against Internet operations. Such attacks are often based on self-replicating programs (worms and viruses) that are transmitted from system to system, consuming prodigious amounts of router processing time and network channel bandwidth. In recent years, some of these worms and viruses have been transmitted without explicitly destructive payloads and yet have been able to disrupt key Internet backbone subnetworks for several days.

Another kind of attack on Internet operations seeks to corrupt the routing tables that determine how a packet should travel through the Internet. In both cases, the intent of the attack is to reduce the normally expected functionality of the Internet for some significant portion of its users—that is, a denial-of-service attack in intent, although not one necessarily based on flooding traffic.

An attacker might also target the Internet's Domain Name System (DNS), which translates domain names (e.g. "example.com") to specific Internet Protocol (IP) addresses (e.g. 123.231.0.67) denoting specific Internet nodes. A relatively small number of "root name servers" underpins the DNS. Although the DNS is designed to provide redundancy in case of accidental failure, it has some vulnerability to an attack that might target all name servers simultaneously. Although Internet operations would not halt instantly, an increasing number of sites would, over a period of time measured in hours to days, become inaccessible without root name servers to provide authoritative translation information. Physical replacement of damaged servers would be achievable in a matter of days, but changing the IP addresses of the root name servers would be more complicated.

## Recommendations: Focus on Terrorists

It is only a matter of time before cyber terror attacks, at present largely a threat, become a reality. Both government and private sector need to focus on preparations. There are a number of measures that must be taken. Build Much Stronger Defenses, More Integrated Emergency Preparedness and Response Systems, and Improve the Processes for Their Use.

The first order of business is to provide indications and warnings that an attack is taking place. This is a difficult area, and intrusion detection has become a particularly active area in research and development. Not surprisingly, detection and notification are more difficult and prone to false positives during the early stages of an attack, before significant damage has been done.

To prevent penetration of the system at risk from the outside, we try to erect barriers and otherwise harden it. Both cyber and physical approaches are necessary. Passwords are the oldest, and still most widely used, cybertechnique. More recent and somewhat widely used techniques are firewalls and proxy servers. Like all forms of cyberdefense, these can be defeated, although it is possible to make them real barriers against many attempted attacks. Physical protection needs to consider several forms of penetration or attempts to isolate the system. These include attacks on electronics using electromagnetic pulses, and attempts to cut cable endings. A wide variety of forms of physical protection are possible, ranging from fences to biometrics.

In the event of an attack there needs to be a system for incident management, mitigating an attack, and damage limitation. A next line of defense is internal compartmentalization and containment. In this instance, the goals are to limit penetration and damage, protect surviving assets, and protect and gather information to help with recovery and response after the attack. Approaches include creating internal physical barriers and cyberbarriers through compartmentalization and need-to-know access controls, intrusion tolerance schemes, setting up decoys, maintaining protected redundancies, and hiding assets. All have both static (pre-positioned and unchanging during the attack) and dynamic variants.

Another approach is automatic or partial shutdown and reallocation. A system that senses it is under attack would start erecting internal barriers that would not be tolerable during normal operations, in an attempt to isolate those parts of the system that had been compromised. It would also involve load-shedding strategies to reallocate surviving capabilities to the most important functions required by the organization. All of this amounts to various forms of real-time reassignment and reconfiguration under **rapid** degradation. Particular attention needs to be given to preserving and collecting information during an attack. This is done most easily if the attack has a clear and precise starting time and backups are made regularly, or if the organization maintains a redundant "shadow" system. More insidious attacks that build up slowly present a much more difficult problem in identifying a state where the system is free from inserted malicious code. It is also important to have strong audit functions to identify when an attack starts and to collect information that might assist in the identification and apprehension of the attacker and help the organization better defend itself against similar attacks in the future.

Organizations should establish security policies and plans for defending against attacks. Special attention should be given to preventing and dealing with insider attacks. Staff should know who to call for help. It might be a good idea to test the plan through the use of exercises. However, most organizations avoid live "fire drills" because they can be expensive, disruptive, and risky in their own right. Many information systems are delicate and their owners are afraid something will go wrong, resulting in the selfinflicted equivalent of a serious attack.

Improve the security of systems that control physical processes (e.g., SCADA).

From the standpoint of counter terrorism, we would imagine that attacking physical targets via control and management systems would result in the kind of mass casualties, damage, fear, and loss of confidence that terrorists favor. Many of these systems are vulnerable to tampering with control signals, especially by insiders.

Increasing the security for DC/SCADA systems poses particularly difficult problems. These systems are often small and self-contained, and have constrained power needs (including backup). Security may not readily fit with the space, real-time, or power requirements. Security measures could also reduce performance or be problematic in the synchronization of other more extensive processes. Additionally, most of these systems are in the private or mixed sectors (for example, airports). Their owners and operators may not have sufficient resources to secure them more effectively.

National governments that are in positions to do so should give priority to protecting the small percentage of cyberspace users who are private owners and operators of digital control and management systems. This would include providing them with various forms of assistance and technology. Particular attention should be given to transportation systems because for decades they have been highly favored by terrorists both as targets and as the means of delivering an attack.

This kind of defensive work is essentially "target hardening". This can be defined as the use of various technologies and products and procedures (for example, those governing outside dial-in or reconstitution and recovery) to protect the information technology (IT) assets owned or operated by an individual or organization.

It is important to notice that many of these recommendations would have more general value than just vs. terrorists (e.g., they would help against accidents, natural disasters, serious crime, and non-terrorist forms of conflict). However, as defense does not involve serious risk or impose a penalty on the attacker, there is also the need to develop deterrents. For this we need laws:

## Design and Implement a Stronger "System of Justice", Especially Its International Dimensions

International cooperation should concentrate on effective intelligence operations. This is an area where a considerable amount of success could be expected, which would create the atmosphere for a long-term international legal framework.

The problems of jurisdiction are greatly compounded by the easy transnational access provided by many components of cyberspace, most notably the Internet. What may be perceived as serious in one country whose cyberinfrastructure may be used as part of a terrorist action may not even make the legal radar screen of others that are part of an attack that crosses multiple sovereign physical jurisdictions. Most countries have given little or no thought to making serious crimes of the various forms of cyberattack, and "without law there is no sin". Seeking widely adopted national laws at least criminalizing attacks against or using the networks is an important objective. Legislating against the support functions to which terrorists put the Internet would be a more distant prospect. The enforcement and prosecution of these laws are also critical elements of cybersecurity.

Given the many technical and evidentiary problems of identifying cybercriminals and prosecuting them, nobody has any delusion that such laws would end criminal or terrorist activities in cyberspace. Nonetheless, they might reduce the enormous amount of malicious "noise" in cyberspace, and this would help make it easier to more readily identify more serious activities. They would also provide a necessary basis for encouraging people to report malicious cyberactivities, and for international cooperation in dealing with several kinds of problem.

## Recommendations: CIIP at Every Stage

Security must become a criterion for any system used for CII from the design stage onwards. The priorities in design have been access and throughput. Added security is not just costly; it may also result in reduced efficiency and functionality. Furthermore, so far there does not seem to be much incentive for people to design or redesign systems to be much more secure. There has been much speculation that the design or redesign of systems will occur only in the aftermath of a "digital Pearl Harbor" or in response to the forces of legal liability or insurance necessities and standards. Even better, security should be a factor to be considered over the entire life cycle of such systems. Organizations should build cadres of capable defenders, and contingency plans (including internationally) for crisis and emergency conditions need to be in place. There could be national-level CERTs or CSIRTs (Cybersecurity Incident Response Teams).

A postdesign and implementation variant is to try to prevent attacks by finding and fixing vulnerabilities before an attacker can try to exploit them. Red teams, test beds, or simulations may be used to do this. Another approach, at least to the often-serious threat of possible insider attacks, is to more thoroughly screen employees with potentially sensitive access.

It is clear that for a number of these measures operational contingencies among owners and operators and their governments need to be established.

## Recommendations: Help Build National and Regional Cybersecurity Capabilities

Harmonization of national laws (as provided for in the 2001 Council of Europe Convention on Cybercrime) is a good first step toward ensuring the availability of legal recourse. This would provide the basis for tracking, identifying, and prosecuting cybercriminals across national boundaries. Considerable efforts are underway today at the regional intergovernmental and international governmental level.3 One goal for which international action would be useful is the more effective coordination and sharing of information and R&D.

## Types of Relevant International Conventions

There is no reason why an international legislative system should not be built up around the new technologies we see today. If we make a comparison with aviation, that was also one hundred years ago a new technology for which no laws existed, yet there is now a very effective worldwide legislative framework for air traffic.

Comparisons with other areas of international cooperation help us to see what kind of work can be done in this area for cybersecurity. There are three types of relevant international convention with multilateral operational dimensions:

### Crime and Punishment

- Define undesirable behavior as criminal.
- Concern with sub-state actors.

The prime example of such a convention is the Council of Europe Convention on Cybercrime (2001).

### Infrastructure Protection

- Define undesirable behavior.
- Concern with sub-state actors.

- Establish standards/best practices.
- Concern with state actors.

Here the prime examples are the Civil Aviation Conventions (1919, 1944, 1963, ...).

## Arms Control

- Control/limit behavior and possessions.
- Concern with state actors.

The prime example: Biological and Toxin Weapons Convention (1972).

## An International CIIP Convention?

For international conventions covering Critical Infrastructure those concerning Civil Aviation may be the most relevant model to follow. The following characteristics are notable:

- They range from issues of aircraft safety to strong laws prohibiting acts against aircraft.
- The laws covering acts against aviation infrastructure are also effective.
- There is an International Civil Aviation Organization (ICAO).
- Since 1944 these conventions have gained near universal acceptance, with 189 countries signing up to them, and the coverage is growing.
- They are supported by other UN agencies and NGOs.

If a CIIP Convention is to become a reality, there needs to be significant and sufficient international concern (the WSIS C5 Action Item could be an indicator here). It is essential that the convention strive for universal sign-up, and this probably necessitates a UN umbrella, perhaps the ITU. A CIIP Convention must be supported by an operational organization that can help build and certify national capabilities.

# 11

# Use of the Internet by Terrorists— A Threat Analysis

## INTRODUCTION

This chapter is designed to analyze the threat posed by terrorists using the Internet for cyberterrorism and other – more general – terrorist purposes. This danger is subject to an ongoing and controversial discussion. Whereas some authors claim that – up to today – not a single instance of cyberterrorism has been recorded, others argue that terrorists already routinely make use of the Internet. One reason for these differences in opinion is that the underlying terms of "terrorism" and "cyberterrorism" are not well defined. In fact, more than 100 different definitions of terrorism with more than 20 definitional elements were identified in a study carried out in 1988. The definitions for "cyberterrorism", in particular, range from very narrow (i.e. using the Internet to attack other systems in the Internet, resulting in violence against persons or property) to very broad (i.e. also including any other form of Internet usage by terrorists or even conventional attacks that are aimed at IT infrastructures).

This chapter will not analyze the different definitions of terrorism and cyberterrorism. Instead, it will give an overview of the use that terrorists can make of the Internet and the advantages that they can gain from this usage. For this reason, in the following text, the term "terrorism" is understood in a broad sense in order to enable a comprehensive examination of possible uses. For an analysis of definitions of terrorism. To analyze the possibilities that terrorists have by using the Internet, it is not sufficient merely to look at confirmed cases of terrorist involvement. Instead, it is necessary to identify possible targets, risks, and other forms of terrorist Internet use. Therefore, this analysis is based on cybercrime- and cyberterrorism literature as well as on specialized security reports and everyday news reports. This broad approach allows an expanded view not only of real occurrences of cyberterrorism and other uses of the Internet, but also of possible future (or undetected current) forms of utilization.

Three different areas of terrorist uses of the Internet are mainly under discussion. With a view to news coverage, terrorist attacks that are carried out via the Internet are especially considered to be "cyberterrorism". These attacks are either aimed at other IT structures, such as individual computers, central servers, and routers or at objects in the "physical world", such as buildings, planes, trains, or even human life (Part 1.). However, these intensely observed and frightening possibilities might not be the most interesting ones for terrorists. Since Internet access is available in many countries, terrorist organizations use the Internet not only to attack, but also to inform, threaten, and attract attention. Finally, the Internet offers to all of its users many interesting possibilities and information that can also be used by terrorists. These possibilities include the exchange of encrypted information between people in countries where censorship and mass surveillance are exercised as well as the obtainment of information about possible targets.

## Attacks via the Internet

Attacks via the Internet have, for a long time, been the domain of cyber criminals who abuse systems for their own benefit, especially to gain monetary income. However, these acts can also be committed with a terrorist intent. To analyze further the possibilities of digital attacks for terrorist organizations, one has to look at the reasons and motives behind engagement in this fairly new field. The attacks themselves are often highly flexible and can be combined in several different ways. This makes it hard to distinguish, for example, a hacking attack that is being committed with the intent to "test" the security of a certain computer system from another hacking attack that is being carried out to shut down the system and create further damage. With respect to terrorist ambitions, however, the attacks can roughly be divided into actions carried out with the intent to attack other IT systems (and perhaps the physical infrastructure that is connected to these systems) and attacks that are carried out with the goal of endangering human life.

## Reasons and Motives for Terrorist Attacks

Since many attacks carried out via the Internet give no explanation for the reasons behind them, it is often not possible to determine whether they are the result of an arbitrary experiment carried out by a user who tried out a program discovered while browsing the Internet or the result of the purposeful aggression of an organized group. Accordingly, in many cases of cyber aggressions, the originator is not known. For this reason, some authors have claimed that – up to now – not a single instance of cyberterrorism has been recorded. Even if it is true that – according to informal sources – many cyberterrorist attacks have already taken place, many (if not most) cases are kept confidential due to the security threat to important infrastructures. However, even if evidence is scarce, the threat of terrorists using (or considering use of) the Internet for their purposes is not unrealistic. This in turn can also be used by terrorists as a form of psychological warfare: cyber-fear is generated by the fact that what a computer attack could do is too often associated with what actually will happen.

## Motivation for Attacks via the Internet

The existence of many different reasons and motives show why the Internet, in general, is interesting not only for the "ordinary" criminal, but also for terrorist purposes:

Attacks that are conducted via the Internet can be launched from anywhere in the world. It is not necessary to be "on site" as it is for a classic bomb attack. Internet connections that are needed for the initialization of the attack are widely available or can be started from most up-to-date mobile phones;

When the attack is set up, it can be launched quickly with hardly any need for further preparation. This makes it possible to react spontaneously to current events ("cyber-revenge");

The speed of many forms of attack is not dependent on the connection speed of the attacker, e.g. in cases of Distributed Denial-of-Service attacks (DDoS attacks). Instead, the connection speed of captured victim computers can be fully exploited. Thus, worms and viruses can spread at the fastest possible rate without the need for any further involvement on the part of the attacker;

Actions committed via the Internet can be kept anonymous and untraceable. Technically, anonymizing services and similar camouflaging techniques, as well as the forwarding of traffic via other hacked systems, can make tracing an attack difficult if not impossible. Furthermore, if traces are being led through different countries, legal problems and differing technical standards in these countries add to the list of problems. Finally, digital evidence can be deliberately forged, thus raising suspicion against uninvolved and innocent parties;

The cost-benefit-ratio is extremely positive: use of the Internet itself is cheap. For many attacks, only a small bandwidth connection is needed, which is affordable in most countries. Damage caused via the Internet, however, can be rather costly. IT experts must continue to be involved in fixing newfound security flaws; furthermore, additional costs arise if damages have occurred and require fixing (e.g. reconstructing IT equipment or repairing physical damage that resulted from a computer breakdown);

Often, attacks are easy to carry out because many targets are poorly protected. Therefore, attackers can choose from a wide variety of interesting targets. If the favored target is not vulnerable to the "weapon of choice", many other targets are still available.

## Terrorist Motivation

The short list above already shows that attacks via the Internet are generally attractive for any criminal organization. However, differences between ordinary criminals and terrorist organizations can be observed when the underlying motivation for such attacks is analyzed. Cybercriminals often conduct attacks simply to gain monetary income or to demonstrate their "virtual power". This can be achieved, for example, by the following:

Circumventing security measures. Attackers can thereby corrupt the integrity and confidentiality of computer systems and data;

Rendering systems useless. This can be followed up by further drastic effects if mission-critical IT systems are affected;

Creating physical harm. This can be the case if critical infrastructures, such as transportation, power, or water facilities that are connected to an IT system, can be manipulated by a perpetrator who has gained access to such a control system. Terrorist organizations, however, typically follow a more long-term perspective.

Their general aim is to achieve a (primarily political) goal with their actions. Therefore, the following actions are of high importance to the organization:

- the generation of fear,
- the creation of economic confusion, or
- the discrimination of the political opponent.

Other reasons, however, can also be an underlying agenda for a terrorist act that is being committed via the Internet, for example:

- the generation of monetary income or
- the gathering of information on a target (either for a conventional or an electronic attack).

Depending on individual motivation, terrorist aggressions can be performed in different ways. As an example, a hacking attack with the intent to shut down an important system at an airport could be made publicly known in order to arouse fear in the population.

However, a hacking attack that is committed in the hopes of gaining information on the automobile route of an important person might be kept secret so as not to endanger future plans for a bomb assassination on that person. In general, it is possible to imagine that all of the general aims mentioned above could also be accomplished with the help of attacks that are committed over the Internet.

## Attacks on IT Systems

Attacks on IT systems can roughly be divided into three different groups. (1) With the help of hacking techniques, access to individual systems can be gained. The system can be subsequently used to shut itself down, gather, alter, or delete information from it, or to conquer further systems that are attached. The latter is especially important with regard to attacks on an infrastructure that is controlled by a computer system. (2) The second approach is not designed to gain access to a computer, but to render it useless.

These so-called "Denial-of-Service attacks" (DoS attacks) are often committed with the help of hundreds or thousands of computers that send (mostly useless) instructions to the victim computer. (3) Finally, a third type of attacks combines one or both of the above-mentioned attacks with a conventional bomb attack.

## INDIVIDUAL HACKING ATTACKS

### Accessing Systems

The first type of attacks is aimed at enabling access to protected data and computer systems. This can be achieved if the victim computer is vulnerable to a security weakness that can be exploited by the attacker. Software and techniques for this purpose can be acquired through different channels: many specialized security forums discuss the known weaknesses of different operating systems and other software. If the designated victim computer is not immune against all current (and known) software flaws (socalled "patching"), this information can be used to gain access to it. However, even if all known patches have been applied to a computer system, this does not mean that the system is protected against all possible attacks. So-called "Zero-Day-Exploits", i.e. software flaws that have not yet been disclosed to the manufacturer (and therefore not yet been patched), can be acquired via the black market. Such software enables access to a system even though the system administrators have followed all publicly known security measures.

Once an attacker has gained access to a computer system, several possibilities lie ahead. First, the system can simply be shut down, thereby making it unavailable to legitimate users. However, the system can be restarted by administrators immediately, giving the attackers only a very short moment of success. Nevertheless, even a very short interruption can be hazardous for some systems, such as control systems for power plants or in medical environments. Furthermore, an outage can be combined with a conventional attack, e.g. to handicap rescue workers after a bomb attack.

Furthermore, the information on a system can be altered, thereby giving it a new meaning, e.g. to mislead people relying on that information, or destroyed. Finally, some attacks can be conducted without anybody noticing, making countermeasures extremely difficult.

## Altering Information

The second possibility is to change information that is being stored on the computer system. This can lead to so-called "defacements" that often take place after a web server has been compromised , . In the case of a defacement, a web page (usually an entry page) is replaced with another page that informs the visiting user that this particular web server has been hacked (and most likely also provides information about who has done it). In doing so, the attackers can easily demonstrate their capabilities and the weakness of the victim. In addition, the impression is created that the attacker will be able repeat his action at any given point in time and even with other, even more highly protected systems. Therefore, defacements of web servers that belong to security agencies, the military, or other important services are popular targets for attackers. The group "Pentaguard", for example, demonstrated its capabilities in 2001 when it simultaneously defaced a multitude of government and military websites in the U.K, Australia, and the United States. This attack was later evaluated as one of "the largest, most systematic defacements of worldwide government servers on the Web". Terrorist organizations had also already used this technique in the past. Al-Qaeda, for example, hacked the website of Silicon Valley Landsurveying Inc. in order to deposit a video file showing the hijacked (and later beheaded) Paul Marshal Johnson. By publishing the link to the stored video, the organization could simultaneously demonstrate its technical as well as conventional dangerousness. In another case, pro-Palestinian hackers used a coordinated attack to break into 80 Israel-related sites and deface them. Instead of defacing a web server, all other information stored on a computer system can also be affected, i.e. deleted or altered. If, for example, vital data, such as the U.S. Social Security database, financial institutions' records, or secret military documents, were able to be irreversibly damaged, grave social disorder and a long-lasting lack of trust in all government institutions could be the consequence. Studies, such as the exercise "Eligible Receiver", and recent attacks have shown that even top-secret military computers and sensitive nuclear research centers are not immune against all attacks.

## Silent Operations

The shutting down of a computer or the defacement of a web page each have the advantage that the success of the attack becomes immediately known to both operators and users of the affected system. However, if an attacker does not aim at a demonstration of his powers, but rather tries to gather information, secrecy is of essence.

Therefore, the third possibility for an attacker to proceed after gaining access to a computer is simply to search for useful information and try to leave few or no traces at all. This form of action also has another advantage: whereas a security flaw that has been detected can be fixed after an intruder has been detected, an unknown security weakness allows the attacker to use it not only once but for a longer period of time. Hence, apart from the above-mentioned "Zero-Day-Exploits", other forms of custommade software are of also interest.

A mode of operation that could also be put to use by a terrorist organization can be observed in a case that a security company has tested . The company prepared USB sticks with a custom-designed, newly developed Trojan horse program that could not be detected by virus scanners. Twenty of these sticks were "lost" on the premises of a credit union. Of these, 15 sticks were found by employees – and promptly connected to the company network where the Trojan started to collect passwords and other valuable information and e-mailed this data back to the offenders. Such an attack would be a powerful way for a terrorist organization to initiate counterespionage.

Another way to introduce such software could be through legal channels. This was observed in the year 2000, when Japan's Metropolitan Police Department used a software system to track 150 police vehicles, including unmarked cars. It turned out that this software had been developed by the Aum Shinrikyo cult – the same group that gassed the Tokyo subway in 1995. It turned out that members of the cult had developed software for at least eighty firms and ten government agencies. The cult had been able to work largely undetected because the software developers were engaged as subcontractors, thus enabling personnel clearance to be easily circumvented.

## Large-Scale Attacks

If the information inside a computer is not of essence, but the aim is simply to make its services unavailable, the use of large-scale attacks might be preferred over a hacking attack. Large-scale attacks are often committed with the help of hundreds or thousands of other computers (so-called Distributed-Denial-of-Service-Attacks or DDoS-Attacks). In these cases, viruses and Trojan horses are used to control other computers.

These computers are turned into so-called "zombies" that are forced to report to a botnet on a regular basis. These zombies are, in turn, controlled by a bot-master that instructs them, for instance, to forward thousands of requests to a particular site in order to make it inaccessible to its users. In 2006, more than 60,000 active bot-infected computers were observed per day. Furthermore, over 6 million distinct bot-infected computers were detected in 6 months. These "zombies" were controlled by less than 5,000 command-and-control-servers . It can therefore be safely assumed that the persons in control of these bot-nets are not hobby hackers, but well experienced and organized groups.

For terrorist groups, however, it is not necessary to acquire these skills or to organize bot-nets by themselves as bot-nets can also be rented. Prices for attacks range from about 150 to 400 US-dollars, depending on the target and the duration of the attack. Some bot-net-operators even offer discounts for multiple orders. Also – as a nontechnical alternative – the same effect as that achieved with a bot-net attack can be obtained if enough human supporters are available who can take over the part of will-less "zombies" in bot-net attacks. This can be observed in an online demonstration that was launched against the German airline "Lufthansa" in 2001. In order to call attention to the involvement of the company in the deportation of illegal alien residents, supporters were asked to open the web page of the company at the same date and time. Over 13,000 people followed the call. The Lufthansa server was unable to reply to the sudden peak of requests so that the web page became unavailable to customers during this time frame. This technique is also known as "swarming", "virtual blockade", or "virtual sit-in" and it shows that even technically non-adept organizations can use the power of distributed attacks against targets in the Internet.

However, for a terrorist organization, the operation of a bot-net could also be an interesting option, since it can be used in a variety of ways. Two main options seem to be realistic: the use of bot-nets for email campaigns and for aggressive attacks on other Internet sites. In the first option, the "zombie" computers can be used to send out massmailings with terrorist content (e.g. propaganda). These mails are difficult to trace back since they do not originate from the computer of the terrorist organization, but from thousands of computers linked to the bot-net. Furthermore, this service can also be rented out to other companies wishing to cover their tracks in order to forward spamemails and willing to pay for this service. Therefore, by using this first option, the botnet can also be used as a source of income for the organization. When using a bot-net for the second option, i.e. utilization for attacks on other targets in the Internet, a terrorist organization can benefit from the large diversification of attackers in a bot-net. Such aggressions can hardly be traced back and, in addition, the defense against such attacks is often not possible.

Manifold examples of the use of bot-nets to bring down other services in the Internet can be found. Among them are actions that can be classified as terrorist or part of a cyber war. For example, six different Hizbollah sites, the Hamas site, and other Palestinian information sites were brought down by a so-called "FloodNet" attack of pro- Israeli hackers. The service virtually "flooded" the respective servers with pings resulting in the unavailability of the servers for all other requests. Even after a relaunch with a slightly different spelling, the sites were still unreachable as the hackers immediately adjusted the attack to the new name. The targets of such attacks can be chosen freely, i.e. any system that is reachable over the Internet can be the victim of a (distributed or simple) denial-of-service-attack. Therefore, the internal and external communication systems of NATO troops were the victim of an attack during the allied air strikes on Kosovo and Serbia as well as the thirteen root servers for the Internet domain name systems (DNS).

## Hybrid Attacks

Many of the attacks described above can result in violence against persons or property and they can generate fear within a population. However, this depends largely on the chosen target and the actual effect that the attack was able to accomplish. Therefore, some authors claim that a conventional bomb attack is – in many ways – easier to plan and conduct and that the results can be better foreseen. However, even in cases of conventional bomb attacks, the losses can be increased if hybrid attacks are launched, i.e. an attack that is aimed at a physical target is combined with one or both of the abovementioned electronic forms of attack.

The bomb attack can be aimed at any given target. For example, it is often chosen to bring forth a high number of casualties. In this case, a supplementary digital attack could be launched that is aimed at the communication devices of police or ambulances in order to hinder an effective coordination of rescue teams , . Another possibility would be for attackers to choose to launch an assault on the economic stability of a country. In this case, a hybrid attack against national financial networks (such as Fedwire or Fednet) or against transfer networks (such as SWIFT) could be launched. It is estimated that such an attack could wreak havoc on the entire global economy .

Another possibility would be to directly attack the infrastructure that forms the basis of the Internet. To achieve this, offenders could assault any system whose operation is of the essence for the functioning of the Internet. One example would be the domain name service (DNS). The DNS is responsible for the translation of domain names (such as www.mpicc.de) into IP-numbers (such as 194.94.219.193). This task is necessary for many transactions, e.g. the opening of a web page or the sending of an email. If an attacker was able to disturb this service, large parts of Internet-based services would be inaccessible. Therefore, a DDoS attack on the thirteen root servers of the DNS in October 2002 was described as an attack against the "heart of the Internet network." However, due to built-in safeguards, no slowdowns or even outages were caused. The same is true for a recent attack which took place in February 2007: even though the aggression lasted for almost twelve hours, the influence was hardly noticeable.

Such attacks against the infrastructure are possible not only by digital, but also by conventional means. For example, many transcontinental data connections rely on transatlantic cable connections between Europe and the United States. Whereas European cable ends are widely spread between many different countries, they are often bundled on the American side (e.g. in New Jersey and Rhode Island). An attack on one or two of these connections could have a serious impact on Internet connections in general. In the past, this was observed when cables were damaged accidentally. For example, after an underground cable between China and the USA was severely damaged, according to a survey, 97% of Chinese users reported problems of accessing foreign web pages and 57% claimed that their life and work was being affected by the damage. Another focus of a conventional attack against IT infrastructures could be to target one or more of the central so-called peeringpoints that interconnect different networks in the Internet.

The German peeringpoint DE-CIX in Frankfurt, for example, is said to handle 80% of German and 35% of European Internet traffic. The London Internet Exchange LINX is the world's largest

Internet peeringpoint. In 2006, it was at the center of a planned assault. However, Scotland Yard arrested suspects beforehand. An MI5-website is reported to have said that "without these services, the UK could suffer serious consequences, including severe economic damage, grave social disruption, or even large-scale loss of life." Since this report is focused on the use of the Internet by terrorists, there will be no further analysis of possible targets for conventional attacks. The examples above show, however, that terrorists can severely damage targets in the Internet even without any technical knowledge.

## Attacks on Human Life

Often, attacks on computer systems are considered less dangerous than conventional attacks with bombs because damages to computers are said to "only" lead to economic losses. However, these days, computers are no longer exclusively used to "crunch numbers" and store huge amounts of data. Instead, a new type of service has quietly evolved: SCADA systems are used to measure and control other systems and can therefore lead to effects not only in the "virtual", but also in the "real" world. Often, these systems are also connected to the Internet – in one way or another: according to informal sources, 17% of SCADA malfunctions are caused by a direct Internet access to the SCADA system . Other possibilities include VPN-, modem- or trusted connections, e.g. remote access to allow maintenance work. Even though such possibilities for remote access are not advisable for security reasons, the need to cut costs and the ability to remotely control several SCADA systems centrally, instead of having one person control one system on-site, led many companies to establish such structures.

Furthermore, many of the control systems are based on standard Windows- and UNIX operating systems. Therefore, some hackers claim that it would take them only about a week to get into most of the existing control systems. The effect of a combination of SCADA systems that are connected to the Internet and security weaknesses could be observed in 2003 when 21 power plants were brought down and other critically important institutions in the United States, including Edwards Air Force Base, the test center for

B-2 and B-1 bombers, also affected. As far as is publicly known, these breakdowns were the result of the W32.Lovsan worm that was using the same port to exploit a weakness on individual personal computers being used by the plants to communicate with each other. The collision resulted in a large power-down in the United States and Eastern Canada.

However, even though 60 million households are said to have been without electricity, no panic erupted; there were only a few injuries, and hospitals and emergency services continued to function properly. Therefore, some authors question whether cyber attacks are really of the same class as conventional attacks carried out with bombs. From a terrorist's point of view, it generally should not matter which weapon is used to commit an attack – as long as the attack is efficient, causes fear in the public, and is repeatable (at least in general) at any given point in time. Therefore, attacks that endanger human life often receive larger media coverage than those that only affect computer systems. Some of these attacks only have a nexus to electronics, e.g. bomb attacks that are triggered by RFID chips contained in newer passports. Other forms of computer attacks that endanger human life have – for the most part – only been discussed and not yet taken place (or this has not become known to the public). Two different options are mainly being discussed: attacks on SCADA systems connected to potentially dangerous machinery with an immediate outcome and those that lead to a long-term effect.

## Attacks with an Immediate Outcome

Most scenarios that are under discussion and that could directly result in lost lives have not yet taken place or they have not become known to the public. The following are especially considered to be potential target scenarios for terrorist attacks with an immediate danger to human lives: launching attacks on hydroelectric dams, tampering with control systems for railways or air traffic, and gaining control over systems supervising power plants.

Probably the most discussed scenario of cyberterrorism with an immediate danger for human lives is an attack on a hydroelectric dam. The consequences of (accidentally) damaged dams have been observed in the past, e.g. when, in 1975, the Banqiao and Shimantan dams on tributaries of the Huang He (Yellow) River in China failed, dozens of lower dams were damaged, and at least 85,000 people died. If terrorists were able, for example, by way of hacking into a SCADA system controlling a dam, to create a similar effect by deliberately opening the floodgates, again hundreds or even thousands of people would be at risk. The vulnerability of such systems could also be observed in 1996, when an individual used simple explosive devices to destroy the master terminal of a hydroelectric dam in Oregon. Although the structure of the dam was not affected by the attack, the power-generating turbines were completely disabled and had to be switched to manual control. However, attacks via digital channels have also been on the rise. In 1998, for example, a 12-year-old was able to break into a computer system that runs Arizona's Roosevelt Dam. Federal authorities afterwards reported that he had complete command of the SCADA system controlling the dam's massive floodgates.

A similar incidence – albeit without a threat to human life – took place in the year 2000, when the police arrested a man who used a stolen computer and radio transmitter to control the sewage treatment in Queensland, Australia. The culprit had manipulated the system over a period of two months, letting hundreds of thousands of gallons of putrid sludge ooze into parks and rivers. According to an employee of the Australian Environmental Protection Agency "marine life died, the creek water turned black and the stench was unbearable for residents." However, the perpetrator's motive was not to generate fear in the public, but to bargain for a consulting contract in order to fix the problems he had caused. Nevertheless, the case shows that physical damage can be caused by manipulating SCADA systems.

It is easy to imagine what could happen if a terrorist were to gain control over a system that is set up to prevent the collision of airplanes. In 1997, a juvenile was able to access the communication systems of Worcester, Mass. Airport. The action disrupted the telephone service to the Federal Aviation Administration Tower at the Airport, the Airport Fire Department, and other related services such as airport security, the weather service, and various private airfreight companies. Furthermore, the main radio transmitter and the circuit which enables aircrafts to send an electronic signal to activate the runway lights on approach were disabled. Fortunately, no accidents were caused by the attack. However, the incident clearly shows the potential danger and the vulnerability of systems that are responsible for protecting human lives. In a worst case scenario, colliding trains or airplanes could possibly cost hundreds of lives.

Finally, other scenarios with the possibility for mass mortality have also had an impact on the discussion about possible targets for cyberterrorists. In particular, the chance of terrorists controlling nuclear power plants or military missile control centers has been a subject discussed by many authors . The above-mentioned power-down of 2003 has shown that digital attacks can indeed have an impact on such systems. However, many of these situations rely on the failure of all other security measures at the same time. Air traffic controllers and pilots are especially trained as regards "situational awareness" and use computers only as an aid. So, for a successful attack, it would be necessary to manipulate pilots and/or controllers as well as intrude into the computer system. Furthermore, military facilities that are able to launch missiles are often not connected to the Internet, but "air-gapped" instead, making a remote launch simply impossible.

There are, however, no grounds for a complete all-clear. One reason is that it is not reasonable or sufficient to distinguish exclusively between "computer only" and "human only" scenarios. If organizations have (or can buy) the aid of an insider – either in the form of active participation or in the form of gathering otherwise protected information – many security measures can be dangerously compromised. The second reason is that the military also makes use of increased connectivity and remote controlling in order to save the lives of soldiers. New weapons are being developed that rely on remote control. For example, semi-autonomous military robots often provide a communication channel for human controllers – sometimes even over the Internet. This, for example, is the case with

"RoboGuard", a guard robot that can be equipped with infrared-sensors and weaponry. Finally, many software products also used by military services rely on civilian technology and established operating systems, thereby opening additional loopholes for security risks.

## Attacks with a Long-Term-Effect

The situations mentioned above can result in a one-time catastrophe. In order to create long-lasting panic and fear within the population, however, long-term effects and uncertainty may be even more suitable for terrorist organizations. Scenarios that are being discussed in this field include the manipulation of machinery, for example, in the production of food or medication. However, it is doubtful whether such scenarios are realistic. If, for example, the production chain of a food company were altered to create poisonous food, it seems likely that quality control would detect changes in the composition at an early stage. In addition, a sudden increase in the use of different ingredients would likely draw attention. Finally, the taste of the altered product would likely change.

Other possible targets include the weapons-production process, where manipulation could lead to useless ammunition. This would be effective especially, because testing is hardly possible and defects would be noticed only after it is too late. However, since these production areas are usually high-risk areas, security measures are high, and production computers are seldom linked to public networks the risk of a digital effect in this area can be considered very low.

## Terrorist-Related Contents

From the beginning, one great strength of the Internet has always been its use for communication. However, widespread success began with the establishment of the WWW and the possibility for everyone to disseminate information. Today, terrorists have also begun to use the Internet not only to launch attacks, but also to exploit it for new possibilities in a "war of ideas." The use of the Internet is especially of interest for the presentation of terrorist viewpoints, the propagation of threats and propaganda, and the possibility to it for fundraising.

## Presentation of Terrorist Views

In general, terrorists and terrorist organizations have to work undercover which makes the communication of their views, aims, and ambitions extremely difficult. "Conventional" ways to spread ideas are leaflets and "mouth-to-mouth" propaganda. However, both alternatives are time-consuming and risky and they do not reach a large group of people. Additionally, terrorists are faced with the problem of how to communicate with (and possibly influence) the media or other people and organizations who might not actively be looking for such information but who would be interested in it once introduced to it.

With the help of the Internet, the situation has changed. Almost every organization of importance now has its own website and the number of terrorist websites is steadily rising: Whereas in 1999, two of 30 deemed foreign terrorist organizations had their own websites (according to the United States Department of State), in 2005 more than 4,500 terrorist-related websites were known to exist. Many websites contain detailed information on leaders, the history of the organization, aims, or recent successes. The information is put together in such a way that the different "target groups", e.g. supporters, enemies, or mass media, can easily find relevant information. Some websites even offer cartoon-style design and children stories in order to reach already the youngest. Also, information is provided in different languages so that even foreigners can compare their media news with the views of the respective organization. The website of the Revolutionary Armed Forces of Colombia (FARC – http://www.farcep.org [last visited: September 2007]), for example, offers information in English, Italian, Portuguese, Russian, and German.

For an overview of terrorist websites and their languages of operation. As regards content, terrorists are not restricted to presenting information on their organization alone. Everything is virtually possible, from a mere presentation of viewpoints to a general glorification of terrorism or justification of recent acts of violence (or threats to perform new acts) even up to and including the incitement of further terrorist acts by the reading audience and recruits. The honoring of "martyrs" and communication with families of terrorists has even already taken place. The website alneda. com, for example, has published the names and home phone numbers of 84 al- Qaeda fighters who have been captured. Presumably, the aim of this action was to allow sympathizers to contact their families and let them know whether they were alive. Other websites contain obituaries of suicide bombers, effectively glorifying them and encouraging others to follow this path. The Internet has therefore become the most important means by which terrorist organizations communicate with their supporters and other interested parties.

The most popular terrorist sites attract tens of thousands of visitors each month . Of course, governments try to shut down such websites and prevent the spreading of information. However, the "censorship resistance" of the Internet is often used. For example, when Jordanian officials removed an article from 40 print copies of The Economist on sale in Jordan, an online copy was printed, photocopied, and faxed to 1,000 Jordanians, thereby circumventing local censors . Furthermore, websites are often stored on servers that are physically located in different countries than the one the organization is acting from. For example, several websites of al Qaeda are physically stored in the USA and Canada.

## Threats and Propaganda

As mentioned above, terrorist websites are not restricted to a presentation of views alone. Instead, terrorists can also use the Internet to send threats to enemies and spread propaganda. The possibility to use multimedia technology especially enables an organization to burn images into the memories of the viewing audience in an impressive way. The assassination of Daniel Perl for example, showed the impact of psychological warfare as conducted by these new means. Also, other more recent, messages are no longer sent as mere text messages. Instead, professional-looking videos are being produced, e.g. in the case of threats against German and Austrian involvement in Afghanistan. These videos were subtitled in German and sent to a website called "Global Islamic Mediafront (GIMF). A high-ranking member of the German Office for the Protection of the Constitution is quoted as having said that this video is seen as a form of "psychological warfare" because it does not make direct threats, but instead creates an atmosphere of unease. Other messages are directly forwarded to TV stations which incorporate the material and broadcast it in their programs. Therefore, some attacks are staged and filmed from several angles at the same time so that the material can be better used for the distribution to the media, websites, and the production of DVDs.

The use of terrorist websites, however, also has two big disadvantages. First, most websites are only visited by people who are actively seeking such information. Therefore, organizations have to find new ways to also reach other people, e.g. mass media. Secondly, websites serve as a "single point of failure": If the website is closed down, all information contained there must be moved to another site and the new name spread among those who wish to visit the site and get information from it.

Terrorists have started to fight both problems and added more decentralized approaches to their arsenal. This makes it harder for the government to control content on the one hand. On the other hand, it also makes propaganda available for those capable of being influenced by it or who are open to the views of the organization but not actively seeking it. It is probably for this reason that many propaganda videos have shown up on video-sharing platforms such as YouTube. They depict terrorism in a glorious light and show assault scenes, bombings (often accompanied by modern music), or speeches by agitators. In addition to videos, Internet radio shows are also being launched. Both, video and radio shows allow organizations to spread their body of thought among young viewers who are vulnerable to such influences and may stumble over such material while looking for a new pop song.

Material and information that is spread via the Internet can also be used to influence public opinion. Whereas, in the past, only a few well-established organizations were able to produce newspapers, magazines, or TV shows, the Internet makes it possible for virtually anyone to launch their own periodicals or otherwise use the power of the media. The cost advantage over traditional mass media greatly helps to promote such journals. Al-Qaeda, for example, has launched a weekly bilingual news show containing world news from a terrorist point of view. Viewers of such online journals often cannot identify the source and evaluate whether the news being broadcast is true or false. This, however, has proven to be a double-edged sword in the past.

On the one hand, organizations were able to express their own views under the guise of a seemingly neutral authority, leading to a seemingly prevailing opinion between many "independent" journals. On the other hand, due also to the quick proliferation of fake communiqués, it was not easy to distinguish real terrorist messages from the statements of non-existent groups for some time.

Nevertheless, the risk remains that traditional mass media – thanks to increasing use of the Internet as a source of stories and illustrated footage – can fall for news sites that are set up especially for this purpose. By attractively presenting viewpoints and opinions, terrorist organizations can at least increase their chances of introducing these opinions into mass media products. In this context, semantic attacks are also being discussed. A semantic attack involves subtly changing the content of the web page of a traditional news site, thus disseminating false information. However, it is doubtful whether these attacks would remain unnoticed.

## Fundraising and Financing

Some organizations have started to use their websites not only to disseminate information, but also to use it as a source of income for financing (fundraising). This can be done, for example, by selling CDs, DVDs, T-Shirts, badges, flags or books. Other websites give instructions on how to donate money to the organization, for example directly by means of credit card or by providing bank account details. By doing so, organizations can establish a link to supporters and candidates for possible recruitment. The same can be achieved, if terrorists gather user demographics, e.g. from personal information entered on online questionnaires and order forms. Users that are identified as potential sympathizers can then be e-mailed and asked to make donations. Since the websites of the organizations themselves are often at the center of surveillance by security agencies, hundreds of support websites commonly appear and disappear. To allow visitors to find further websites, they are often link by web rings. Yahoo for example has pulled dozens of sites in the Jihad Web Ring, a coalition of 55 Jihad-related sites.

## Use of the Internet for Other Purposes

The third sector that is of interest to terrorists, apart from attacks carried out over the Internet and the dissemination of information, is the use of the Internet for seemingly harmless tasks such as sending e-mails or visiting web sites. However, the following section will show that even these simple tasks can be beneficial to a terrorist organization if they are carried out via the Internet. This is especially true for the individual communication between terrorists and terrorist groups and the use of the Internet as a planning and supporting instrument.

## Individual Communication

The general benefits of the Internet, such as speed, low cost-level, and wide accessibility, apply especially if it is used for communication purposes. The use of the Internet to communicate goes back to the roots of the Internet itself. Therefore, many tools and programs are in existence and their functionality has already been widely tested. In general, communication can be divided into text-based tools on the one hand, that can either be used in realtime ("chatting") or in delayed mode (e.g. email), and voice-based systems on the other hand.

Text-based systems, such as email, have the advantage that they are widely available and that many companies usually offer these services free of charge. Additionally, they do not require a lot of bandwidth, making it possible to send and retrieve information even over older mobile phones or in areas where Internet-connections are limited. Since email services are offered free of charge by many different companies, terrorist organizations can rely on them and refrain from building up their own service. For example, the organizers of the 9/11 attacks had opened multiple accounts on largely anonymous e-mail services such as "Hotmail." . Text-based, real-time systems, such as IRC, allow for a fast (and largely unsupervised) conversation of two or more persons who are online at the same time. If, however, this is not the case, delayed applications that use a process-and-store mechanism (as with email) have a great advantage: messages can be stored and retrieved at any given point in time; terrorists neither have to be online all the time, nor do they have to entrust third parties with the task of accepting personal messages for them. Finally, many encryption tools have been developed and are freely available for this service. Voice-based systems, however, allow for even faster communication than textbased real-time systems.

Voice-over-IP systems (VoIP) have enjoyed great success since the free-of-charge software "Skype" was introduced. Lately, many manufacturers of messaging systems (such as AIM or Microsoft Messenger) have also included a voice function into their products. Therefore, it is of no surprise that VoIP software has been found in connection with al-Qaeda cells.

## Encryption and Anonymity

Information that is exchanged over the Internet is – by nature – digital. This allows for easy encryption and also for opportunities to remain anonymous. With regard to the latter, anonymity services and open proxies can be used. However, in many cases, terrorists must anticipate that their message will be intercepted. Therefore, they must either disguise the message itself or use conventional encryption techniques. To hide a message, two techniques are especially being discussed. The first is to hide the message with the help of steganography. In this case, a message is hidden inside a picture, sound file, or any other file. This file can then be put on any public website, e.g. a photo could be put on a classic photo site such as webshots.com. Afterwards, other members of the organization could download the picture and decrypt the message. The entire process is concealed because no one (except for the terrorists) knows that the file contains more information than initially appears. Furthermore, the course of action is completely inconspicuous because it is an everyday event to up- or download a picture from a photo site and does not draw any attention to itself. Some authors claim that the use of steganography is only a myth. However, even if this technique is not proven, there is a possibility that it could be used by terrorists as well as anybody else. Furthermore, also other techniques could be used to secretly pass messages that cannot be noticed or deciphered by observers. If, for example, code words or certain signals are being agreed upon between different terrorists, it would be sufficient to use this code word in an inconspicuous context. Therefore, experts currently argue whether the color of the beard of Osama Bin Laden in his latest video is a secret message for his followers. Similar techniques were already used by the group of terrorists conducting the attack on 9/11. The message from Mohammed Atta to the other attackers stated that "19 confirmations for studies in the faculty of law, the faculty of urban planning, the faculty of fine arts, and the faculty of engineering" were obtained. This message could be sent without attracting any attention, even if it was intercepted. For the well-informed, however, the references to the various faculties revealed the different targets for the assassins.

Another method of preventing the content of a message from being revealed is the use of a free mailer e-mail account. To begin with, the use of a free mailer account itself offers a great degree of anonymity and protection in itself, especially if more than one service is used (either alternatively or simultaneously). However, to protect the content of an e-mail, the account is used in an unconventional way: instead of logging in, writing, and sending an e-mail, the password is not known to just one person but to two – sender and recipient. The sender logs onto the account and writes, but does not send, the message. Instead, the message is saved as a draft. Later, the recipient logs onto the same account and reads the message in the draft folder. By means of this technique, the message never leaves the system, so that no traces of an e-mail remain on any system. Thereby, governmental filtering systems were successfully circumvented for a long time. In the meantime, however, this technique is known to secret services around the globe. Therefore, if conventional messages (i.e. unencrypted or not in other ways protected) are being exchanged in this way, terrorist conversations can still be tapped. More difficulties arise, however, if this technique is not used with email accounts, but with online repositories. These storage places accept all kinds of different files, e.g. plain text file, encrypted files, or the above-mentioned seemingly harmless files that contain further information hidden inside.

But even if terrorists decide to send messages as proper e-mails (e.g. because there was no safe channel to exchange the password for the e-mail account), they can do so confidently because any message can be encrypted. Apparently, terrorists are already using all the possibilities that computers and networks offer, "starting from encryption techniques to password-protected repositories somewhere in the virtual world."

This statement by the President of the German Federal Police (Bundeskriminalamt) Jörg Ziercke was confirmed when thousands of encrypted messages were found by federal officials on the computers of arrested Al-Qaeda terrorists Abu Zubaydah and Ramzi Yousef; the latter of which was tried for the previous bombing of the World Trade Center. Good encryption programs are available to the public as opensource software. Thus, terrorists can be sure that no hidden "backdoor" is contained in the program. Furthermore, if the right encryption parameters are used, even up-to-date technology is not able to decrypt the message without the proper key.

Yet, apparently not all terrorists use encrypted messages. For example, the organizers of the 9/11 attacks indeed used e-mail, but did not see the need to encrypt their messages. In some cases, this might not be careless, but the intended purpose. If, for example, terrorists want the content of their communication to become known, they send it in unencrypted form in the hopes that the message will be intercepted by the appropriate authorities. Since it is common knowledge that the surveillance of telecommunication is on the rise, such information could be purposefully disseminated in order to conceal other – real – attack plans that concentrate on other targets.

## Planning and Supporting

According to a terrorist training manual, public sources can provide up to 80% of all required information on an opponent.

Officials agree and state that the combination of all unclassified information available in the Internet "adds up to something that ought to be classified". Terrorists can therefore heavily rely on publicly available information in the Internet for the planning of attacks and for the support of their mission. Examples of this field of application are especially the use of publicly available information and the collection of specialized information for training purposes.

## Publicly Available Information

An often cited example of publicly available information which is useful for terrorists is the satellite maps that are provided, for example, by Google, Microsoft, or NASA. In former times, these images were only available to experts. Now, they are a common good and accessible for anybody, including terrorists. In the eyes of governments around the world, at least part of such information poses a threat to national security because it allows the examination of otherwise protected areas from a bird's eye view. Therefore, it is reasonable that officials have begun to ask providers of digital maps to disclose certain – security-relevant – information, e.g. defensive fortifications or military development and production areas. But even maps of publicly accessible areas can be of interest because they can easily be combined with other data, such as street names. As a result, for example, escape routes can be planned with great precision, even before a territory is inspected in person.

In many cases, the information that is contained on the website of possible targets (e.g. companies or government institutions) is also of interest to terrorists. In one case, for example, maps, time schedules for shuttle busses, and a copy of the official telephone directory of a military base were available via the official website. This information could be gathered by terrorists and used for the preparation of a conventional attack. The same is true for much other information that can be accessed via the Internet. For example, reports of security weaknesses in airports or transport companies could draw the attention of terrorists to possible targets. In summary, the amount of sensitive data that can be discovered at the various corporate websites can be constituted as "a gold mine for potential attackers.". According to some authors, terrorist organizations have even started to use databases to gather, sort, and evaluate the details of potential targets in the United States. Actual findings on terrorists' computers have shown that publicly available information of all kinds are indeed being downloaded and used for planning purposes.

## Training

Since so much information that can be abused is available over the Internet, some authors claim that the Web has become "an open university for jihad". Some information that is of great interest – especially for new terrorists – has even been precompiled, e.g. information on bombs, poisons, or many other dangerous goods. The "Mujahadeen Poisons Handbook", for example, contains various "recipes" for homemade poisons and poisonous gases for use in terrorist attacks. Comparable information can also be found in other collections, such as the "Terrorist's Handbook", the "Anarchist Cookbook", the "Encyclopedia of Jihad", the "Sabotage Handbook", and the famous "How to make Bombs", all of which are freely available. Modern terrorists amend these handbooks by adding extra information, e.g. on hostage taking, guerrilla tactics, and special bombs. Some excerpts, e.g. from the virtual training manual of al-Qaida Al Battar, have been published by the U.S. Department of Justice. The danger that appears to originate from many of these compilation should, however, not be overestimated. Even though the documents are clearly labeled, many of them contain the same information that can be found in most standard chemistry books for university students. Then again the Internet offers some advantages over traditional libraries. For example, contents can be gathered without causing any suspicion and without attracting a librarian's attention. Furthermore, new information can be added at any time and collections can be mirrored between different locations. This (and the possibility to use anonymity services for retrieving the information) enables terrorists to circumvent censorship and deletion.

## Support

As explained above, the Internet can serve as a huge library for terrorists. Combined with the possibilities to interact fast and anonymously with each other new opportunities for a support between terrorists and terrorist groups arise. This can happen in three different ways: (1) supporters find instructions on what contributions are currently needed by an organization; (2) organizations offer help to individuals; and (3) organizations help each other. The first possibility is that individuals support a terrorist organization. This can happen in many of the ways that are being described above, e.g. through financing. But also support of electronic attacks has already taken place. Recently, for example, software called "the electronic jihad program" has been discovered on jihadi web-sites. The program can be downloaded by interested followers. It is designed as to allow individuals to easily participate in attacks on different web sites over a windows-like interface. In order to encourage other users, usernames of participants and the hours spent for attacking websites are being collected and put on public "high score"-lists. The publishers of this software obviously hope that with a spreading use of the Internet continually more users engage in such a form of "electronic jihad."

The second form of support goes into the opposite direction, i.e. terrorist organizations support individuals in their efforts. This form of support can especially take place in the above mentioned way of compiling information for special purposes like instructions on hostage taking or on building bombs. This form of support is seemingly on the rise. Al-Qaeda, for example, is said to run a "massive and dynamic online library of training materials" which is supported by experts who can answer questions either on message boards or in chat rooms. Topics that are covered in this database are said to range from weapons and poisons to navigation instruments and even to camouflaging and masquerading. Such a "terrorist's helpdesk" could enable small groups of terrorists all over the globe to act fast and competent. Information on the third form of support – support between different organizations – is hardly available. However, at least the technical infrastructure is available that allows loosely interconnected groups to maintain contact with one another. Even terrorist groups that fight for different political goals and that are located in different geographical areas could communicate with each other and exchange information, such as on weapons or tactics.

## Conclusion and Recommendations

The assessments in the literature on the danger of terrorists using the Internet range from "imminent threat" to an "exaggerated cyber angst". This, however, is mostly due to the fact that no common definition of cyberterrorism exists. Most authors would probably agree that terrorists have begun using the Internet at least for communication purposes. Only a few, however, would describe this as a form of cyberterrorism. Based on the broad approach that is being followed in this chapter, for a realistic assessment of a terrorist use of the Internet one has to look at the skills terrorists have shown up to today, the protection of the possible targets and services described above, and the results that are possible if terrorists choose to actually use the Internet.

## Skills

Often, those who claim that cyberterrorism is not a real threat state also that terrorists lack the necessary skills for an electronic attack. This is true insofar as attacks in security- relevant areas indeed require highly developed computer skills that exceed common user know-how by far. Therefore, some experts assume that it would take from two to four years of preparation for a structured cyber attack against multiple systems and networks. For a "complex coordinated cyberattack, causing mass disruption against integrated, heterogeneous systems" even six to ten years would be needed . The current generation of young terrorists, however, has – as least partly – been growing up in a digital world. Seized computers of al-Qaeda, for example, show that they are becoming increasingly familiar with hacker tools that are freely available over the Internet. Also the above-mentioned use of encryption and communication tools as well as the design and setup of web sites confirm this observation. But even if the terrorists themselves were not yet ready for an attack, this is no reason for an all-clear. With the above-mentioned interconnection and the fact that much information on security issues is available on the Internet terrorists can gain this experience in only a short time. Furthermore, skill and information can also be acquired on the free market. The Islamic fundamentalist group "Harkat-ul-Ansar", for example, has attempted to buy cyber attack software from hackers in late 1998 . Also the above-mentioned "Zero-Day exploits" are available for anybody who is willing and able to spend between $ 1,000 and $ 5,000. The same is true for computers that can be used in a DDoS attack. In this case, prices range only from $ 150 to $ 400, depending on the target and duration of the attack. However, some authors doubt if organizations have enough money for large strikes. After evaluating the results of a governmental test for a "Digital Pearl Harbor", for example, officials stated that terrorists would have to spend about $ 200 million for appropriate resources. But in this calculation it has to be considered that several terrorist- sponsoring nations might want to become involved. They can either invest money in terrorist organizations, provide know-how and resources, or aid external efforts by contributing their own personnel. The U.S. Department of State, for example, lists several designated state sponsors of terrorism . Other countries are known for the training of hackers for national defense purposes or keeping specialized departments within their intelligence services. Summarizing it can be stated that different terrorists and terrorist organizations have demonstrated their newly gained experiences with technology. This is especially true for the presentation of terrorist contents and the use of the Internet for other purposes. A large cyber attack that was verifiably committed by terrorists has – up till now – not yet taken place. However, it has to be assumed that terrorists can either use their own skills or cooperate with different parties in order to launch digital strikes.

## Possible Results

When looking at the results that are possible one has to differentiate between the use of the Internet for the distribution of contents or similar forms of utilization and the use for a digital attack.

## Common Use of the Internet

The use of the Internet for buying airline tickets or gathering information on a certain building is in essence a legitimate use of the Internet regardless of the underlying motivation and intention . Therefore, the direct result of terrorists using the Internet for the above mentioned purposes is hardly noticeable. However, the indirect consequences are not marginal. Especially the possibility to stay in contact from almost any place in the world and the chance to do so without being noticed by intelligence services is a great benefit for terrorists and terrorist organizations. Furthermore, the tracing of suspects is being seriously hindered if anonymity services and encryption techniques are being used.

## Use for Digital Attacks

The attacks that can possibly be launched over the Internet have been illustrated above. Especially the latest attacks on the country of Estonia in 2007 have shown that a well planned attack can bring down major commercial banks, telecommunication services, name servers, and even ATMs all at the same time. In essence, according to Estonian Defense minister Jaak Aaviksoo, the national security of an entire nation was threatened by this particular attack.

However, terrorists will carefully assess how much time, personnel, and money is needed for a certain attack and what the outcome will be. A scenario that results "only" in the unavailability of (computer or other) services is likely to be put aside since the outcome is a common phenomenon even without computer attacks. Other scenarios that are able to create public fear and extensive media coverage on the other hand will be considered by terrorists in greater depth.

But then again, terrorists will consider the efforts that it takes to carry out such attacks. Often, a conventional attack can be carried out with greater ease – and it can be easily repeated (whereas a computer-based attack is a one-time threat if the security hole can be fixed afterwards). For example, a cyber attack on a transportation system is possible – but the same (or even greater) result can be created with the use of explosives. The same thought applies also to many other scenarios.

From this point of view a sole large digital attack executed by a terrorist organization seems rather unlikely, because the effort would exceed the possible outcome. It does seem likely, however, that followers are incited to start attacks by themselves. This, for example, seems to have happened in the case of the attack against Estonia: Hackers and "script kiddies" alike were instigated in chat rooms to initiate DoS attacks against Estonian services at the same time. The second possibility that seems likely are the above-mentioned hybrid attacks. These can be used in conjunction with a conventional attack in order to increase the number of casualties. In these cases the preparation is often easy or can be bought, e.g. if DDoS attacks are used.

## Level of Protection

Most experts agree that some of the worst and scariest results of digital attacks are only possible, because many targets are only poorly protected. In a recent study, for example, U.S. authorities were audited on the implementation of the Federal Information Security Management Act of 2002 (FISMA) that defines IT-security measures such as secure password management or access control. The overall rating for all government agencies was a school grade of "D

Interestingly enough, the Department of Homeland Security, which is also responsible for the coordination of state cyber security, received an "F". Indeed, it failed the test three times in a row. But also other governments around the world were found to be vulnerable to cyber attacks. Computers at the Chancellery and three ministries in Germany, for example, have been infected with spy programs that allegedly were installed over the Internet by Chinese army hackers.

However, it is not the public sector alone that is to be blamed. More than 80 percent of critical infrastructure systems are privately owned. Many of these systems are also easy targets and not adequately protected. A survey conducted in 1997, for example, found that then 40 percent of water facilities allowed their operators direct access to the Internet, and 60 percent of the SCADA systems could be connected by modem. Additionally, even in power plants configurations were detected where all control systems were set to the same password. Furthermore, even actual attacks on the systems were often not detected. In the above-mentioned case of 2000 when a consultant broke into the control system of sewage treatment in

Queensland, Australia, it took over 40 attempts to actually unleash the raw sewage. Not one of the unsuccessful attempts, however, was noticed by the people managing the infrastructure.

## Recommendations

From the analysis carried out above, mainly three different recommendations can be derived. They regard the awareness towards security issues, the communication paths between countries and different institutions, and the dealing with terrorist contents.

## Security Awareness

Especially the results of the last section show that a severe problem lies in the level of protection at the different sites. Unprotected systems – especially if they are responsible for valuable infrastructure, services, or data – pose a just too tempting target for cybercriminals as well as for terrorists. Therefore, a strong initiative should be started to incite the public and the private sector to invest more time, money, and care into security measures.

In the public sector, several instruments have been introduced that were targeted to either test security level of public institutions or to raise their awareness towards security issues. The well known test called "Eligible Receiver" that was conducted in 1997, for example, was able to point out several serious vulnerabilities in the military's computer network. Other tests have led to similar results. With a view to a raised awareness towards security issues, the U.S. FISMA is a good example. Through this act public institutions are forced to inspect and adjust their measures at regular intervals. Similar initiatives could lead to better results also in the private sector. Currently, many companies might not be aware of their importance for the economy as a whole – or at least they do not act according to this role. According to Richard Clarke a typical company devotes only one quarter of one percent of its information technology budget to cyber security or – as he puts it – "slightly less than they spend on coffee". Today, these figures have changed slightly, but still more than half of the companies that answered to the CSI survey of 2007 stated that they spent 5% or less.

A possible initiative could – as a first step – classify companies according to their endangerment. If – according to this classification – high- and medium-risk businesses would also be audited (comparable to FISMA), this again could have two positive effects: First, it would be known, which companies are responsible for certain critical infrastructures. In the U.S. alone, for example, some 5,700 companies are deemed to be essential to national security. Secondly, it would become known which dependencies between these companies currently exist. Thirdly, due to the auditing, also companies in the private sector would have to increase their security level constantly.

## Communication Paths

The second recommendation against digital attacks concerns the communication between different institutions in the case of an attack. Most cybercrime cases involve not only resources in one, but in many different countries or institutions at the same time. Therefore, fast and efficient communication is of the essence to fight digital attacks. Several initiatives have been made so far to strengthen this sharing of information in the event of a digital attack.

Article 35 of the Convention on Cyber Crime by the Council of Europe, for example, asks the member countries to introduce contact points that are available on a 24 hour, 7 day per week basis in order to ensure immediate assistance for the purpose of investigations or proceedings concerning criminal offences related to computer systems and data. This 24/7 network is an important step towards fast communication paths between different countries.

Similar activities, however, are needed not only between countries, but also between the different institutions within each country. In the U.S., for example, the National Infrastructure Protection Center (NIPC) was created in 1998. Its mission is to provide "a national focal point for gathering information on threats to the infrastructures, and providing the principal means of facilitating and coordinating the federal government's response to an incident, mitigating attacks, investigating threats, and monitoring reconstitution efforts.". To accomplish this mission, the NIPC believes that it is necessary to build a "coalition of trust amongst all government agencies, between the government and the private sector, amongst the different business interests within the private sector itself, and in concert with the greater international community."

In essence, fixed communication paths have to be established between (1) different countries (e.g. through the 24/7 network of the Council of Europe), (2) between the different institutions and services in the public sector, and (3) between important companies in the private sector and institutions in the public sector. As a guide on what companies have to be considered "important" in this context, the infrastructure definition of the NIPC can be taken into account. It defines infrastructure as "those physical and cyber-based systems essential to the minimum operations of the economy and government, including telecommunications, energy, banking and finance, transportation, water systems, emergency systems, both governmental and private".

## Terrorist Contents

The final recommendation regards the interaction with terrorist contents, e.g. websites and training materials. It might sound provocatively, but the (young) history of the Internet shows that all efforts to censor and control media and communication are doomed to fail. Technically, it is almost impossible to effectively hinder websites or to block communication between terrorists – especially if encryption technology or other methods to obscure their communications are being used. Additionally, all of these efforts threaten civil liberties and the freedom of law-abiding citizens. Finally, it is still unclear how the valuation of crimes and ethics in different countries can safely be combined.

Therefore, countries should refrain from enacting ineffective control methods of a purely symbolic nature that seriously infringes the freedom of information rights and that can lead to the development of uncontrolled surveillance. Instead, advantage should be taken of the situation that terrorists communicate over open channels. This can be used, for instance, to register activities, assess the size and possibly future actions of terrorist groups.

# 12

# The Reliance of Al-qaeda on the Internet

"We were underestimating the amount of attention [al Qaeda] was paying to the Internet." Roger Cressey, chief of staff of President Bush's Critical Infrastructure Protection Board Jihadism according to al Qaeda (as opposed to the classical reified conception of Jihad) is a thoroughly modern phenomenon. The Internet, that most contemporary of media, has become the leading platform of al Qaeda's communication, propaganda, recruitment and networking. Al Qaeda is using hundreds of Jihadist websites, forums, chat rooms, electronic boards and blogs. One can certainly reach the conclusion that without the Internet, al Qaeda would not be able to function and survive. As Ayman al- Zawahiri, al Qaeda's spiritual and religious leader, argued:

"We must get our message across to the masses of the nation and break the media siege imposed on the jihad movement. This is an independent battle that we must launch side by side with the military battle."

The findings reported here come from a more general research project hosted and funded by United States Institute of Peace that summarized nine years of monitoring terrorist presence on the Net. The population for this study was defined as the Internet sites of terrorist movements as they appeared in the period between January 1998 and September 2007. We applied a systematic content analysis to the accumulating archive of terrorist sites. Throughout the years of monitoring the terrorist presence in the Net, we learned how to locate their new sites, how to search in chat rooms and forums of supporters and sympathizers for the new "addresses" and how to use links in other organizations' websites to update our lists. This was often a Sisyphean effort, especially since in certain instances (e.g., al Qaeda's websites) the location and the contents changed almost daily.

The present report, one of numerous publications on the project of monitoring and analysis of the terrorist presence on the Internet, focuses on the terrorist entity that leads, in terms of amount as well a sophistication, terrorist abuse of the Net, namely al Qaeda.

## Al Qaeda Goes Virtual

Al Qaeda (Arabic for "The Base") traces its roots to the Afghan resistance to the Soviet invasion of Afghanistan in 1979. In 1982 Osama bin Laden joined the anti-Soviet resistance. He went to Afghanistan, where he joined the mujahedeen and established his own military camps. In 1988, bin Laden established al Qaeda, at first not as a terrorist organization but as a network of foreign soldiers who had come to Afghanistan, so that the soldiers' relatives could track them. In 1989, when the Russians withdrew from Afghanistan, bin Laden returned to Saudi Arabia; however, the Saudi government placed him under house arrest and then forced him to move to Sudan. While in Sudan, bin Laden formed his alliances with militant groups from Egypt, Pakistan, Algeria, and Tunisia, as well as sending fighters to Chechnya and Tajikistan. In 1996, under American pressure, Sudan forced bin Laden and other members of al Qaeda to leave, and they moved to Afghanistan, where they stayed until the U.S. attacks on the Taliban in 2001.

Given the transnational makeup and illicit nature of al Qaeda's operations, the Internet has complemented the organization's "fuzzy" structure and served its needs handily. The Net is becoming a major weapon in al Qaeda's bid to win supporters to its cause, keep its decentralized structure, galvanize its members to action, and raise funds.As Middle East expert Paul Eedle argues, "The Web site is central to al Qaeda's strategy to ensure that its war with the U.S. will continue even if many of its cells across the world are broken up and its current leaders are killed or captured. The site's function is to deepen and broaden worldwide Muslim support, allowing al Qaeda or successor organizations to fish for recruits, money and political backing. The whole thrust of the site, from videos glorifying September 11 to Islamic legal arguments justifying the killing of civilians, and even poetry, is to convince radical Muslims that, for decades, the U.S. has been waging a war to destroy Islam, and that they must fight back."

A widespread network of Web sites is used to feed directions and information from those at the top of al Qaeda to supporters and sympathizers around the world. Lectures, taped announcements, videos of terrorist attacks, guidebooks, and manuals are being spread by al Qaeda's Web sites, forums, chat rooms, and online bulletin boards. With Net access spreading swiftly across the Middle East, the audience for the online campaign is steadily growing. According to Eedle, "The Internet is an ideal tool for a network like al-Qaeda. It is not a matter of a few radical-sounding messages posted on the odd bulletin board; it's a very wide array of Internet sites and message boards … Al Qaeda has much wider ambitions than just setting off explosives. It is trying to mobilize the whole Muslim world against the West." Many of the sites associated with al Qaeda gain credibility by demonstrating in various ways their close links with the organization. Certain "fingerprints" in graphics and text clearly indicate whether the sites indeed have ties with al Qaeda. Evidence of direct links between al Qaeda and some of the Web sites is sometimes subtle to detect, but in many cases there is little doubt that this group is the source of the material. However, al Qaeda openly acknowledges the importance of the Internet as a propaganda tool, as it did on one of its numerous websites:

"Due to the advances of modern technology, it is easy to spread news, information, articles and other information over the Internet. We strongly urge Muslim Internet professionals to spread and disseminate news and information about the Jihad through e-mail lists, discussion groups, and their own Web sites. If you fail to do this, and our site closes down before you have done this, we may hold you to account before Allah on the Day of Judgment ... We expect our Web site to be opened and closed continuously. Therefore, we urgently recommend any Muslims that are interested in our material to copy all the articles from our site and disseminate them through their own Web sites, discussion boards and e-mail lists. This is something that any Muslim can participate in, easily, including sisters. This way, even if our sites are closed down, the material will live on with the Grace of Allah."

The online propaganda strategy of al Qaeda, like its approach to online planning and coordination, takes advantage of the speed, anonymity and interactivity of the Internet. Al Qaeda's sites are maintained by group members and supporters who are in direct contact with the members. Many sites are registered or hosted in Europe, Asia, or even the United States (according to a July 2004 survey, 76 percent of Islamic terrorist Web sites are hosted by American companies).

Many of these Web sites are anti- American and anti-West: "The Muslims know that America only wants to fight Islam and to liquidate everyone who acts according to the Islamic Shariah, because America knows that the biggest danger to it and for the Jews is Islam and its believers," states the Azzam Publications site that features more than four dozen celebratory biographies of "Foreign Mujahideen Killed in Jihad." The Azzam Publications site promotes the book edited by the convicted mastermind of the 1993 World Trade Center attack, Sheikh Omar Abdel Rahman, and another written by bin Laden's mentor, Abdullah Azzam. The Al-Maqdese site markets the book called *Strengthening the Legitimacy of the Ruin in America*, which uses Islamic juridical arguments to justify the September 11 attacks.

## Al Qaeda's Dynamic Presence on the Net

One weapon against terrorists' use of the Internet is direct assaults on their Web sites; however, all efforts to prevent or minimize al Qaeda's use of the Internet have proved unsuccessful. In the late 1990s, when this project began, al Qaeda had one Web site (www.alneda.com). Today, though the original site was hacked, al

Qaeda is present in hundreds of Web sites. If an al Qaeda site is taken offline by a counterterrorism agency, by the Internet Service Provider hosting it, or by hackers, it will reemerge on the server of another service provider. U.S. officials were searching the Internet for the reappearance of alneda.com, the original Web site used as a mouthpiece by al Qaeda terrorists. It was registered in Singapore and appeared on Web servers in Malaysia and Texas before it was taken off at the request of U.S. officials. Then it changed its name and URL every few days, forced to move from server to server by citizens who complained to the ISPs hosting the sites. Then, in late 2002, al Qaeda lost the Internet domain: it expired and was acquired by a private citizen. The Alneda site operators tried to reappear by using various server accounts that had no associated domain name. When that failed, they started posting the Alneda site as a "parasite." Sheikh Yousef Al-Ayyeri, who operated this site, exploited a known "bug" in a program called cPanel, found on many Web servers. This flaw allowed him to install his site as a "parasite" on an existing and legitimate site. Thus, the Alneda site was posted on the hijacked Web site until someone noticed and got the ISP to remove the illegal site. When it was removed, the process started again. This pattern of Alneda's presence on the Net began in the end of September 2002 and continued until April 2003.

In April 2003 al Qaeda's Web site reemerged, this time named "Faroq," flying the banner of Alneda. Although the new site and other al Qaeda sites moved regularly, various informal means were used to pass on details of the site's new locations, including via e-mails, chat rooms, and announcements or links on other groups' Web sites. The new Web site, faroq.com, began as an al Qaeda site focusing primarily on fighting the United States in Iraq but then transformed itself into a more general site, including reposting content from the original Alneda site. Today, being on the run, al Qaeda's organization is even more virtual, which often means more dependent on the Internet to spread propaganda and plot operations. This reliance on the free access and use of the Net is also one of the main reasons why, despite the many blows that it received since 9/11, the organization's operational capabilities have not truly diminished.

## THE ADVANTAGES OF THE NET FOR AL QAEDA

Al Qaeda's marginalized status vis-à-vis the Western media is partly a consequence of what Phillip Hammond refers to as 'the media war on terrorism'. Bemoaning this 'media siege', al Qaeda as well as other terrorist groups have turned to the Internet as their principal ideological and practical channel of communication. Thus, proliferation of terrorist websites demonstrated an exponential growth from 12 websites in 1998 to over 5,500 in 2007. By its very nature, the Internet is in many ways an ideal arena for activity by terrorist organizations. Most notably, it offers:

- easy access;
- little or no regulation, censorship, or other forms of government control;
- potentially huge audiences spread throughout the world;
- anonymity of communication;
- fast flow of information;
- interactive communication;
- inexpensive development and maintenance of a web presence; and
- a multimedia environment (the ability to combine text, graphics, audio, and video and to allow users to download films, songs, books, posters, and so forth).

Al Qaeda is using the Internet for various purposes, targeting various audiences. Our studies have identified at least eight different uses that can be grouped into two categories: communicative and operational uses. Let us explain and illustrate some of these al Qaeda uses of the Net.

### The Communicative Uses

From the communicative perspective, terrorism has often been conceptualized as a form of psychological warfare, and certainly al Qaeda has sought to wage such a campaign through the Internet. For instance, al Qaeda uses the Internet to spread disinformation, to deliver threats intended to instill fear and helplessness, and to disseminate horrific images of recent actions. The Internet—an uncensored medium that carries stories, pictures, threats, or messages regardless of their validity or potential impact—is peculiarly well suited to allowing even a small group to amplify its message and exaggerate its importance and the threat it poses. Since September 11, 2001, al Qaeda has festooned its websites with a string of announcements of an impending "large attack" on U.S. targets. These warnings have received considerable media coverage, which has helped to generate a widespread sense of dread and insecurity among audiences throughout the world and especially within the United States. Interestingly, al Qaeda has consistently claimed on its websites that the destruction of the World Trade Center has inflicted psychological damage, as well as concrete damage, on the U.S. economy.

Another popular communicative use of the Net is for publicity and propaganda. Until the advent of the Internet, terrorists' hopes of winning publicity for their causes and activities depended on attracting the attention of television, radio, or the print media. The fact that terrorists themselves have direct control over the content of their websites offers further opportunities to shape how they are perceived by different target audiences and to manipulate their image and the image of their enemies. Thus, the most visible part of al Qaeda's online presence involves the spread of propaganda. For its online propaganda al Qaeda is using its media production branch, called As-Sahab Foundation for Islamic Media Publication (As-Sahab means "The Cloud" in Arabic). This organization uses modern technology to produce its video statements to the world, using semi-professional hardware. In addition to being released in Arabic, some published videos come with English or other language subtitles, while more recent productions include videos in English and German. Al Qaeda is also operating online radio and television broadcasting and an additional online production facility—the Global Islamic Media Group (GIMF), an al Qaeda mouthpiece group. Many terrorist groups, among them Hamas and al Qaeda, have undergone a transformation from strictly hierarchical organizations with designated leaders to affiliations of semi-independent cells that have no single commanding hierarchy.

Through the use of the Internet, these loosely interconnected groups are able to maintain contact with one another—and with members of other terrorist groups. The Internet connects not only members of the same terrorist organizations but also members of different groups. For instance, dozens of sites exist that express support for terrorism conducted in the name of jihad. These sites and related forums permit terrorists in places such as Chechnya, Palestine, Indonesia, Afghanistan, Turkey, Iraq, Malaysia, the Philippines, and Lebanon to exchange not only ideas and suggestions but also practical information about how to build bombs, establish terror cells, and carry out attacks. Thus, al Qaeda has became an online "terrorist Internet Service Provider" linking together various elements of the worldwide Jihadist communities. To pursue this objective, bin Laden and his deputy Ayman al Zawahiri set up a unique structure whose essence was to provide a global virtual network linking together thousands of disparate human, financial, military, intellectual and technical resources. Thus al Qaeda became "the Jihad's Franchise", using the Net to link terrorist groups that range from Algeria's "Groupe Islamique Armé" (later becoming GSPC) to Pakistan's "Jaish Muhammad", the Chechen rebels, the Iraqi insurgents or the al Qaeda cells in Lebanon or Indonesia.

## Al Qaeda's Cyber-Propaganda

Al Qaeda's propaganda is reacting to every major event, attempting to benefit from disasters or scandals. Even the blackout in the Northeast and Midwest of the United States in the summer of 2003 was used by al Qaeda's communications: Al Qaeda's Abu Hafs Brigades posted online their announcement claiming responsibility for "Operation Quick Lightning in the Land of the Tyrant of this Generation," referring to the blackout. This was the third communiqué by this group: In previous postings they accepted responsibility for the downing of an airplane in Kenya and for the bombing of the Jakarta Marriott Hotel on August 5, 2003. The new communiqué assured readers that the operation "was carried out on the orders of Osama bin Laden to hit the pillars of the U.S. economy" as "a realization of bin Laden's promise to offer the Iraqi people a present." The included text warned, "Let the criminal Bush and his gang know that the punishment is the result of the action, the soldiers of God cut the power on these cities, they darkened the lives of the Americans as these criminals blackened the lives of the Muslim people in Iraq, Afghanistan and Palestine. The Americans lived a black day they will never forget. They lived a day of terror and fear ... a state of chaos and confusion where looting and pillaging rampaged the cities, just like the capital of the caliphate Baghdad, and Afghanistan and Palestine were. Let the American people take a sip from the same glass."

Another online channel used to promote the ideological legitimacy of global jihad is the Web site of al Qaeda's Center for Islamic Studies and Research. This Web site has published the bimonthly virtual magazine *Sawt al-Jihad*, or *The Voice of Jihad.*15 The new magazine focuses on the use of violence as jihad's only way.16 The "editorial" by Sheikh Naser al-Najdi entitled "Belief First: They are the Heretics, the Blood of Each of Them Is the Blood of a Dog," calls for the killing of every American: "My fighting brother, kill the heretic; kill whoever's blood is the blood of a dog; kill those that Almighty Allah has ordered you to kill … Bush son of Bush … a dog son of a dog … his blood is that of a dog … Shut your mouth and speak with your other mouth—the mouth of the defender against his attacker. Rhetoric might cause retreat."

Al Qaeda is also targeting women on the Net and attempts to recruit women for terrorist attacks. One of the articles posted on al Qaeda's website, entitled "Umm Hamza, an Example for the Woman Holy Warrior," tells the story of a female martyr, the late Umm Hamza, as told by her husband: "Umm Hamza and Martyrdom: Umm Hamza was very happy whenever she heard about a martyrdom operation carried out by a woman, whether it was in Palestine or Chechnya. She used to cry because she wanted a martyrdom operation against the Christians in the Arabian Peninsula." The article also carries a copy of a letter handwritten by Umm Hamza shortly before her death. On August 26, 2004, al Qaeda launched its online women's magazine called Al- Khansa, named after an early Islamic poetess who wrote eulogies for Muslims who died while fighting the "infidels". The Web site also gives advice on raising children to carry on the

Jihad, how to provide first aid for a family member injured in combat and descriptions of physical training women need to prepare themselves for fighting. The main goal of the magazine seems to be teaching women married to Islamists how to support their husbands in their violent war against the non-Muslim world. One of its first articles reads: "The blood of our husbands and the body parts of our children are our sacrificial offering."

## The Operational Uses

Beyond communications, al Qaeda is increasingly using the Internet for operational purposes. Following the loss of Afghanistan as a sanctuary and training ground, al Qaeda moved to cyberspace, posting thousands of pages of its training manuals online. From the making of an IED or deadly chemical weapons to the staging of an ambush, the Internet has now become al Qaeda's "virtual training camp". The Net is used by terrorist organizations for data mining: they can learn from the Internet about the schedules and locations of targets such as transportation facilities, nuclear power plants, public buildings, airports and ports, and even counterterrorism measures. According to Secretary of Defense Donald Rumsfeld, speaking on January 15, 2003, an al Qaeda training manual recovered in Afghanistan tells its readers, "Using public sources openly and without resorting to illegal means, it is possible to gather at least 80 per cent of all information required about the enemy".

Specific targets that al Qaeda-related websites have discussed include the Centers for Disease Control and Prevention in Atlanta; FedWire, the money-movement clearing system maintained by the Federal Reserve Board; and facilities controlling the flow of information over the Internet. Al Qaeda websites use maps, diagrams and photos of potential targets downloaded from popular web sites such as Google Earth. One captured al Qaeda computer contained engineering and structural architecture features of a dam, which had been downloaded from the Internet and which would enable al Qaeda engineers and planners to simulate catastrophic failures. In other captured computers, U.S. investigators found evidence that al Qaeda operators spent time on sites that offer software and programming instructions for the digital switches that run power, water, transportation, and communications grids. Like many other political organizations, terrorist groups use the Internet to raise funds. Al Qaeda, for instance, has always depended heavily on donations, and its global fund-raising network is built upon a foundation of charities, non-governmental organizations, and other financial institutions that use websites and Internet-based chat rooms and forums. The Internet can be used not only to solicit donations from sympathizers but also to recruit and mobilize supporters to play a more active role in support of terrorist activities or causes. Recruiters may also use more interactive Internet technology to roam online chat rooms and cyber cafes, looking for receptive members of the public, particularly young people. Electronic bulletin boards and user nets (issue-specific chat rooms and bulletins) can also serve as vehicles for reaching out to potential recruits. The SITE Institute, a Washington, D.C.-based terrorism research group that monitors al Qaeda's Internet communications, has provided chilling details of a high-tech online campaign launched to recruit fighters to travel to Iraq and attack U.S. and coalition forces there.

## Conclusion

Al Qaeda represents the worst that globalization and advanced community technologies have to offer. Al Qaeda is a virtual "network of networks", a Jihadist franchise marketing its messages of death and destruction on the Internet. Even if we witness the demise of al Qaeda, we are not likely to witness the demise of its spirit and appeal. In a briefing given in late September 2001, Ronald Dick, assistant director of the FBI and head of the United States National Infrastructure Protection Center (NIPC), told reporters that the hijackers of 9/11 had used the Internet, and "used it well." Since 9/11, al Qaeda operatives have only sharpened their Internet skills and increased their web presence.

How should democratic societies respond to the challenge of online al Qaeda? At least two principles seem clear. First, we must become better informed about the use of the Net by al Qaeda as well as other terrorists, and better able to monitor their activities. Those uses are numerous and, from the terrorists' perspective, invaluable. Hence, it is imperative that security agencies continue to improve their ability to study and monitor terrorist activities on the Internet and explore measures to limit the usability of this medium by modern terrorists. The growing familiarity with terrorist online discourse may guide us to use the same Internet to challenge the culture of doom and death with an alternative discourse, with the voice of hope and humanism.

Second, while we must thus better defend our societies against terrorism, we must not in the process erode the very qualities and values that make our societies worth defending. The Internet is in many ways an almost perfect embodiment of the democratic ideals of free speech and open communication; it is a marketplace of ideas unlike any that has existed before. Unfortunately, as this report has shown, the freedom offered by the Internet is vulnerable to abuse from groups that, paradoxically, are themselves often hostile to uncensored thought and expression.

The use of advanced techniques to monitor, search, track, and analyze communications carries inherent dangers. Although such technologies might prove very helpful in the fight against cyber terrorism and Internet-savvy terrorists, they would also hand participating governments, especially authoritarian governments and agencies with little public accountability, tools with which to violate civil liberties domestically and abroad. It does not take much imagination to recognize that the long-term implications could be profound and damaging for democracies and their values, adding a heavy price in terms of diminished civil liberties to the high toll exacted by terrorism itself.

# 13

# Cyberterrorism and International Cooperation

## DEFINITION OF CYBERTERRORISM

While the discussion of what constitutes cyberterrorism is presented under the second main heading, the definition of the term is given here to introduce the concept. Cyberterrorism can simply be defined as coercing others for a political cause, while using computing resources in cyberspace. "More comprehensively, cyberterrorism refers to the convergence of terrorism and cyberspace. It is generally understood to mean unlawful attacks and threats of attacks against computers, networks, and the information stored therein when done to intimidate or coerce a government or its people in furtherance of political and social objectives" (Denning 2000). To clarify the difference between information warfare and cyberterrorism, it should be understood that cyberterrorism can be a component of information warfare, in other words, information warfare encompasses cyberterrorism (Taylor, Caeti, Loper, Fritch, and Liederbach, 2004, p. 20).

According to Ron Dick, Director of NIIPC in 2002, cyberterrorism means any "criminal act perpetrated through computers resulting in violence, death and/or destruction, and creating terror for the purpose of coercing a government to change its policies" (as cited in Berinato, 2002).

By combining the above concepts, cyberterrorism may also be defined as the politically motivated use of computers as weapons or as targets by sub-national groups or clandestine agents intent on violence, to influence an audience or cause a government to change its policies" (Wilson, 2003, p. 4).

In her article, "What Is Cyberterrorism?" Conway defines the term cyberterrorism as "premeditated, politically motivated attacks by sub-national groups or clandestine agents against information, computer systems, computer programs, and data that result in violence against noncombatant and targets" (2002, p. 436). By this definition, Conway excludes cybercrime activities, including stealing credit card information, sending emails with pornographic content, or hacking a Web site. Some researchers in this area characterize an act as cyberterrorism only if the act results in destruction, death, and/or injury, and creates fear among the public (Denning 2000, Conway, 2002). Furthermore, some also claim that we have not witnessed the destructive aspect of cyberterrorism yet, and therefore they suggest that cyberterrorism does not exist at all (Denning, 1999).

In terms of witnessing cyberterrorism, the claim might be considered to be an accurate one; however, there is also evidence indicating that terrorist organizations have been considering attacking information infrastructures and other communication networks by engaging in cyberterrorism (Devost 1995). In their article, "In Defense of Cyberterrorism: An Argument for Anticipating Cyber-Attacks," Brenner and Goodman attempt to answer the question "why has cyberterrorism not yet manifested itself?" As an answer, they review the literature. The conclude that for some people, the reason why international terrorists have not mounted cyber attacks yet is that they do not have the capability in terms of the technical background. That explanation is called the "there are not enough good terrorist hackers theory," which claims that the terrorists do not have the computer expertise to launch such attacks, and this perspective gives the target countries, in particular, Western countries, the comfort of thinking that they are safe (Brenner and Goodman, 2002, p. 46). Brenner and Goodman consider two problems with respect to that theory: First, this theory ignores the fact that the countries where the terrorists are active have the sophistication that is necessary to launch cyber attacks against the information infrastructure of other countries. For example, the Pakistani hacker groups, G-Force Pakistan and The Pakistani Hackers Club and the Sri Lankan Internet Black Tigers, a special unit of Sri Lankan Tamil Tigers of Tamil Eelam, are credited with executing attacks that seem to be a cyberterrorism campaign (Brenner and Goodman, 2002, p. 47).

The second problem with the theory is that it underestimates the imminent possibility that terrorists can recruit "hacker mercenaries" who have the expertise and motivation to launch cyber attacks if they are paid (Brenner and Goodman, 2002, p. 48). Another explanation of why we have not seen cyberterrorism is that the leaders of the terrorist organizations come from an older generation; therefore, they may not see that type of attack as an alternative (Brenner and Goodman, 2002, p. 48).

Another perspective for defining cyberterrorism is presented by Devost, Houghton, and Pollard. They define information terrorism as the "intentional use of a digital information system, network or component toward an end that supports or facilitates a terrorist campaign or action" (1997). The importance of such a definition is reflected in their statement that cyberterrorism is the "nexus between criminal information system fraud or abuse, and the physical violence of terrorism" (1997). They are fully aware of the fact that one of the most important aspects of defining terrorism is to include politically motivated violence instead of defining the term with actions which may have nothing to do with violence. However, with this definition, they want to "allow for the inclusion of pure information-system abuse" as a new face of terrorism (as cited in Conway, 2002, p. 437). Of course that kind of approach results in including cybercrime activities within the context of cyberterrorism only if they are politically motivated.

In addition to these perspectives, a guide prepared by the Federal Emergency Management Agency (FEMA) discusses the concept of cyberterrorism and presents its own perspective as to what it is. According to the FEMA, in order for an attack to be qualified as cyberterrorism, it should cause violence against property or person, or "at least cause enough harm to generate fear" (FEMA, 2002).

Also, FEMA reveals the distinction between cybercrime and cyberterrorism (2002): "Cyberterrorism is distinct from computer crime, economic espionage, and "hactivism," although terrorists may employ any of these forms of computer abuse to further their agendas. The weapons of cyberterrorism computers differ from weapons of mass destruction such as biological agents, chemical agents, and radiological agents in that they don't directly cause death and injury. However, acting indirectly, they can cause serious consequences to individuals, businesses, industry, government, and the public at large. Depending on how they are used, they can lead to injury and death." The definition offered by the FEMA has an important component which underlies the definition of terrorism and cyberterrorism. An action that generates fear in the public may become a means for terrorists; in other words, a politically motivated attack which results in a tremendous amount of fear and panic in the public may well be characterized as cyberterrorism, even though it does not lead to physical injury or death.

The fact is: "Anyone who could learn to fly a commercial airliner could probably acquire the expertise to penetrate one of our critical information systems" (as cited in Brenner and Goodman, 2002, p. 45). It is not a reasonable assumption that today's terrorists do not have the capability of carrying out cyber attacks. Cyber attacks by individuals, such as hackers and other criminal entities, provide strong evidence that the Internet can be a tool for terrorists who attempt to exploit every possible means available to them for their cause.

## Cyberterrorism as a Force Multiplier

Conventional terrorist tactics, such as car bombings, assassinations, suicide bombings, kidnapping, and hijacking may never be replaced by cyber attacks. However, as a force multiplier, cyberterrorism can create more effect if it is executed in concert with other traditional terrorist actions. A good example can be the scenario created by CSIS involving the detonation of a bomb as a conventional terrorist act and a denial of service attack as a force multiplier (Cilluffo, 2000).

Brenner and Goodman analyze the characteristics of cyberspace and the advantages that it provides for terrorists and other criminal entities. The first characteristic of cyberspace is that "cyberspace is borderless" (Brenner and Goodman, 2002, p. 12). As the former CIA Director George Tenet affirms, cyberspace gives terrorists the operational flexibility and greater security which can be capitalized on in many ways, including establishing networks with other terrorist organizations and members, communicating between members, and facilitating use of the Internet as a propaganda mechanism (as cited in Brenner and Goodman, 2002, pp. 13-14). Also, cyberspace enables terrorists to attack multiple targets at the same time, which can increase the significance of the attack. An interesting perspective by two authors, Brenner and Goodman, is that cyber attacks can act as "terror multipliers," which is a term for force multiplier (2002, p. 26). Terror multiplier can be explained as the effect of a cyber attack which is created by the anonymous nature of the attack source, and its unknown consequences.

Terrorists will attack vulnerable targets, as opposed to the well-protected ones, in order to be successful in their actions and create appropriate conditions which will serve their cause. Vulnerability represents one of the most important concepts of this research. Therefore, the next section focuses on the definition and detailed explanation of vulnerability.

## Typology of Cyberterrorism

There are different approaches in terms of the typology of cyberterrorism. For example, Collin (1999) identifies three types of cyberterrorist acts: Destruction, alteration, and acquisition and retransmission. Grabosky et al. (1998) also identifies three major forms of cyberterrorist acts: destruction of the files, impeding accessibility to data files by encrypting it, and significantly overloading a system, thereby impairing the system's capability.

Another classification of cyberterrorism, "information operations," is presented by Zanini and Edwards (2001, p. 41). The term they used, in fact, has the same meaning as "cyberterrorism." According to Zanini and Edwards (2001, p. 41), there are three types of offensive activities terrorists can use: First, terrorists can use information technologies such as the Internet for perception management and propaganda. Second, by using the Internet and other computer networks, terrorists can carry out disruptive attacks. Finally, they can use the networks for destructive purposes (2001). Perception management and propaganda involve both influencing public opinion and recruitment of new members. The final type of attack is the destructive attack, which is carried out to cause actual destruction of virtual and physical systems, including power, water, or traffic control systems (2001, p. 45). However, some analysts argue that since these attacks may not result in loss of human life they may not produce the same emotional reaction as traditional attacks do (Denning, 2001). On the other hand, Ballard et al. conceptualized a more comprehensive typology of cyberterrorism called "cyber incident typology" (Ballard, Hornik, and McKenzie, 2002, p. 1009):

## International Cooperation as a Tool to Confront the Cyberterrorism Threat

Cooperation with other countries must be a central part of building cyber security (Lewis, 2003, xii). However, "The Internet does not yet have the Web of cooperation that has been built up elsewhere" (Lewis, 2003, p. xii). There are reasons behind this lack of cooperation. First of all, it is new to some states, secondly, some states may not know what is needed, and finally, it touches on many sensitive issues ranging from economic competition, privacy, and access, to national security (Lewis, 2003). In particular, the difficulty with respect to national security and cyber security is that it is always a question as to the extent to which free states are willing to cooperate with other nations in national security issues while they may be required to advertise their own vulnerabilities (Lewis, 2003, p. xix). With advances in technology, financial and banking systems, telecommunication networks, aviation systems, and air traffic control become more reliant on computer and telecommunication networks, which serve many countries but are not controlled by a single country. Therefore, it may be reasonable to claim that it may be easier to facilitate international cooperation in critical infrastructure protection by starting with areas where the transnational connections are very large, such as financial services (Lewis, 2003, p. xix).

## Models of International Cooperation

According to Miyawaki (1999), "The ease with which the origins of cyber attacks can be hidden, and the fact that cyber attacks on one nation can come from anywhere on the globe, mean that cybercrime and cyberterrorism are truly international threats." Ever since terrorism and other types of transnational criminal activities became the main topics in the international arena, the term 'cooperation' has become a focal point for every government. In particular, bilateral and multilateral cooperation have been shown as the most effective method to respond to transnational cybercrime and cyberterrorism. The next section will present strategies, attempts, and efforts with respect to countering cyberterrorism and cybercrime.

Lukasik presents a detailed analysis of responding to transnational cybercrime and cyberterrorism. Lukasik asserts that in order to have a successful global response, the following elements should be in place:

- A common terminology between parties involved in the incident to include identification of the intruder's *modus operandi*, the technical attack details, and the identification of the targets
- Knowledge of the technical skills of all parties involved in resolving the incident
- Knowledge of existing agreements on how incidents of a variety of types are to be handled
- An understanding of the common and conflicting societal issues surrounding the incidents (2001, pp. 152-153).

Later he lists the critical elements that have to be in place in order to have what he calls a "framework for international cooperation":

- Broad membership, consisting of both the world's most technologically advanced nations as well as developing nations, all of whom share the benefits and the risks of global information architectures

- A voluntary and non-coercive environment based on concepts of consensus and practical experience
- Open technical standards that prevent the manipulation of information technology for unilateral gain
- An open organizational structure that provides opportunities for all constituencies to express their concerns
- A mechanism for providing continuous monitoring of actions that can adversely impact privacy
- Mechanisms for reviewing the state of information technology and its practical implementations to enable the international framework to remain relevant in the light of changing capabilities and requirements
- Mechanisms that can assist in building trust relationships globally
- Funding arrangements that can assist less developed nations in meeting their responsibilities to protect the information commons (2001, pp. 176-177). In terms of international cooperation, there are different forms of relationship among governments and their related law enforcement agencies. These cooperative efforts are:
    1. Formal bilateral cooperation: Mutual legal assistance treaties (MLATs)
    2. Informal bilateral cooperation: Individual police contacts (inter-agency cooperation), CERTs, etc.
    3. Formal multilateral cooperation: Council of Europe
    4. Informal multilateral cooperation: G-8, OECD, APEC, CERT collectives.

The necessity for multilateralism emerges because countries have different rules to regulate extradition and legal assistance as well as different substantive laws that govern computer crime (Barkham, 2001). "Operational efforts to prevent and respond to computer attacks must be global" and so far, the most effective international cooperation to respond to cyber attacks have been bilateral in nature (Vatis, 2003, pp. 1-2). There are advantages and disadvantages of all of these four types of cooperation. For example, Vatis presents some of the obstacles facing MLATs as follows: First of all, the scope of the MLATs is narrow in terms of the number of the countries. For example, the U.S. State Department has mutual legal assistance in criminal matters treaties (MLATs) in force with 19 nineteen countries. Secondly, most of these treaties do not cover cybercrime specifically or do so in general terms (Vatis, 2003, p. 2). Finally, application of the MLATs can be time-consuming since these may involve more paper work and other bureaucratic procedures. This final obstacle may not be a major problem for traditional crime when the issue is physical evidence; however, in cybercrime, time is significant since it may take a few minutes if not seconds to destroy evidence or lose track of the criminals (Vatis, 2003, p. 3).

In addition to the issues discussed above, there are more fundamental issues involving international cooperation. First of all, the growth of computer technology and reliance on these types of technologies may differ from country to country. In other words, some countries have not yet seen such crime while others may have experienced many such crimes; therefore, while some countries may have substantive and procedurally clear laws regarding cybercrime and cyberterrorism investigation, others may not have a clue as to what these concepts represent (Vatis, 2003, p. 3). The second important reason is that it may become very difficult to distinguish cybercrime from information warfare, given the fact that many countries are developing cyber techniques for fighting a war or intelligence purposes (Speeches and Testimony, 1998). Vatis considers bilateral cooperation to be more feasible and gives some of the examples:

- In February and March 1998, more than fifty civilian, governmental, and private sector computer systems in the U.S. were affected when intruders penetrated at least 200 unclassified U.S. military personnel and other government computer systems. The timing of these attacks coincided with an increase in the U.S. military presence in the Middle East. The NIPC, working closely with the Israel's law enforcement, identified two people in Cloverdale, CA, and individuals in Israel who were the true perpetrators

- In February 2000, the NIPC received reports that CNN, Yahoo, Amazon.com, e-Bay and other sites had been attacked through Distributed Denial of Service (DDOS), in which intruders took over the networks. The investigation has been carried out by the NIPC with the cooperation of the companies. The attacks have been traced to Canada. The NIPC has worked with the Royal Canadian Mounted Police (RCMP), and to arrest a juvenile, called "Mafiaboy,"was arrested
- In May 2000, individuals and companies around the world were attacked by the "Love Bug" or "I LOVE YOU" virus. The NIPC investigated the incident and identified the suspect by tracing the attack to the Philippines. The FBI, working closely with the Philippines' National Bureau of Investigation, identified the suspect, Onel de Guzman (2003, p. 7)

These are real world examples of bilateral cooperation between law enforcement agencies from two different countries. They are promising in the sense that they prove that working together creates results.

Cuellar focuses in one article on the importance of the international treaty in terms of responding to cybercrime and cyberterrorism. He summarizes the effect of a treaty with respect to its political consequences which may advance the underlying goals of security and safety: a) deterrence of specific offenses: treaties among states allow for extradition and prosecution, which will marginally enhance deterrence against cybercrime and cyberterrorism. In other words, cyber offenders in general will be deterred from committing cybercrime since jurisdictional difficulties in the investigation of the offense will be removed with treaties. b) International cooperation for legal cooperation: A treaty will encourage cooperation between signatory countries' law enforcement entities. c) Enhancing prospects for technical cooperation beyond the boundaries of the treaty: Since the treaty will be a starting point for having an international consensus as to which actions define cybercrime or cyberterrorism against civil aviation, eventually law enforcement and other entities responsible for investigating and prosecuting cybercrime and cyberterrorism will go beyond the confines of the treaty (Cuellar, 2001, p. 121).

## Public and Private Cooperation

"The Internet and other aspects of the information infrastructure are inherently transnational" (Sofaer and Goodman, 2001, p. 2). The transnational nature of cybercrime and cyberterrorism requires that the public and the private sectors work together and cooperate.

"The most active international cooperation for cyber security has been in law enforcement," however, there has not been large scale cooperation outside of law enforcement" (Lewis, 2003, p. xix). For example, even though critical infrastructure protection has a law enforcement component, issues can go beyond the capacity of the law enforcement and it becomes an issue of national security (Lewis, 2003, p. xix). "Cyberterrorism and cybercrime could also overlap in damaging ways; groups can steal credit card numbers or important data to damage economies and for their own gain" (Lewis, 2003, p. xv). Localized law enforcement efforts toward cyber criminal activities are at a disadvantage in an interconnected world due to the limited jurisdiction that every law enforcement agency has. Nevertheless, Lewis is of the opinion that "cyber attacks are far less damaging than physical attacks" (Lewis, 2003, p. xiv).

The next section focuses on the efforts aiming at responding to cyberterrorism and cybercrime. The examples are both of national and international level cooperation between law enforcement agencies as well as other international entities. They also include public-private cooperative efforts.

# MULTILATERAL LEVEL INTERNATIONAL COOPERATION

## Group of 8

The Group of 8 (G-8) countries is composed of the U.S., the United Kingdom, France, Germany, Japan, Canada, Italy, and Russia. The leaders have been meeting annually since 1975 to discuss issues of importance, including crime and terrorism, and the information highway (Group of 8, 2003). The G-8 Subgroup on High-Tech Crime was founded in 1997. In January 1997, the G-8 also set up a "24-Hour-Contact-Group" to facilitate law enforcement communications for investigations (Group of 8, 2003). This type of network enabled group members to foster speedy communications between and among the members which allow them to preserve digital evidence until legal processes can be started (Vatis, 2003, p. 3). The idea is to produce global agreements so that there cannot be digital havens where anybody can plan and execute illegal business (Hancock, 2003).

The G-8 also held meetings between law enforcement and industry representatives, and through these meetings the G-8 aims to foster cooperation, not only among the law enforcement group members, but also industries so that each party can present their concerns, experiences, and visions (Vatis, 2003, p. 5). These activities have had several impacts, including being a model for larger formal multilateral efforts, and identifying difficulties that individual states and multilateral entities may encounter (Vatis, 2003, p. 5).

The G-8, in their meeting in 2000, published the Okinawa Charter on Global Information Society, and indicated its commitment to the creation of international cooperation to target cybercrime (G7-G8 Summit in Okinawa, 2000). This meeting created another task force—the Digital Opportunity Taskforce (dot force)—in order to integrate its efforts into a broader international approach. To this end, it was decided that the dot force would convene as soon as possible to explore how best to secure participation of stakeholders. This high-level task force is in close consultation with other partners and in a manner intended to be responsive to the needs of developing countries.

Efforts made by the G-8 states demonstrate the importance of cooperation at the international level which may lead to the creation of a deterrent for the criminals, in the sense that the investigation and prosecution of the criminal act will be swift and certain. The G-8 held a meeting in Paris, France, in May 2003, and ended up with three significant decisions with respect to critical infrastructure protection: To combat this threat, they determined that they needed unprecedented global cooperation to protect their information infrastructures, including computer network and communication systems. They also saw the need to respond to terrorist and criminal threats against them (Meeting of G8 Ministers of Justice and Home Affairs, 2003).

## Council of Europe (CoE)

The Council of Europe (CoE) is an intergovernmental organization, which is made up of forty-five European countries. In addition to these countries, states such as the U.S., Canada, and Japan have observer status (Council of Europe, 2003). In 2001, the CoE drew up a Convention on Cybercrime, and non-European countries, such as the U.S., Canada, and Japan, participated in the drafting process. The underlying reasons behind having a convention are described by the CoE (International Working Group, 2002). It was drafted:

- Considering that the aim of the Council of Europe is to achieve a greater unity between its members;
- Recognizing the value of fostering co-operation with the other States parties to this Convention;
- Convinced of the need to pursue, as a matter of priority, a common criminal policy aimed at the protection of society against cybercrime, inter alia by adopting appropriate legislation and fostering international co-operation;
- Conscious of the profound changes brought about by the digitalization, convergence and continuing globalization of computer networks;
- Concerned at the risk that computer networks and electronic information may also be used for committing criminal offences and that evidence relating to such offences may be stored and transferred by these networks;
- Recognizing the need for co-operation between States and private industry in combating cybercrime and the need to protect legitimate interests in the use and development of information technologies;

- And believing that an effective fight against cybercrime requires increased, rapid and well-functioning international co-operation in criminal matters.

The purpose of this convention was "to make criminal investigations and proceedings concerning criminal offences related to computer systems and data more effective and to enable the collection of electronic evidence of a criminal offence" (International Working Group, 2002).

According to Weber, the Convention on Cybercrime establishes three general principles to international cooperation. First, international cooperation will be provided among the states "to the widest extent possible". Second, the obligation to cooperate extends not only to the crimes established by the treaty, but also to the collection of electronic evidence whenever it relates to a criminal offense. Third, the provisions for international cooperation do not supercede preexisting provisions of international agreements on these issues (2003, p. 433).

The CoE has taken a more comprehensive approach by publishing and refining a Draft on Cybercrime (Sofaer, 2001). The Draft includes a detailed description of the concepts, computer system, computer data, and data traffic (Convention on Cybercrime, 2001). The Draft also includes several provisions which criminalize some of the activities in the cyberspace.

The significance of that convention is that, once in force, all countries that ratified it, including those who are non-member observer states, are required to standardize their laws to comply with the provisions of the Convention (Westby, 2003). Especially those countries which are signatory states are required to adopt such domestic laws in order to establish minimum standards (Council of Europe, 2001). In Budapest, on November 23, 2001, the CoE opened the treaty for signature by the member states and by non-member states, including the U.S. As of December, 2002, there were 32 thirtytwo signatories and it had been ratified by Albania and Croatia (Weber, 2003, pp. 429- 430).

Of course, there was some criticism directed towards the Draft of the Convention regarding the issue of basic human rights and information freedom. For some, the Draft was "contrary to well-established norms for the protection of the individual ... that it improperly extends the police authority of national governments ... that it will undermine the development of network security techniques ... and that it will reduce government accountability in future law enforcement conduct" (Ever, 2000). Some even said this treaty will "kill the Internet" (Davis, 2003, p. 217).

Nevertheless, the convention addresses deterrence as a necessary function and it aims at swift and efficient law enforcement efforts toward cybercrime detection, investigation, and prosecution, all of which will protect "confidentiality, integrity, and availability of computer systems" (Baron, 2002, p. 268). The treaty of the CoE on cybercrime is important for a number of reasons. "The Council's approach recognizes that accomplishment of this goal is predicated upon finding solutions to the lack of criminal statutes, the lack of procedural powers, and the lack of enforceable mutual assistance provisions that result from the jurisdictional gap in cybercrime regulation" (Weber, 2003, p. 430).

## European Union (EU)

The European Union (EU) emerged from three organizations formed in the 1950s by Belgium, West Germany, France, Italy, Luxembourg, and the Netherlands: the European Coal and Steel Community (ECSC), the European Atomic Energy Community (Euratom), and the European Economic Community (Sussmann, 1999, p. 479). "The EU is, in fact, unique. Its Member States have set up common institutions to which they delegate some of their sovereignty so that decisions on specific matters of joint interest can be made democratically at the European level" (The European Union at a Glance,. 2003). Currently there are more than twenty-five member states within the EU. With respect to cyber security and critical infrastructure security, the EU has published several documents. It has also created entities to respond to the challenges of critical information infrastructure security.

Among these efforts, in April 1998, the European Commission prepared a study called COMCRIME which focused on security of information infrastructures and combating computer-related crime (Cybercrime European Commission, 2004). In January, 1999, the European Parliament and the Council adopted an action plan on promoting safer use of the Internet by combating illegal and harmful content on global networks. In 2001, the European Commission prepared a document entitled "Network and Information Security: Proposal for a European Policy Approach," in which the following four conditions were presented as key conditions in order to be successful in responding to cybercrime and information infrastructure vulnerabilities (Cybercrime, European Commission, 2001):

- The adoption of adequate substantive and procedural legislative provisions to deal with both domestic and transnational criminal activities.
- The availability of a sufficient number of well-trained and equipped law enforcement personnel.
- The improvement of the co-operation between all the actors concerned, users and consumers, industry and law enforcement.
- The need for ongoing industry and community-led initiatives.

Another significant effort by the EU is the eEurope 2005 Action Plan which was approved by the European Council in June, 2002 (Council of Europe, 2002). The central component of the eEurope 2005 Action Plan is information infrastructure protection (Westby, 2003), and it stresses "the importance of ensuring the appropriate security of networks and the information that is transmitted through them for individuals, business, administrations and other organizations" (Council of Europe, 2002).

In terms of important agencies of the EU with regard to critical information and infrastructure protection, there is the European Network and Information Security Agency (ENISA). The objectives of the ENISA are to facilitate and intensify European coordination in the area of information security, provide the highest security of the information infrastructure systems for the members, and to create common understanding of information security among the member states in the EU (Information Society, 2003). "The management board of the Agency will be composed of five representatives appointed by the Council, five by the Commission, two by the European Parliament, as well as four industry and two consumers' representatives" (EU News Report, 2003). The agency has a budget of 24 million euro over a five-year period and it is intended to help the Commission and the member states cooperate more efficiently in their responses to information security and network problems such as viruses and unauthorized interception of communications, computer crashes, and information technology (IT) network failures (EU Business, 2003).

## United Nations (UN)

The United Nations (UN) has increased awareness of information security, in particular, computer related crimes. In 2000, the Tenth United Nations Congress on Crime Prevention and the Treatment of Offenders was held in Vienna, Austria. In sum, the meeting emphasized the importance of internationally coordinated efforts toward preventing and responding to threats against information systems and cyber security.

In addition, it was emphasized that the exchange of technical and forensic expertise between national law enforcement authorities was crucial for faster and more effective investigation of such crimes (Tenth United Nations Congress, 2000). Furthermore, in different meetings, the members of the UN expressed their concerns about the threat of cybercrime and cyberterrorism, and proposed training programs about cyberterrorism for the national law enforcement agencies (Security Council 4,792nd Meeting, 2003).

## Asia Pacific Economic Cooperation (APEC)

APEC was formed in 1989 in response to the growing interdependence among Asia- Pacific economies, and since then APEC has become the primary regional vehicle for promoting open trade and practical economic cooperation (TIA Online, 2002). Asia Pacific Economic Cooperation (APEC) established the Telecommunication and Information Working Group (APEC-TEL), which provides coordination between the governments, private sectors, and business of the 21 twenty-one APEC members (Westby 2003, p. 103).

The Fifth APEC Ministerial Meeting on Telecommunications and Information Industry was held in May 2002 in China and the members of the APEC declared the need for economies to promote the development of advanced, secure and reliable information infrastructures and expressed their commitment to improving the multilateral and bilateral cooperation in the APEC region in developing telecommunications regulatory policies, and information and network security (APEC Shanghai Declaration, 2002). They also made clear that it is very important to establish a legal basis to address the criminal misuse of information technologies and law enforcement cooperation in combating that misuse (TELMIN 2002).

## Organization for Economic Co-operation and Development (OECD)

The Organization for Economic Co-operation and Development (OECD) defines cyber security in their Guidelines for the Security of Information Systems as "the protection of the interest of those relying on information systems from harm resulting from failures of availability, confidentiality, and integrity" (OECD, 2002). The Guidelines for the Security of Information Systems and Networks states that due to increased interconnectivity, information systems and networks have now become more vulnerable to a growing number and a wider variety of threats, which explains one of the fundamental issues in information security (OECD, 2002). By stating "... participants, as appropriate to their roles, should be aware of the relevant security risks and preventive measures, assume responsibility and take steps to enhance the security of information systems and networks," the OECD put the responsibility on the shoulders of every member in the organization (OECD, 2002). The OECD Council adopted nine important principles to develop "the culture of cyber security" (OECD, 2002).

## Interpol

Interpol is the abbreviation for the International Criminal Police Organization. It was established in 1956 to enhance globally and facilitate cross-border criminal police cooperation (Interpol, 2003). Currently, there are 181 countries in over five continents that participate. Interpol is the largest international police organization, which serves as an entity to help member countries with their investigations involving international crimes.

Interpol, among other crimes, focuses on the misuse of information technologies under the name of information technology crime (Interpol, 2003). Interpol has created parties of information technology crime in regions around the world. Instead of establishing a new division, Interpol gathered "working parties" or experts from members of national computer crime units (Interpol, 2003). Currently there are five major working parties that Interpol works with: a) European Working Party on Technology Crime, b) American Regional Working Party on Information Technology Crime, c) African Regional Working Party on Information Technology Crime, d) Asia- South Pacific Regional Working Party on Information Technology Crime, and e) Steering Committee for Information Technology Crime (Interpol, 2003). Among these working groups, the European Working Party on Technology Crime, formed in 1990, has shown significant achievements, some of which include the compilation of the Computer Crime Manual, now called the Information Technology Crime Investigation Manual (ITCIM), a best practice guide for the experienced investigator, numerous training courses in order to share its expertise with other members, a rapid information exchange system which essentially consists of two elements, and preparing training video / CD-ROM for international law enforcement (Interpol, 2003).

## European Police Office (Europol)

The Council Act of 26 July, 1995, signed up the Convention on the establishment of a European Police Office (Europol Convention, 2003), which was established to improve police cooperation between the member states to combat terrorism, illicit drug trafficking, and other serious types of international crime. It became fully operational in 1999 (Area of Security, 2003). "The official inauguration of Europol in 1998 … marked a new watershed of EU cooperation in the field of "Justice and Home Affairs" … which reflects a shift in the direction of supranationalism and away from Europe's long-standing intergovernmental approach to international law enforcement" (Occhipinti, 2003, p. 1). Europol has also the following principal tasks (Europol 2003):

- To facilitate information exchange between member states;
- To obtain, assemble and analyze information and intelligence;
- To notify the authorities of the member states without delay of information concerning them and of any relations identified between criminal offenses;
- To assist investigations in the member states;
- To keep a computerized system of collected information.

In other words, Europol can serve as an effective mechanism in terms of investigating crimes involving information technologies, such as cybercrime and cyberterrorism. "It is important to emphasize that Europol will not have executive authority, and it is important that Europol should not be viewed as a European equivalent of the Federal Bureau of Investigation in the United States. Nor will Europol take over from, or place any type of restraint on, national counterterrorist agencies" (Marotta, 2001, p. 18).

However, according to Occhipinti, recent developments indicate that the nature of collaboration on policing in the EU has become more supranational and the EU will move even closer to having a supranational form of police cooperation, "including a role for Europol that increasingly resembles that of the U.S. FBI" (2003, p. 238).

## Policy Implications

This study strongly emphasizes the importance of cooperation in response to the threats coming from cyberspace. In particular, countries with high level of vulnerabilities need to be involved in cooperative efforts not only with those countries that are highly vulnerable, but also with other countries with lower levels of vulnerability. Given the fact that a cyber attack can be launched from anywhere, the source of such an attack does not necessarily have to be a country with a high level of technological development. This brings us to the issue of having a vested interest in expanding an alliance to include many countries with a variety of different backgrounds. In terms of a theoretical discussion, any country concerned with cyberterrorism should embrace the double approach. That is, while taking every necessary step to ensure the safety of their critical infrastructures, they should also make every effort to achieve an inclusive partnership/alliance with other countries.

To achieve such an overwhelming task, different venues should be sought, including formal and informal cooperation. Cooperation may involve both formal and informal relationships, and the effectiveness of both may vary depending on the case in question. While the desired relationship should be formal cooperation, it has drawbacks, most notably time-consuming bureaucratic procedures, although time can be crucial for law enforcement and other national security agencies. Particularly, investigating cyberterrorism does not allow the luxury of spending time going through bureaucracy. On the other hand, while informal mechanisms are efficient in terms of time, in some countries, informal cooperation may not be approved by their governments. Therefore, in responding to cyberterrorism or cybercrime, both informal and formal cooperation should be put into practice, while efforts are made to lessen the bureaucratic procedures, and this can be achieved by bilateral agreements.

Awareness is another milestone toward achieving real, concrete cooperation. Developing awareness at the domestic and international level toward cyberterrorism and cybercrime will help concerned parties to work with other countries. Recognizing existing or potential risks will motivate countries to start to take necessary measures to respond to cyberterrorism and cybercrime, to include legal, technical, and political procedures.

Another important issue with respect to policy is the legal discrepancies and/or lack of legal measures targeting cyberterrorism and cybercrime. While countries amend new laws or update the existing ones to compensate for the gap stemming from new trends in responding to cyberterrorism, they also should try to establish a consensus as to what cyberterrorism constitutes and what the general procedures should be in terms of handling investigations and prosecution of cyberterrorism related incidents. Conventions, such as the Council of Europe Convention on Cybercrime—even though there are some questions about articles in the Convention

Treaty—is an ambitious attempt toward achieving such a consensus. In terms of facilitation of cooperation at the national and international levels, a number of entities can play important roles. In particular, institutions such as CERT and FIRST can be instrumental in carrying out informal and formal bilateral and multilateral cooperation. In the area of cyberterrorism and cybercrime such an activity at the informal level among private or public institutions can lead to formal cooperation since informal processes can guide the development of a culture of cooperation. Moreover, entities such as G-8 and OECD can lead other non-member countries toward developing a certain level of awareness. While these entities do not have operational branches, they can set the standards for future applications and strategies for themselves and be examples for other countries. On the other hand, institutions such as the UN and the Council of Europe can be more active organizations since they have more member states. Also the members can be obliged to fulfill the requests from these multilateral entities, which can be vital to achieving consensus.

In addition, developed countries can offer technical and legal assistance to other countries; in other words, developed countries can expand the response policies by supporting other countries. One way to accomplish a sound cooperation is to identify regions and focus those areas. Countries such as Turkey can be a center in the Middle East, including the former Soviet republics. Turkey can work with experts from the U.S. and other European countries to train law enforcement in the region in the area of terrorism and cybercrime. Given the fact that Turkey has a long history of struggle against terrorism and organized crime, the experience can be utilized toward advancing regional countries' abilities and understanding of how to handle terrorism, in particular, cyberterrorism and cybercrime.

Other critical and rather sensitive issues are national sovereignty and jurisdiction. National sovereignty is a political issue that may be an obstacle since countries have every right to claim their sovereignty when it comes to investigating cyberterrorism. Respectively, the issue of jurisdiction becomes a legal issue when investigating cyberterrorism and cybercrime, both of which are transnational in nature. To overcome these two critical issues, existing applications from other areas can be considered. Aviation is one of those areas that involve internationally recognized and implemented regulations worldwide. Agreement in such an area can be a model for cyberterrorism and cybercrime initiatives. Another application is the "European Arrest Warrant" which can give a clue as to how the international community will overcome issues of jurisdiction.

Of course the author of this study does not imply that we need to have such a system; however, the European Arrest Warrant can be taken as an example. In terms of overlaps between cybercrime techniques and cyberterrorism, the study suggests that cybercrime techniques are readily available tools for terrorists to exploit. More importantly, technology provides ample opportunity for terrorists to expand their operations and establish new networks with other terrorist organizations. Cyberspace gives terrorists new tools to recruit new members and to support their activities financially. The C-F-R-P factor is very critical in terms of responding not only to cyberterrorism, but also to traditional terrorism. The C-F-R-P factor can, in fact, be monitored by law enforcement and can be used to identify possible recruitment techniques, possible new recruits, and finance sources. Also, it can provide invaluable information in terms of communication. It is true that not every terrorist organization uses the Internet for communication; nevertheless, communication on the Internet can provide leads for further investigations.

## Recommendations

Cooperation is very critical in terms of responding to cyberterrorism. Cooperation at the national level includes law enforcement and private sector. Sometimes overlaps in terms of the responsibilities and authorities between different law enforcement agencies may cause confusion. To avoid such an event, law enforcers should establish a coordination center that will not be a supervisory unit, but a unit which will facilitate coordination and collaboration between layers of bureaucracy. This is particularly important in countries like the U.S., where there are numerous law enforcement agencies with a number of laws giving authority to them. Also, implementations, such as the U.S.'s Secret Service Electronic Crime Task Force, should be expanded across the world.

The most important aspect of such programs is that they create a sense of trust between law enforcement agencies and the private sector. Of course, the purpose of these programs should be to share the concerns and support each other. Finally, increasing awareness of vulnerabilities to cyberterrorism and cybercrime can be facilitated by training of law enforcers and the public. At the National level, documents, such as the National Strategy to Secure Cyberspace, published by the U.S., indicated the importance of national and international levels of cooperation to respond to threats coming from cyberspace. It also emphasizes the importance of cooperation and collaboration between the public and private sector to respond adequately to cyber threats. It is true that a document, alone, may not be effective, but it may describe the path to be followed.

While there are numerous issues regarding how to achieve sound international cooperation, the first step toward it involves believing in establishing international cooperation. In other words, countries should spend time and energy establishing a general consensus as to what they should do to achieve real cooperation. Based on the research results, while multilateral cooperation is desirable, bilateral agreements are considered as more achievable than multilateral agreements. Therefore, countries should focus on establishing more bilateral agreements; they also should explore new venues to set up multilateral cooperation. To achieve real cooperation at the international level, countries should practice real coordination and exchange of intelligence. Formal bilateral and multilateral agreements and organizations achieve some level of cooperation, but bureaucracy and other obstacles may slow down the procedures which are very critical in investigating cybercrime. To solve that problem, countries should look for ways to practice informal cooperation at least among the law enforcement agencies.

Moreover, legal measures play a very critical role in responding to cybercrime and cyberterrorism. Laws and conventions, such as the Council of Europe Convention on Cybercrime, are useful tools to facilitate cooperation. In order to respond to this kind of transnational crime, having a common definition of the crime is vital. Recognizing the importance of defining a crime according to its unique characteristics will not only ease the investigation procedures, but also enable cooperation with other countries. Therefore, countries should again attempt to come up with internationally accepted definitions of terrorism, cybercrime, and cyberterrorism.

Finally, we need to find new strategies and tactics to respond to the overwhelming problems we face today. The global nature of the issues such as cybercrime and terrorism requires global responses. It is necessary to look for a radical approach. Globalization of crime, in fact, asks for globalization of law enforcement. This statement may sound overambitious; however, given the extent and complexity of cybercrime and terrorism, it may be underestimating the seriousness of these problems if we claim otherwise.

## THE NOTION OF CYBER TERRORISM

The word "terrorism" comes from the Latin word "*terrere*" which means "to frighten". In very general terms we can view terrorism as any concerted action (or threat of action) undertaken in order to provoke fear.

No common understanding of this notion has been reached on an international level. Often, a uniform definition of terrorism will not even exist across the various concerned agencies of a given country. Such is the case with the United States, where the range of definitions is currently applied.1 Therefore the legal notion of terrorism can only be explained on the basis of certain characteristics and types of action.

It is agreed in general that terrorism seeks to spread fear across a society, the actions taken tend to be large, deadly and spectacular. Therefore it is not difficult to imagine death, injuries or major loss of property as possible results of a terrorist attack. It becomes more complicated when we try to combine terrorism with the notion "cyber", as often the use of information and communication technology serves other, maybe less vital, interests of the society, such as informational privacy, freedom of information or access to public services.

The expression "cyber terrorism" is about an intentional negative and harmful use of information technology for producing destructive and harmful effects. The consequences of a network or information system may be different. In a society like Estonia a denial-of-service attack is likely have decreased the functionality of public eservices as its consequence. The perception of fear therefore needs to be measured by certain characteristics of the specific society, such as dependence on ICT, and potential conflicting interests and interest groups prepared to use extraordinary measures for pursuing their aims.

Obviously, there is not a reasonable basis for talking about any international agreement or consensus in terms of the expression "cyber terrorism". However, as the dependence on ICT is growing, and technology carries with it new possibilities for terrorist action, the discussion on these topics needs to go on.

## THE EXISTING INTERNATIONAL LEGAL FRAMEWORK

### The United Nations

As mentioned above, there are several legal instruments dealing with different types of terrorist activities. The UN-banned terrorist actions include: Offences Committed On Board Aircraft, Unlawful Seizure of Aircraft, Crimes against the Safety of Civil Aviation, Crimes against Internationally Protected Persons, Taking of Hostages, Unlawful Use of Nuclear Material, Unlawful Acts against the Safety of Maritime Navigation, Unlawful Acts against the Safety of Fixed Platforms Located on the Continental Shelf, Making of Plastic Explosives for the Purpose of Detonation, Terrorist Bombings, Financing of Terrorism and Nuclear Terrorism. In addition to the above, the United Nations has launched a global strategy to fight terrorism, in which it seeks to help its member states develop the capacity to take the fight forward. Perhaps the most important is the ongoing coordination work done pursuant to Security Council Resolution 1373. The UN web site gives an excellent overview of its approach. We might note, however, that despite all of this work, the United Nations has not developed a single working definition of terrorism. Instead, the UN has worked ad hoc. One could argue that the method of developing legal instruments that the United Nations has used fails because it is too focused on building a consensus about already employed existing methods used by terrorists. It cannot lead the fight against new methods (such as cyber terror). Thus, we might consider using the United Nations experience as an argument to avoid an overly reactive (rather than proactive) approach to coping with terrorist threats.

## The Council of Europe

The CODEXTER (Committee of Experts on Terrorism) pursues its work regarding the analysis of international law and action against terrorism. The work of the CODEXTER is currently focusing, inter alia, on the use of the Internet for terrorist purposes, the notion of cyber terrorism, enhanced co-operation between the Council of Europe and its member States and Interpol, as well as on the consideration of possible work concerning false identity information as a challenge to immigration authorities. In the CODEXTER framework the Council of Europe has proposed possible legal responses to cyber terrorism. Professor Sieber outlined in particular:

(a) the harmonization of national substantive criminal law and of national procedural law;

(b) the improvement of international co-operation; and

(c) other important aspects, such as, inter alia, the duty to protect infrastructures/data security certifications and preventive monitoring of data.

As regards the option of cutting off internet resources, in CoE opinion such a restriction would be difficult to establish as various means of communication exist. However, such an option could be applied as a sanction, for example, to a particular server used as a safe harbour for terrorists.

Limited results could be achieved with national filtering techniques. Even if traffic goes through central server (as in China and Iran) the flow could be controlled for the general public but there would be many ways to avoid it. Newsgroups are also used for the diffusion of messages of a terrorist content. Furthermore, it would be difficult to reach an international agreement on what constitutes illegal content as the current definition of terrorist content is very vague.

The main common problem of existing international instruments is the insufficient number of states parties. This is especially true with respect to the Cyber Crime Convention (ETS No. 185), as well as to the Convention on the Prevention of Terrorism (CETS No. 196), which are the most important international instruments for fighting cyber terrorism and other terrorist use of the Internet.

At present, serious threats to commit terrorist acts are not adequately covered either by this Convention or by other Council of Europe conventions, and this deficit is not fully compensated for by the instruments of other international organizations. Considering the effects of threats to commit terrorist acts, we believe that there is a need for action in this area – possibly in the form of a protocol to the Convention on the Prevention of Terrorism.

Regarding the possible updating of ETS No. 185, this Convention should be evaluated with regard to its ability to cover technological advances, particularly in the area of forensic investigative techniques (such as online searches or the use of key logger software). In the fast-paced technological environment of cyber crime, such evaluations, which frequently lead to revisions and updates, are an absolutely normal process, especially when dealing with high risks such as those posed by terrorism. Should a decision to amend the Convention be taken, the possibility of excluding the political exception clause for some of the Convention's offences might also be considered, especially in serious cases of data and system interference. It is necessary for countries to make sure that their domestic statutes on data and system interference provide sanctions appropriate for cases involving terrorist attacks against computer systems. Indeed, "effective, proportionate and dissuasive sanctions" are already required by the Cyber Crime Convention, and it can be left to national legislatures to achieve this result by means of sentencing rules, aggravated offences on data interference, or infrastructure offences.

Professor Sieber has proposed that international efforts should focus on developing repressive and preventive measures that target the dissemination of illegal content on the Internet and that are both effective and respectful of civil liberties. This could be done either with a special focus on illegal terrorist content or in a more general way that would encompass other types of illegal content as well. As far as substantive law is concerned, this would also require harmonized rules regarding the responsibility of Internet service providers.

The necessary developments in the areas of criminal procedure and international co-operation would require specific regulations based on technical control mechanisms on the Internet that do not unduly inhibit the free exchange of information. In his opinion, the Council of Europe, with its long tradition of balancing security interests in criminal matters with the protection of human rights, would be the ideal institution to tackle the difficult problems posed by the development of such international standards and procedures for regulating illegal content on computer networks.

## OSCE

OSCE activities on cyber terrorism include the Joint OSCE-CoE Expert Workshop and Ministerial Council Decision no. 3/04 "Combating the Use of the Internet for Terrorist Purposes". The OSCE supports the view that existing legal instruments could provide a basis on which to fight terrorist-related use of Internet, but this legal basis was not used sufficiently. Thus, adherence to international instruments, in particular to the Convention on Cyber Crime and the CoE Convention on the Prevention of Terrorism, must be promoted. There is significant difference in national approaches – in some countries "content" offences are considered terrorist offences; in others they imply interference with the right to the freedom of expression, which is of the utmost importance. There are other possible actions for the monitoring of sites of a terrorist content: the setting-up of hotlines, similar to those set up for child pornography websites, interstate exchanges of information and the restricted use of filtering, e.g. by educational institutions. As for requests from other states for co-operation, there should be two options for dealing with requests – if a country cannot close a website on the grounds of national legislation, it should at least collect information.

## The European Union

The role of the EU in addressing cyber terrorism issues is significant in that the EU law has internet as an object of regulation: the issues of ISP liability, fighting against spam, personal data protection, etc., have been regulated in many EU countries directly because of the influence of the relevant directives.

Recently, there have been attempts to also regulate on cyber crime and cyber terrorism issues: The communication on cyber crime sets out the future approach of the EU-wide combat against cyber crime. The policy aims to include improved operational law enforcement cooperation; better political cooperation and coordination between Member States; political and legal cooperation with third countries; awareness raising; training; research; a reinforced dialogue with industry and possible legislative action.

## Other Developments

As regards different countries, the US has developed substantial means for prevention and prosecution of cyber terrorist acts. However, the actions of the US, as of several other nations (France, UK, Austria, Pakistan, India), which have invested in developing a sound framework against cyber terrorism, are directed mostly to internal cooperation and a national legal framework. Some useful ideas may also be derived for international cooperation.

The U.S. has stressed that the key threat to cyber security originates in the relentless criminal attacks by organized criminals, individual hackers and non-state actors, including terrorists. From this perspective, the benefits of cyberspace can best be protected by focusing both on the effective criminalization by States of the misuse of information technology and on the systematic national implementation of measures designed to prevent damage to critical information infrastructures no matter the source of the threat; what the U.S. calls the creation of a global culture of cyber security. In this view, all parties (government, business, civil society) are aware of their responsibilities and act appropriate to their roles to ensure cyber security. An attempt to impose borders in cyberspace as a direct challenge to democratic principles that could easily be used by governments to justify restrictions on the free flow of information and the peaceful use of information technology.

14

# The Internet as a Tool for Intelligence and Counter-terrorism

The internet is crucial to the daily operations of the radical groups making up the global jihad. The internet supplies the jihad movement with its recruiting and propaganda interface, as well as the means for ideological growth and the exchange of ideas. The jihadi online presence is literally the physical brain of the global jihad movement. The very openness and accessibility of this medium provides the intelligence community with a wealth of material for foundation intelligence and analysis. This resource has been neglected in recent years due to lack of qualified researchers and linguists. The key to countering these problems may lie in harnessing the power of the private and academic sectors as unofficial research arms of the counter-terrorism community.

## INTRODUCTION

The uses made of the internet by terrorist organizations and extremists groups is nothing new. The terrorists use the net for the same reasons—and in the same ways— that we all use the net: for marketing, for communications, command and control, for intelligence gathering and datamining. Analysts have been bemoaning this fact for almost a decade, noting all the while that intelligence agencies consistently lag behind the terrorists in the use of the web. These complaints are legitimate, and highlight a central difference in both attitude and aptitude between terrorists and their more institutional opponents.

At present, intelligence agencies are focusing most of their efforts on the threat posed by the larger jihad movement, also referred to as the salafist jihad movement or the global jihad. For the purposes of this paper, I will use the later term, with the stipulation that the global jihad refers not only to the loose network of radical organizations and cells currently under scrutiny by the intelligence community, but also to the larger social movement espousing the jihad ideology. Without this social movement, the global jihad would not be the threat that it is.

Moreover, without the internet, the radical groups making up the global jihad's cadre of militants would remain a widely dispersed and isolated group of cells that happened to claim the same historical roots. It is the internet which has "globalized" the jihad movement. The network of global jihad is a product of the communications revolution. But of course, the same can be said of Microsoft. The internet has changed the way large organizations operate, be they multinational corporations or political movements. The internet is a facilitator of globalization and the global jihad is by definition a global movement.

The internet supplies the jihad movement with more than its recruiting and propaganda interface. It also provides the organization with the means for ideological growth and the exchange of ideas. Without free and open communication, a movement of this size breaks down. The jihadi online presence is literally the physical brain of the global jihad movement. The very openness and accessibility of this medium provides the intelligence community with a wealth of material for foundation intelligence and analysis. This resource has been neglected in recent years due to lack of qualified researchers and linguists. The key to countering these problems may lie in harnessing the power of the private and academic sectors as unofficial research arms of the counter-terrorism community.

## The Internet as Training Camp: To Shut Down or to Tune In?

A common refrain over the past few years has been the constant complaint that the terrorists are "winning the battle in cyberspace."

They're technologically creative, highly mobile, unfettered by either moral or bureaucratic constraints. They've got websites out there to fight their battle for the hearts and minds of supporters and potential supporters, to terrify their enemies, and in general "win friends and influence people." And of course, you can't shut them down. If you close down a website, assuming that you can persuade the service provider to do this, then you can be sure it will just pop up again somewhere else.

It was some time before the analysts began suggesting that, instead of engaging in the futile effort to close down websites, we should make full use of the potential to learn about our enemy from what they say about themselves, and even more importantly, among themselves. After all, a good intelligence agency should make a point of reading everything that the enemy writes, squeezing every drop of information on the opponent's psychological state, tactical capabilities, and strategic planning. This is what intelligence agencies do. Only it wasn't being done—or wasn't being done very well—with regard to the vast publishing empire of the internet. And with good reason. The sheer number of websites out there dealing with stuff that we should know about is daunting. Its content is ever changing. And of course there are linguistic issues, as well as cultural issues. To really make sense of it all would require the services of a veritable army of qualified personnel, and would be far beyond the budgetary—not to mention the bureaucratic—capabilities of most intelligence agencies.

But such an army of personnel does exist, even if it's a modest and rather irregular army. Independent research bodies and individuals have been monitoring terrorist websites and listening in on jihadist forums for years. Some of these people are contributors to the current volume—people like Gabi Weimann, who catalogued terrorist websites long before it became fashionable to bemoan the terrorists' subversion of the internet; or the folks at MEMRI, who've been translating relevant documents for years. Aharon Weisburd has been sleuthing into the identities of the jihadi webmasters and forum posters. The Arizona Artificial Intelligence Lab has pioneered new tools for finding out who's who on the "jihadnet," and analyzing their methods of persuasion. Note that all of this has come from the private sector. Smart governments realize the usefulness of these skills early on, and have taken some steps to make effective use of them. Arizona's AI Lab has been the beneficiary of more than $20M in research funding from federal agencies.

And of course, government think tanks and institutes are also dealing with jihadi materials more and more. Of particular note, the Combating Terrorism Center (CTC) at West Point has done some outstanding analysis work in applying what is learned on the web to concrete tactical operations. Some the examples cited here of intelligence gathering from Islamist online materials come from *Stealing al-Qaida's Playbook*, by Jarret M. Brachman and William F. McCants of the CTC. Just to give a taste of what such analysts have come up with over the past two years, I would like to present some examples of how open source datamining can clue us into how the "bad guys" think, and what to do about it.

## Intelligence from the Web

Before going further, I would like to review briefly what good intelligence is and is not. Intelligence is not "news". Governments often press intelligence agencies into service as open source news monitoring agencies, insisting on getting up-to-date reports on things that are covered by the mainstream wire services. This kind of pressure is often detrimental to the agencies' primary tasks, which is providing an insight into fundamental processes. Yes, an intelligence agency should be up to date with what's going on in a particular sphere of interest. But intelligence gathering is not meant to be news reportage.

## At its Best, Intelligence Leads to Understanding

Properly understood, intelligence-gathering should lead to a fundamental understanding of what is going on in the sphere of interest, who the main players are, and who their friends and enemies are. With regard to a specific opponent, this intelligence should include what the opponent is doing and what the opponent is thinking. This is called "foundation intelligence", and without it, an intelligence agency is no more than an under-funded and under-staffed news agency.

## Understanding Leads to Predictions

Proper foundation intelligence can lead to a better understanding not only of how things are likely to unfold in the sphere of interest, but also what effect contingencies outside of that sphere may have on events. Extrapolation from foundation intelligence is the work of professional analysts, who provide the crucial link from foundation intelligence to tactical intelligence. Essentially, good foundation intelligence helps to formulate answers to the following questions regarding the opponent

- What are they saying?
- What can we learn from it?
- What should we do about it?

While the Internet is unlikely to be a lucrative source of reliable tactical intelligence, it is a goldmine for foundation intelligence. This kind of intelligence deals with the following basic issues regarding the opponent:

- Ideology. What are their core beliefs? What divisions are there in the movement?
- Strategy. What are their ultimate goals and overall game plan?
- Tactics. By what methods do they propose to reach these goals?
- Structure. How do they make decisions, and who makes them?

## What We Learn from Jihadist Websites and Forums

The real heart of the global jihad is expressed online. This is the venue where ideas are hashed out, dissent is either neutralized or accommodated, and strategies and tactics are discussed. For the most part, we don't expect to find online discussions of actual attack planning. But we can learn how ideology and opinion are shaping in the larger Muslim community who form the jihad's target constituency and who supply the movement's pool of recruits. In essence, Al-Qaida's flight into cyberspace was necessitated by the destruction of jihadi training camps following the September 11 attacks. The movement's leaders have had to turn to cyberspace as a way of maintaining contact with a geographically dispersed constituency. However, the use of the web as a primary venue for discussion was not only mandated by necessity, but was also a matter of choice. Since its inception, the global jihad has relied very heavily on the internet and the nature of online communities to further its aims.

## Ideological Lessons

The jihad movement's internet presence is most felt in ideological discussion. The web is essential to the movement's ideological development, as well as to the actual dissemination of this ideology to potential recruits and supporters. Such freely accessible discussions offer analysts a window into the jihad movement at both the "grass roots" level and the level of its top-level leaders. Senior ideologues, as well as mid-level operatives and up-and-coming scholars write on these sites. This is intelligence straight "from the horse's mouth."

Downing and Méese of the CTC point out that a fair amount of the jihad's key doctrinal literature is available online, in addition to documents that have been captured by the intelligence agencies of different countries.

One of the best ways to learn about al-Qa'ida is to read the papers, manuals, and other documents which al-Qa'ida leaders have written to guide and discipline their own enterprise. Many of these documents have been captured by military and law enforcement forces and can provide insight into the way the organization works. Other key references are readily available on the World Wide Web.

They emphasize that the more access is provided to these documents, the more benefits will accrue to the counter-terrorism community as a result. As archives of translated jihadi documents become more accessible to analysts, the understanding of the movement's key ideology, strategy, and motivation is growing. What is interesting is that such analysis is increasingly coming from the private and academic sectors. An example of how analysis is leading to a greater understanding of the jihad movement's vulnerabilities comes out of the Combating Terrorism Center (already mentioned in full). In *Stealing al-Qaida's Playbook*, Jarrett Brachman and William McCants demonstrated how "jihadi strategic studies" can be used to identify and exploit the weaknesses of the jihadi movement. The authors point out that the key to defeating the global jihad from an ideological point of view is to understand its ideology from the inside out: who the main ideologues are, and the significant issues that unite and divide the movement. The authors note that jihadi leaders are remarkably open and blunt when discussing who their biggest competition is and what their public relations vulnerabilities are. In a sense, members of the jihadi movement have put their team's playbooks online. By mining these texts for their tactical and strategic insights, the United States will be able to craft effective tactics, techniques, and procedures to defeat followers of the movement.

I'd like to give a few brief examples of the kind of intelligence that can be gleaned from examining some of the strategic dialogue of the global jihad movement. The following examples are from *Stealing al-Qaida's Playbook.*

## Example 1: Abu Bakr Naji, The Management of Barbarism, 2004

Abu Bakr Naji is one of the more prolific Al-Qaida ideologues of the new generation. He is well-read and articulate, and his works are cited on numerous jihad websites, a testament to the high regard in which he is held by the movement. In *The Management of Barbarism*, Naji presents a thoroughgoing analysis of his own movement's strengths and weaknesses, as well as those of his opponents. Obviously, such an analysis is useful for us in that it allows us to see how our enemies see themselves. But no less important is the information they give us as to how they see us. This point is well illustrated by the examination of Naji's writings. Brachman and McCants studied The Management of Barbarism; below are some key points from Naji's work, as cited by Brachman and McCants.

- Naji urges fellow jihadis to study Western works on management, military principles, political theory, and sociology, in order to borrow strategies that have worked for Western governments and to discern their weaknesses.
- The jihadis cannot defeat the United States in a direct military confrontation. Rather, the clash with the United States is more important for propaganda victories in the short term, and the political defeat of the US is viewed as a long-term goal, as American society fractures and its economy is further strained.
- Naji also discloses weaknesses in the jihadi movement and the problems that predictably confront such an entity, such as difficulties in resolving chains of command, ferreting out spies within the organization, and reining in overzealous recruits.
- There is concern that the momentum of the movement may be slowed by clerics who challenge its legitimacy and siphon off its recruits among the youth.
- Naji observes that the jihadi movement has often split over theological differences.

## Example 2: Abu Qatada, Between Two Methods, 1994

Another example of the vulnerability of the jihad movement given by Brachman and McCants comes from Abu Qatada's work, *Between Two Methods*. Abu Qatada is scathing in his criticism of a popular Saudi cleric, Rabi'al Madkhali, a serious rival of the salafi movement: "This man is content to claim that he is a Salafi so that he can be an imam for some inexperienced boys whom he feeds slogans and shimmering phrases." Jihadi ideologues are very open about which Muslim religious leaders they most fear.

Brachman and McCants point out that although a specific enemy may no longer be a threat, by understanding why he was a threat in the past, we can look for—and perhaps exploit—similarly threatening enemies in the present. Why was Madkahli a threat? To begin with, he was a quietest, and was supported by the Saudi government. More importantly, his popularity and outreach were such that he was able to draw off young recruits from the more radical movements.

## Lessons Learned

What do we take away from these examples? Perhaps the most salient piece of information we gain is "what worries them." Naji openly discusses some of the vulnerabilities of the jihadi movement from an ideological perspective. From his discussion, we see that the movement is vulnerable to ideological splits and knowledgeable clerics who "call them" on their interpretation. What does Naji say should be done about it? His suggestion is to co-opt religious clerics to back the jihadi's interpretations. Where this is not possible, he suggests that rival clerics either be intimidated into silence or killed.

For his part, Abu Qatada provides us with some keys as to what sort of rival cleric is the greatest threat to the movement. The answer seems to be one who manages to appeal effectively to the same target audience, the youth, and yet who espouses a program directly at odds with that of the jihad movement.

## Strategic Lessons

The term "jihadi strategic studies" was coined by Thomas Hegghammer and Brynjar Lia, of the Norwegian Defense Research Establishment in Oslo, to refer to books and articles on the strengths and weakness of the jihadi movement and those of its enemies. Hegghammer noted that the Internet has become a vital venue for terrorist cells to organize and "brainstorm" about tactics in a decentralized way. This allows sleeper cells to operate virtually autonomously, deriving their inspiration and operational direction from texts published online by individuals on other continents. Hegghammer argues that it is online that "...you really get the early signs of the ideological developments, which are later going to affect us, or might affect us, physically."

At the same time, the increasing use of the internet as the central brain of the movement has also made the movement more transparent to onlookers. Terrorist/Jihadi thinking is public and susceptible to infiltration. Hegghammer encouraged counter-terrorist agencies to create an "atmosphere of paranoia" on these websites, by posting fraudulent texts and subverting the readers' trust in the literature.

## Example: "Jihadi Iraq, Hopes and Dangers"

Hegghammer and Lia analyzed a document on the Internet, "Jihadi Iraq, Hopes and Dangers", which detailed how terror attacks ahead of Spain's general election could drive Madrid to pull its troops out of Iraq and thus harm the US-led coalition. Brynjar Lia came across the document in December 2003 on a website called "Global Islamic Media." According to Hegghammer and Lia, "The main thesis proposed in the document is that America cannot be coerced to leave Iraq by military-political means alone, but the Islamist resistance can succeed if it makes the occupation of Iraq as costly as possible—in economic terms—for the United States."

Their analysis led them to see in the document a blueprint for driving a wedge between coalition members.

The document therefore offers a number of specific "policy recommendations" in order to increase the economic impact of the insurgency and the jihadi campaign in Iraq. The most important of these recommendations consists of trying to limit the number of American allies present in Iraq, because America must not be allowed to share the cost of occupation with a wide coalition of countries. If the mujahidin can force US allies to withdraw from Iraq, then America will be left to cover the expenses on her own, which she cannot sustain for very long. The intermediary strategic goal is therefore to make one or two of the US allies leave the coalition, because this will cause others to follow suit, and the dominos will start falling.

The document's anonymous author emphasized that: ...It is necessary to make utmost use of the upcoming general election in Spain in March next year. We think that the Spanish government could not tolerate more than two, maximum three blows, after which it will have to withdraw as a result of popular pressure. If its troops still remain in Iraq after these blows, then the victory of the Socialist Party is almost secured, and the withdrawal of the Spanish forces will be on its electoral programme. A few months later, on 11 March—just prior to the elections—Madrid was rocked by a series of train bombings that killed 190 people. Partly as a result, Spain's conservative government, which supported the Iraq war, lost the vote to the opposition Socialists, who later pulled Spanish troops out of Iraq.

It would be hard to believe that the bombers were unaware of the "Hopes and Dangers" document, given its depth of detail and its widespread distribution. In fact, as pointed out by Lia and Hegghammer, the "nom de terror" chosen by an alleged Al- Qaida video spokesman after the attack—Abu Dujana, a warrior and contemporary of Mohammed—matches one mentioned in the "Hopes and Dangers" document. Further evidence that the bombers had considered the political effect of their actions was provided by the behavior of an alleged ringleader of the Madrid attacks. A cell phone on an unexploded bomb led Spanish police to Jamal Zougam within a day of the bombings. As the *New York Times* reported: "When Mr. Zougam arrived in court after five days incommunicado, he reportedly asked the clerks, 'Who won the elections?'"

## Lessons Learned

The "Hopes and Dangers" document is one example of the kind of basic intelligence that is freely available on the Internet. What can be learned from this example of jihadi strategic studies and the way it was put to practical use? One of the most obvious messages is that the new generation of jihadi strategists place a greater emphasis on pragmatism, and less on ideology. The "Hopes and Dangers" document provides a cool analysis of political realities, with fewer references to historical battles and quotes from the Quran. Eschewing flowery rhetoric and exaggeration, it goes to the heart of current events and possible consequences. Clearly, Al-Qaida's future ideological leadership is evolving in the direction of greater professionalism.

## Tactical Lessons

Just as the jihad uses the web for ideological discussion and dissemination of ideas, tactical discussions and training materials are also freely available online. Among the intelligence that can be gleaned from these documents is information on the tactics they see as effective, the weapons they favor and why, and perhaps even more importantly, their assumptions regarding the effectiveness of these weapons. The following two examples are from Brachman and McCants's *Stealing al- Qaida's Playbook*.

## Example 1: Abu Mus'ab al-Suri

Abu Mus'ab al-Suri (aka Mustafa Setmarian Nasar) has made a study of failed jihads in the contemporary world. He identifies various reasons for such failures, including:

- The co-operation of local governments in countering jihads, and the failure of the jihadists to organize simultaneous attacks in neighboring countries. Suri cites as an example the co-operation of Syria with Jordan, Iraq and other neighbors during the 1960s to 1980s. He suggests that if the neighboring states had been struggling against their own jihads, they would not have been so quick to assist Syria.
- The failure to consider the influence of ethnic minorities and tribes, or the possibility that these populations may be co-opted by the state.
- The failure to provide jihadi fighters with a sense of personal connection to their leaders, or with the vision that they too may become leaders.
- The failure to gain popular support from the Muslim majority; Suri identifies the role of propaganda as being crucial in this regard.
- The insufficient involvement of Muslim clerics. Suri argues that clerics' involvement is essential for developing new local jihad groups.

## Example 2: Abu Bakr Naji

Abu Bakr Naji suggests various ways in which the jihad movement could be strengthened. He outlines three stages for establishing the Khaliphate, beginning with the bombing of crucial targets in order to draw the local security forces in around these centers. The ensuing chaos would allow jihad leaders to assume control of the more remote regions, and from there the jihad administrators could network towards establishing a Khaliphate in that country. Naji also suggests that low-ranking jihadists should not be allowed to launch their own attacks, other than small to medium ones. He argues that major attacks such as 9/11 must be organized only by the High Command, since the wrong attack at the wrong time would undermine the movement. Naji notes that mass-scale Muslim support is of prime importance, and that already the Muslim public is wary of the jihadists' use of violence, and may view the jihadists as trouble-makers. Without Muslim support, Naji cautions, new recruits cannot be found. Finally, Naji argues that the education of young people is only complete when they participate in jihad. He views the education provided by Muslim religious leaders as being of lesser importance, while jihad involvement is seen as providing essential training. The involvement of youth in jihad is viewed as a further step towards establishing the "global Islamic resistance" and, ultimately, the global Khaliphate.

### Lessons Learned

One way to counter the jihadis' tactic would be by helping local surrogates establish their own enclaves in those regions left unprotected by security forces. Local ethnic groups can play a role in preventing security vacuums from forming. The jihadis and the counter-terrorism community are competing for the same audience; however, public opinion is more important to the "irregular" side in a low intensity conflict. For this reason, a greater emphasis must be placed on psychological and information operations in the sphere of influence, in order to undermine the popular support on which the jihad movement is dependent.

## COUNTER-ATTACKS

### Terrorism Websites as a Key to Efficacy

As mentioned, the jihad relies heavily on the web for the dissemination of information from the upper echelons, as well as for discussion at all levels. Statements by the leaders of the movement should be considered a useful input for intelligence analysis. Content analysis of such statements may give some hint of intentions, although there is a significant amount of bluster, hype, and misdirection present in much of these statements. Context analysis may therefore be of greater utility. This kind of analysis can determine what the person making the statement *thinks that his followers want to hear.* Thus, context analysis can provide some measure of the "temperature" of the "street." This is a useful input to foundation intelligence, as well as an aid to determining the focus of tactical intelligence gathering. Special attention should be given to the language, focus, and design of jihadi websites. The languages used can tell us who the jihadis see as their primary audience for recruits. In some cases, this points to perceived vulnerabilities among the targeted group. But it can also tell us who the jihadis *would like to have* as recruits—who can be of most use to them. For example, European Muslim converts are increasingly the focus of "narrow casting" on jihadi websites. Another point of consideration is the imagery and design of the sites. These sites are frequently the work of some of the best and brightest of the new generation jihadi recruits. They know their audience, and they know what techniques are likely to be effective. With this in mind, we can say that imitation is the sincerest form of counterterrorism! But it isn't only the style of outreach that can be copied. Here too, a bottom-up approach can yield benefits that would be unthinkable for top-down institutionalized responses. Web designers from the jihadis' own target audience can be recruited by the counter-terrorism community to build a counter-offensive. The success of this kind of campaign depends on working at the "grass roots" community level. The main allies of the counter-terrorism community will be those singled out for recruitment by the jihadis themselves. Terrorists and counter-terrorists are competing for the same audience. The techniques used successfully by both sides will reflect this. Psychological Operations

Analyst Stephen Ulph of the Jamestown Foundation has been monitoring jihadi forums, with a special emphasis on those dealing with the situation in Iraq, the new training ground for the jihadi movement. In July 2005, Ulph noted how news of ongoing discussions between the US military and the Iraqi insurgents was affecting traffic and commentary on jihadi forums: The news evoked considerable notes of distress on the jihadi forums. On the al- Qal'a forum one signing himself al-Sharif al-Idrisi, noted, on June 28, the similarity of this potential development with the situation in Afghanistan, "when those fleeing the Tora Bora caves were met by the Pakistanis not intent on helping them but in selling them to the Americans. We pray God that this doesn't happen to our brothers in Iraq." This kind of commentary highlights a key weakness as perceived by the jihadi militants themselves—their vulnerability to betrayal by the wider society in which they operate. Such fears are, of course, easily played on. One obvious stratagem for exploiting this sense of paranoia would be to "feed" news of betrayals to local news media, then cast blame in the relevant forums upon elements within the organization, or in rival organizations.

Ulph also noted that the news of meetings between coalition leaders and insurgents was met with denial by many: At the same time strenuous denials were being posted on the internet forums that any such meeting took place, including from groups said to have participated in the talks. One posting on June 30 appeared on the al-Qal'a forum signed by The Islamic Army in Iraq, the Army of the Mujahideen and the Army of Ansar al-Sunna. It expressed exasperation at Ayham al-Samarrai's "lies and America's games" and swiftly pointed to the impending peril for the Islamist mujahideen in Iraq: "its intentions are to split the ranks of the mujahideen … to divide the Iraqis from non-Iraqis ... to pull the rug from under the mujahideen … How can a heroic mujahid Muslim brother in any country be a foreigner?"

What is significant here is the perceived motive of these "American games," namely, "to split the ranks of the mujahideen … to divide the Iraqis from non-Iraqis ... to pull the rug from under the mujahideen." One can gain a good deal of insight into the state of insecurity of the opponent from this sort of posting. Obviously, one forum posting or internet statement does not give an indication of the psychology of a whole organization. However, if monitored on an ongoing basis, the total compendium of such statements can provide a real "feel" for the psychological state of the opponent.

And if "being sold out" is what they fear, then by all means, one should play up any and every possible case of such a sell-out, and milk it for all it's worth. The potential of such suspicions to turn the opponents' forces against his own is indicated by the continuation of the same statement quoted by Ulph above: With America's designs being "to return the Baathists to power, in the name of the resistance" the statement accused Iyad Allawi of "giving orders to the Baathist Ayham al-Samarrai to intrigue against the mujahideen and the resistance ... So we proscribe the life of Ayham al-Samarrai, and declare him to be a target of the mujahideen in general and in particular of all members of the three groups (The Islamic Army in Iraq, the Army of the Mujahideen and the Army of Ansar al-Sunna). ... Anyone who allows himself to be seduced into doing what the fantasist Ayham is doing will share the same fate." In other words, whether correct or not, the suspicions served to drive a wedge between the organization and its perceived enemies. Ulph points out that if the same suspicion can be cast upon elements within the organization, instances of "red on red" firing between opponent groups will be seen to increase.

## Countering Recruitment and Propaganda

The global jihad movement, like any other major social movement, depends on a broad base of support. Positive public opinion from within its constituencies is a must, not only for bringing new recruits into its cadres, but also for garnering support for its less obviously goal-driven activities. As has been pointed out by Yoav Mimran, one of the key values of Muslim societies is social unity and harmony. Anyone seen as sowing discord or endangering public order is likely to be seen as an enemy of the public good, no matter how otherwise worthy are his goals. Brachman and McCants have noted that the movement "declines in popularity when it is perceived to be attacking fellow Muslims, causing public disorder, damaging critical national industries, or engaging in sectarianism."

They point out that one effective point of counter-attack would be to "harness the power of the 'Shayma Effect' [referring to an incident where an Egyptian schoolgirl was killed in a jihadi attack], broadcasting images of jihadi attacks that have killed Muslim children.

The authors point out, however, that any such campaign must be managed very much "from the rear" and by proxy. To this we may add that an institutionalized campaign can never have the same power or reach as a genuine "grass roots" campaign among the potential constituency of the opponent. Only when we are able to inspire local actors to join the fray will such a media counter-offensive really be effective. A government-sponsored campaign, no matter how skillfully managed, is no substitute for the participation of local bloggers, media people, and commentators.

## Undermining Trust

From articles which are available online regarding the training of activists, we can learn of areas that the jihad movement itself sees as weaknesses, the better to exploit them. For example, a number of articles have been posted warning forum posters of possible digital interception, and suggesting ways of getting around the problem. In other instances, internal debate can point to potential splits within the movement, or to a lack—or perceived lack—of leadership. In addition, these kinds of debate can show what issues are of greatest concern to the jihadis themselves.

## Example 1: Divide and Conquer

In fact, the penetration of Islamist forums by counter-intelligence agencies has resulted in the arrests of several key figures. These may include the arrests of forty mujahideen in Saudi Arabia, and the arrests of the attackers of the Abqaiq (Buqayq) oil facility. Most certainly, the arrest of the infamous "internet jihad" Irhabi007 was due to a fairly common lack of attention to basic security procedures online.

A significant spin-off of such events is the mistrust and confusion which abounds on jihadist forums in their wake. During the first half of 2005, Stephen Ulph and other researchers at the Jamestown Institute noted a spate of warnings and debates which appeared on jihadist forums. The warnings were to the effect that forum participants should not enter certain websites—not even as a visitor—for fear of being identified by the "dogs in intelligence" (cited by Ulph, as posted on the Syrian site "Minbar Suriya al-

Islami"). The debates concerned the authenticity of certain jihadist forums, or of site administrators or participants who were suspected of being counter-intelligence spies.

The end result is that jihadists' confidence in their ability to dodge state control via the use of Internet forums has dropped significantly in the past couple of years. Despite the jihadist forum administrators' best efforts to use proxies and to conceal participants' identities, this kind of confidence may not be all that easily recovered.

## Example 2: Encourage Sectarianism

According to Ulph, "the pool of experienced, credible ideologues may be draining" amongst jihadist supporters. Ulph has noted that in the wake of the kidnapping and assassination of the Egyptian ambassador to Baghdad, al-Zarqawi's Al-Qaida group was criticized by the two main Egyptian militant Islamist organizations. These detractors argued that Al-Qaida in Iraq was more focused on destroying the Shi'a and Kurd populations than it was on fighting the enemy occupier.

They also suggested that the organization was unable to learn from its past mistakes, and that it was causing "the average Muslim" to feel alienated from Islamist groups in general. The latter criticism was echoed by Abu Muhammad al-Maqdisi of the al-Tawhid wal-jihad movement, who argued that the true nature of jihad was being distorted by al-Zarqawi and other mujahideen in Iraq. In addition, criticisms regarding the London bombings were posted on jihadi forums by Abu Baseer al-Tartusi. These kinds of criticisms are particularly important since they have been publicly aired by members of the Muslim community.

In both instances cited above, internal debate and dissent can work to undermine the confidence of the jihadis in their own organizations. This drop in confidence can affect the organizations' infrastructure, as in the case of the perceived use of Internet forums by counter-terrorism operatives; alternatively, confidence in the leaders themselves may be affected, as in the case of the criticism of Zarqawi.

# Bibliography


Allison, Graham: *Nuclear Terrorism: The Ultimate Preventable Catastrophe*, New York: Times Books, 2004.

Basrur, Rajesh M., and Hasan-Askari Rizvi: *Nuclear Terrorism and South Asia*, Albuquerque, NM: Sandia National Laboratories, February 2003.

Friedman, G.: *The Future of War of Cyber Crimes*, N.Y., Random House, 1996.

Hoffman, Bruce: *Inside Terrorism and Internet Crime*, New York: Columbia University Press, 1998.

Hoffman, Bruce: *Cyber Crime with Internet*, New York: Columbia University Press, 1998.

Huntington, S.P.: *Crimes Vs. Terrorism*, N.Y., Vintage Books, 1964.

Kaplan, David: *Computer Virus Attack*, New York: Crown Publishers, 1996.

Keane J.: *Democracy and Cyber Crimes*, London, Verso, 1988.

Laquer, Walter: *The New Terrorism: Fanaticism and the Arms of Mass Destruction*, Oxford: Oxford University Press, 1999.

Laquer, Walter: *Terrorism Attack from Computer Hacking*, Oxford: Oxford University Press, 1999.

Posen, B.R.: *The Sources of Cyber Crime*, Ithaca, 1984, Cornell Univ. Press.

Rhodes, Richard: *The Making of the Atomic Bomb*, New York: Simon and Schuster, 1988.

Rosen, P.: *Policy of Cyber Laws*, Ithaca, Cornell University Press, 1996.

Schroeer, Dietrich: *Science, Technology, and the Cyber Crimes*, Ontario: John Wiley & Sons, 1984.

# Index